IMAGES
of America

THE LAND OF ORLAND

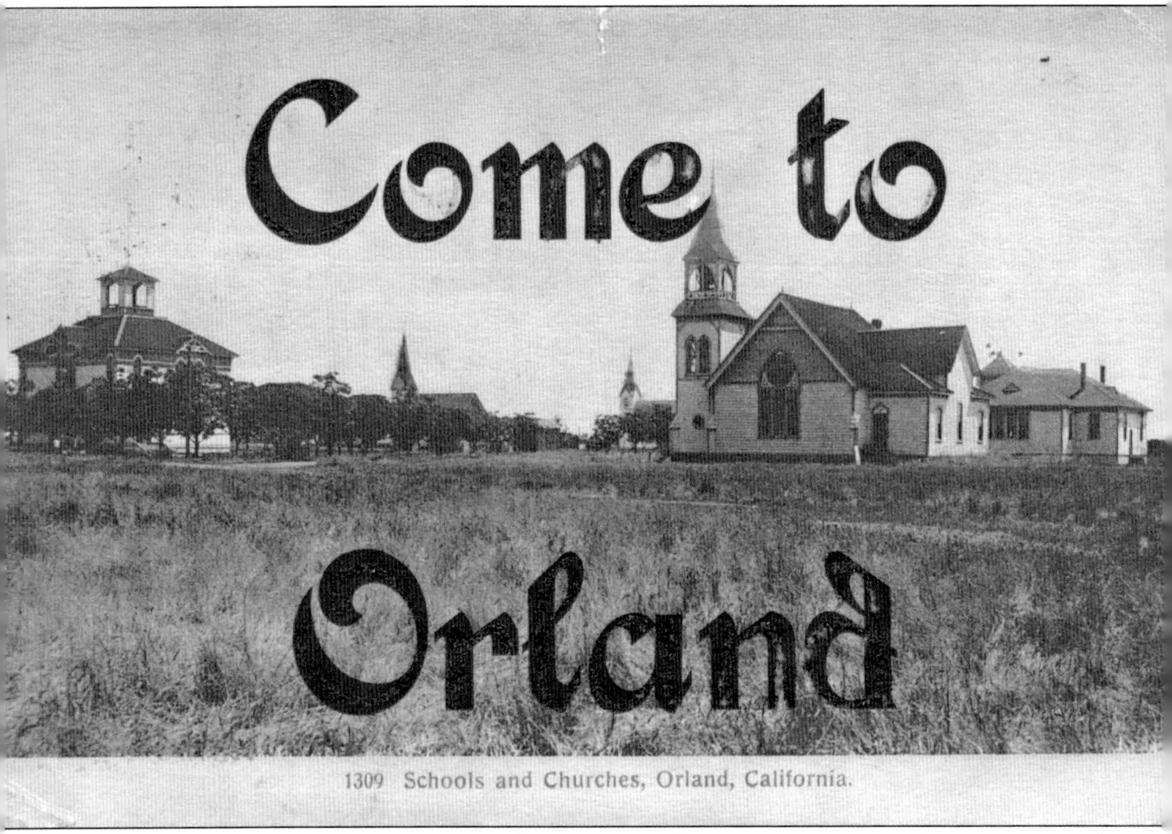

The Orland Promotion Club approved at their October 10, 1910, meeting the acquisition of 3,000 postcards for "boosting" Orland. Every person in the Orland area was urged to secure a few of the free postcards to send to their friends and relatives living in other states. Buildings pictured from left to right are Orland Grammar School, Orland Methodist Church, St. Dominic's Catholic Church, Orland First Baptist Church, and Orland High School. (Courtesy author's collection.)

ON THE COVER: This photograph was taken on May 25, 1947, while volunteers loaded a full truckload of clothing collected during the successful local drive. The community-wide committee established that 10,000 pounds of clothing, shoes, bedding, and sewing material would be the Orland goal for overseas relief through the Church World Service organization. Representatives from Orland Kiwanis, Rotary, Lions, Legion Auxiliary, City Council, and church women's groups were part of the steering committee. The Al Wickland and Son showroom at the corner of Walker Street and Highway 99 West was the collection center, and Virgil Flores agreed to truck the goods directly to the Richmond (California) shipping center. Pictured here, from left to right, are (first row) unidentified, Rev. Robert Rankin, Hazel Thode, Myrtle Tillotson, Nellie Long, unidentified, and Nelda Sweet; (second row, on the truck) unidentified and J. A. Russell. (Courtesy Orland Alumni Association.)

IMAGES
of America

THE LAND OF ORLAND

Gene H. Russell
for the Orland Historical and Cultural Society

ARCADIA
PUBLISHING

ISBN 978-0-7385-5617-8

Published by Arcadia Publishing
Charleston, South Carolina

Printed in the United States of America

Library of Congress Control Number: 2007936580

For all general information, please contact Arcadia Publishing:
Telephone 843-853-2070
Fax 843-853-0044
E-mail sales@arcadiapublishing.com
For customer service and orders:
Toll-Free 1-888-313-2665

Visit us on the Internet at www.arcadiapublishing.com

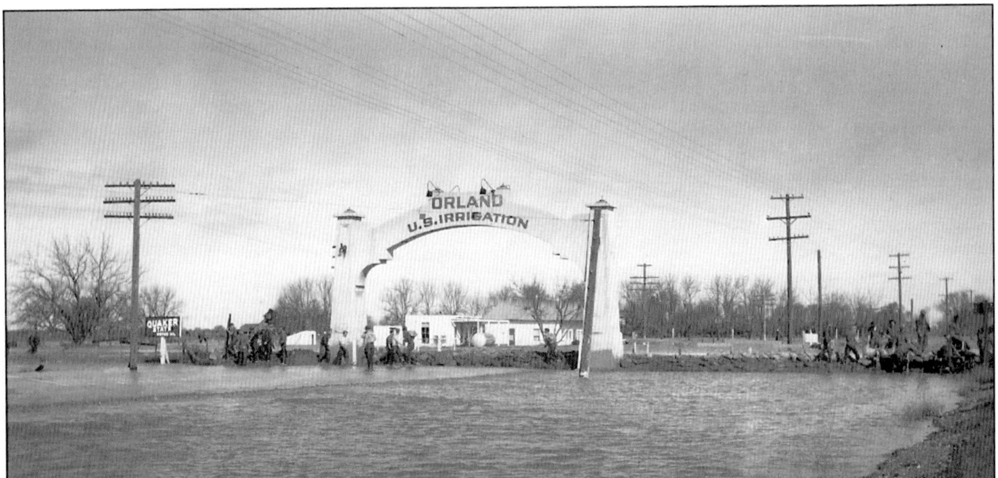

The Orland highway arch has been an endearing symbol for the community since it was built in the summer of 1926 by John Berlinger Sr. Model T Ford trucks were used to haul the Stony Creek gravel to the site one yard at a time. Bessie Mecum was the moving spirit behind the arch and presented the idea to the chamber of commerce and the town trustees for their approval. A second arch at the south entrance to Orland was planned but never built. Pictured is the arch during the February 1940 flood with Civilian Conservation Corps (CCC) boys building a sandbag barrier to keep the water from getting higher in town. (Courtesy Orland Historical and Cultural Society.)

Contents

ACKNOWLEDGMENTS

The majority of the images reproduced in this book are from the archival library housed at the Alta Schmidt House Museum and owned by the Orland Historical and Cultural Society. Many of these invaluable photographs were generously donated to the society by the Les Jacobs and Don Keene families—Orland newspaper editors and publishers from the 1910s into the 1960s. These photographs and those owned by the author do not carry a credit line after the caption.

Individuals who furnished pictures or assisted with information included Carol Baugher, Ed Berkland, Tom Birch, Bill Boot, Jack Bucke, Anna Canon, Paula Crowell, Joe and Shirley Erickson, Ruth Falkner, Greg Gebhart, Charles Gee, Bruce Gilmore, Evelyn Gleason, Mark Guilford, Fay Hanson, Landy Hardy, Ken Hibdon, Shirley Hodge, Bob Jacobson, Alexander and Norman Johansen, Louie Johnson, Fred Kronsbein, Arthalyn Kublick, Diana Mason, Trish Nissen, John Nopel, Joanne Overton, Marjorie Reimers Palmer, Berta Ramsey, Ruth Reimers, Judy Serrano, Jim Slyh, Bob Strawn, Earle Swift, Jose Torres, George and Lana Trovao, and George Vonasek.

The California State Library History Section, the California State Railroad Museum Library, the Orland Alumni Association, the Orland Free Library, the Orland Unit Water Users' Association, and the Special Collections at California State University, Chico, were additional sources of valuable information and vintage images of Orland. Their professional assistance and cooperation was most appreciated.

Special thanks are gratefully extended to Eletta Jacobson, Jay Russell, and Shirley Russell for their support, research assistance, creative talent, and technical expertise in the preparation of this limited collection of 220 classic Orland photographs.

The Orland Historical and Cultural Society is also indebted to all who participated in this project. To share pictures from family photo albums with the community at large is commendable and gives all interested in local history additional insight into the heritage of the land of Orland. In addition, the society wishes to acknowledge the unnamed amateur and professional photographers who took the pictures we now enjoy.

INTRODUCTION

The experimentation and practical development of photography was taking place at almost the exact same time that Granville Perry Swift and Frank Sears were exploring the future land of Orland on the banks of Hambright and Stony Creeks. These early pioneers probably never heard of the daguerreotype (1837) that would have captured the likeness of grizzly bears and elk on the valley floor, the Native Americans in their struggles over disease and starvation, and the first efforts of neighbors to carve out a homestead in the untamed Sacramento Valley. This task to document the decades of 1840 through 1870 would be left to later generations with new gadgets that captured light on glass plates and later celluloid using the newly patented box cameras.

Unfortunately, much of the Old West had vanished from view and was lost before the first cameras came to capture pictures of the Orland area. The earliest photographs in this book, for example, date from the 1880s and 1890s. Close examination of the buildings in the early baseball photograph printed on pages 122–123 gives an indication of the "scattered" appearance of the new village of false-front businesses interspersed with clapboard dwellings. The photographer, facing north, was standing in the area of Mill Street between Fifth Street to his left and Fourth Street to the right. The Bank of Orland and the two-story white IOOF (International Order of Odd Fellows) building are visible in this early-1890s view of the business district. We have to use our imaginations to visualize Orland's three-story floor mill, the first jail and first schoolhouse, the record-setting flood of 1878, the salmon spawning in Stony Creek, the mule teams bringing loaded wagons from the dock at Monroeville traveling across the dusty Colusa plains to Newville, and the earliest attempts to change from barren dryland farming to fertile fields and orchards.

At the dawn of the 20th century, several attempts to form local irrigation districts had been abandoned because of financial difficulties. In 1902, there was renewed interest in the reclamation of Sacramento River and tributaries like Stony Creek with the passage of the Reclamation Act and the creation of the Reclamation Service. Orland visionaries used the Sacramento Valley Development Association to open discussions with the federal government to request a local irrigation project.

In February 1906, the Orland Unit Water Users' Association was formed, and by that July, a survey party was busy at work in the western foothills on Little Stony and Big Stony Creeks. Four months later, the East Park Dam site 60 miles southwest of Orland had been selected for the first federally funded irrigation project in the West. Boom times were just around the corner.

The Stanley Contracting Company of San Francisco submitted the winning bid, and construction on the curved, thick-arch structure began when laborers, concrete men, teamsters, engineers, inspectors, and an occasional photographer went to work in the spring of 1909. The resulting photographs offer an amazing look at construction methods on the wedge-shaped slab containing 12,200 cubic yards of concrete. Limited space in this publication prevents showing but two of these vintage photographs.

In the exhilarating years of growth following the completion of East Park Dam, wooden buildings in the business section of town were replaced with reinforced concrete structures, over

100 new homes were built, and the population of Orland increased from 600 in 1910 to 2,000 in 1912. The farm population increased almost 250 percent as land values (and land speculators) increased dramatically.

Booster club brochures produced and disseminated during these years contain numerous photographs depicting irrigation water flowing in the canals and laterals to the alfalfa fields and the orchards of oranges, lemons, grapefruits, prunes, apricots, pears, peaches, figs, almonds, and walnuts. It was profitable to be a farmer on the Orland Project!

Orland's farming culture had undergone a revival because irrigation was now possible for the barren, depleted alluvial soils after decades of overplanting and dryland farming. The addition of federal irrigation to a long growing season of 262 days made for a community of small farmers where almost every crop tried would soon show a profit. By the late 1910s, the Bureau of Reclamation's Orland venture was known as "the project of no regrets."

In addition to the two creameries, feed and alfalfa mills, a 750-foot warehouse, and a packinghouse for oranges and almonds, Orland could now support commercial photographers with a downtown studio. One of the first of these professionals was John Thomas, who was regarded as an "expert" with an "enviable reputation." His imprint is found on many of the classic photographs from the 1910s and early 1920s. A favorite technique used by Thomas and other photographers was to take their equipment to the roof of the Bank of Orland building or the two-story Victorian school and make "aerial" or bird's-eye views of the community.

Thomas was followed by Peter Richter, who worked out of his Walker Street studio. He is remembered for disappearing under the hood of his large view camera and taking hundreds of class pictures on the steps of the grammar and high schools during the 1930s and 1940s. These photographs are a valuable part of the community's heritage and are housed at the Orland Historical and Cultural Society's archival library. Other Orland professional photographers include John Andres, Mayhew Studios, Roy Wilgus, Harry Harder, Al and Betty Rotting, George Keck, C. L. "Lee" Swann, Joe Winter, Dennis Brown, and Christine Korling-Torres.

The projected crossing of the Newville-Monroeville Road by the northward-bound railroad gave rise to the village that became Orland in 1875. Like all railroad towns in the upper Sacramento Valley—of which Orland is one—there is an interesting history worthy of documentation in word and picture. The photographs that have survived the pre-railroad era are few in number. During the dryland farming era, photography became more practical, resulting in classic pictures of early farming and the emerging town. Most families in the agricultural community would have a few photographs, most likely of relatives. The irrigated-lands era is noted for the proliferation of photographers and cameras, and the means to record the events and activities of life in rural America and to purchase prints for the family photo album. Collectively, images from these three eras make up the visual history of the land of Orland. A sample of this rich history is found in the photographs selected for this special place among the Images of America series.

One

The Early Years

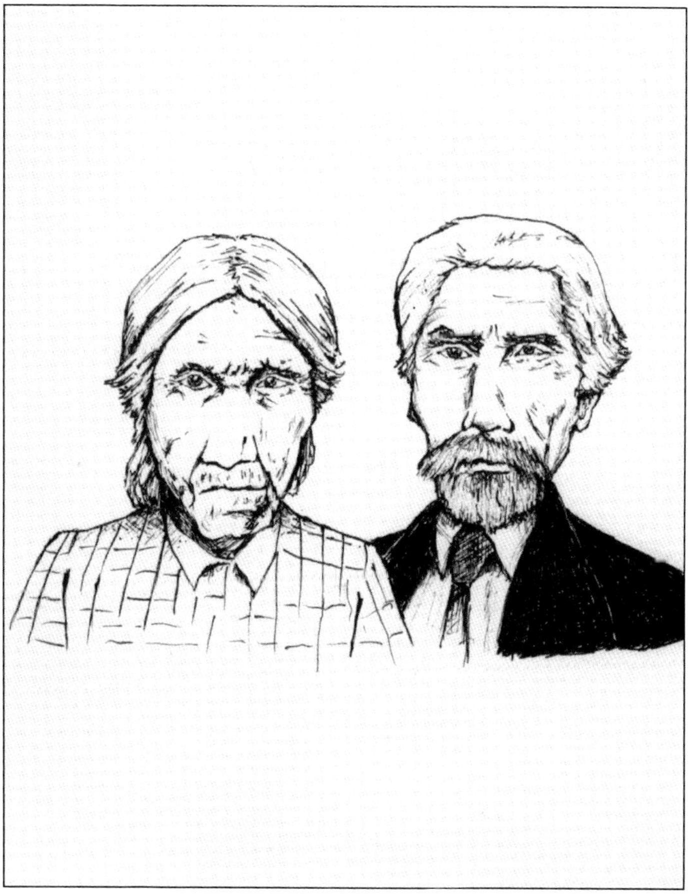

Anne and "Indian Jim" Brown were two of the best known and most respected Native Americans in Northern California. They also were among the last surviving members of their respective tribes. Anne was born and raised on the banks of Stony Creek, a member of the Central Wintun (Nomlaki or Grindstone tribe), and was one of the helpers or housekeepers at Granville Swift's adobe house on Hambright Creek. Anne and Jim, a member of the Concow tribe that lived along Butte Creek, lived seven miles west of Orland and were happily married for nearly half a century. Jim was a peacemaker between the whites and the native people. He died April 15, 1922, and Anne passed away on October 28, 1927.

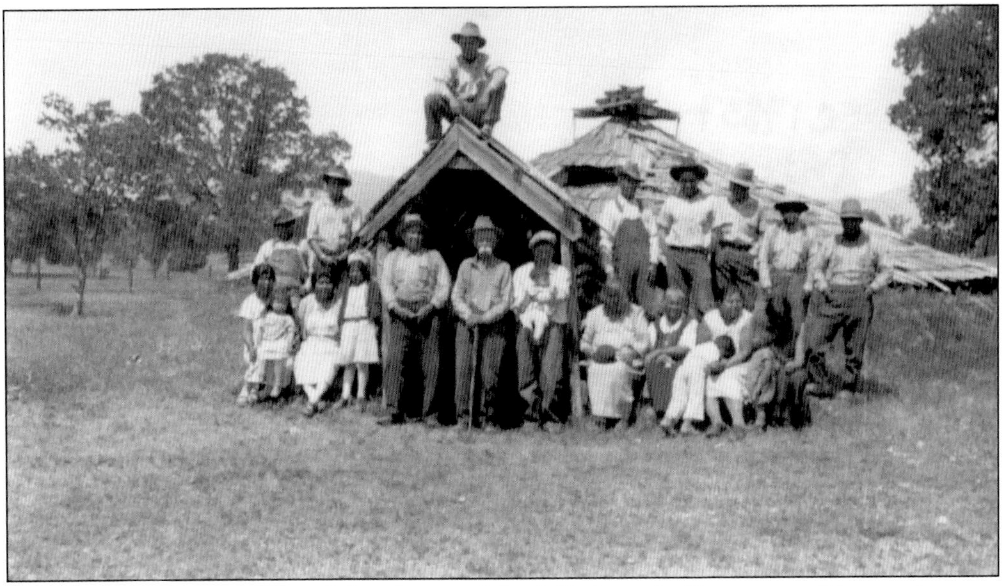

The Central Wintun inhabited the plains and foothills from the Sacramento River to the crest of the Coast Range. They lived in small independent tribes and subsisted on acorns, nuts, wild fruits, roots, seeds, fish, deer, elk, rabbits, and other small game. They were hunter-gathers lacking agriculture, written language, and domestic animals—except the dog. The Wintun were averse to fighting but fond of dancing. Pictured are members of the Grindstone Rancheria in front of their dance house in 1932. (Courtesy Ethel Baker and Special Collections, Meriam Library, California State University, Chico.)

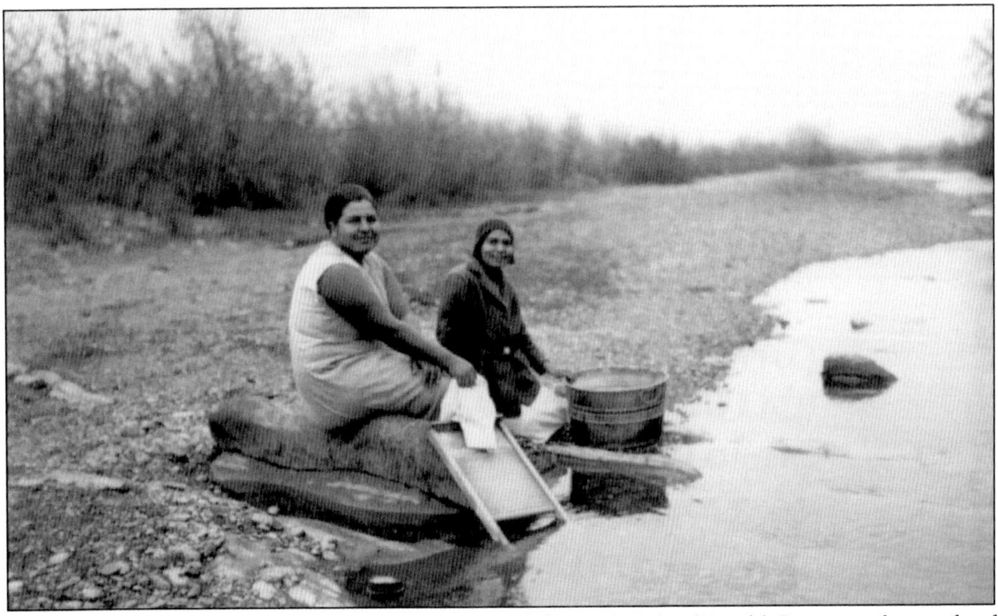

This picture was taken by Don Keene in 1932 and shows Amelia (Smith) Burrows, first wife of Wallace Burrows, and her daughter-in-law Anita (Cook) Burrows, laundering clothes in Stony Creek. The Grindstone Rancheria is located at the point where Grindstone Creek flows into Stony Creek five miles north of Elk Creek. (Courtesy Ethel Baker and Special Collections, Meriam Library, California State University, Chico.)

Capt. Granville Swift was born in Kentucky on May 1, 1821. He was an accomplished outdoorsman when he started west in 1841. Swift worked for John Sutter as a hunter and supplied meat, furs, and hides for his Nueva Helvetia colony. By the mid-1840s, Swift and his cousin Franklin Sears had selected a huge tract of land extending over most of the western valley floor from Stony Creek south to Cache Creek. (Courtesy Earle Swift.)

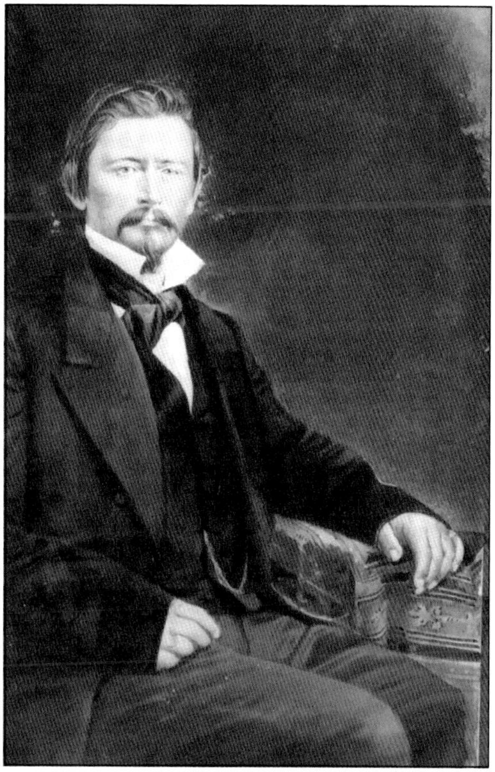

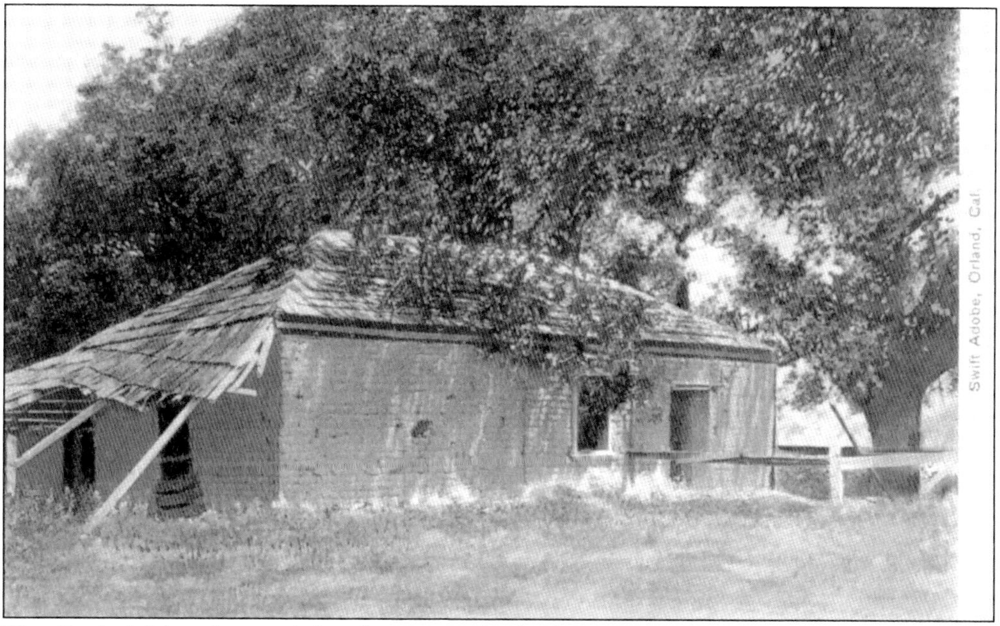

The Swift Adobe, the area's first home, was built about 1847 by Granville Swift and located north of town under majestic valley oak trees along the south bank of Hambright Creek. The 30-by-20-foot building was made of yellow adobe found on the north side of Stony Creek. The home was in good shape until 1886 when livestock began knocking down the porch and treasure seekers started undermining the adobe walls.

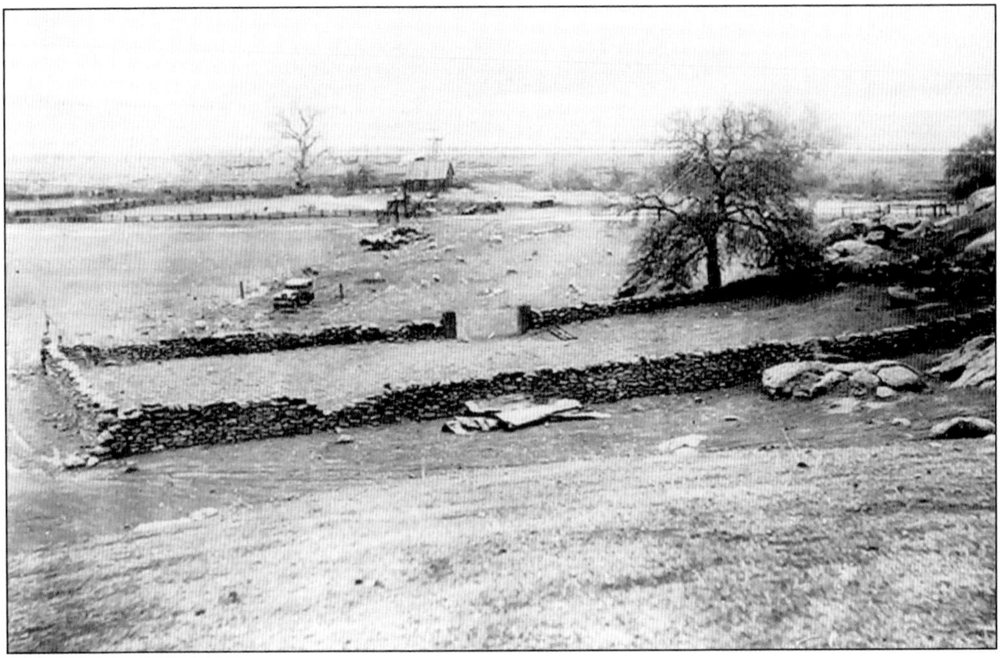

Granville Swift is credited with building the Stone Corral 10 miles west of Maxwell as a holding area for wild horses. By the late 1840s, Swift, with the help of his Native Americans, had gathered a vast herd of cattle and horses, and had some acreage planted in wheat and barley. The Stone Corral was designated State Historic Landmark No. 238 in 1936. (Courtesy Earle Swift.)

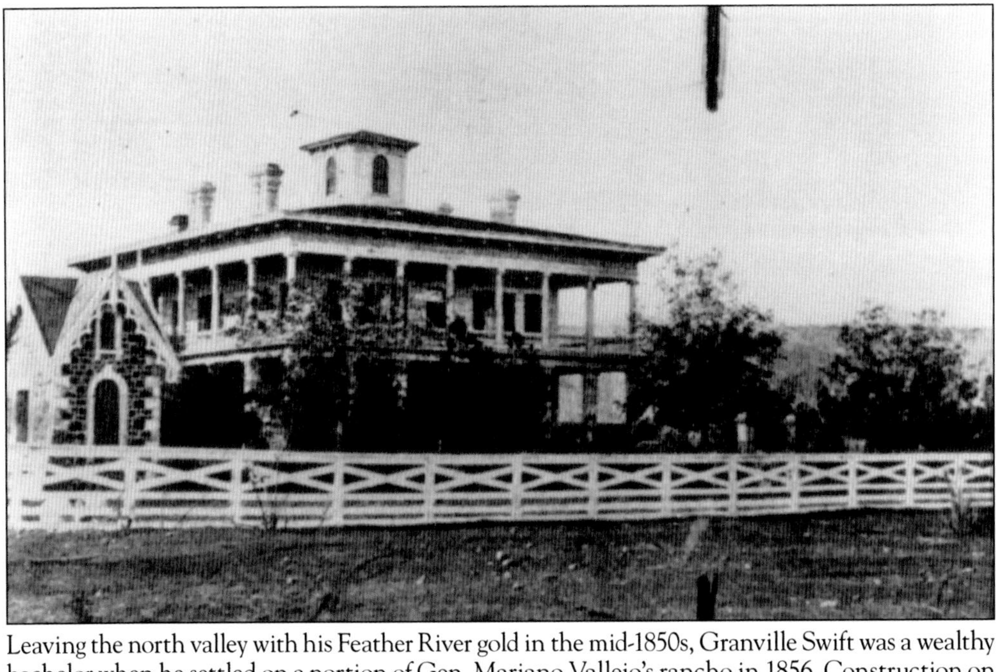

Leaving the north valley with his Feather River gold in the mid-1850s, Granville Swift was a wealthy bachelor when he settled on a portion of Gen. Mariano Vallejo's rancho in 1856. Construction on his three-story "palace in the country," known as Temelec Hall, started on June 19, 1858, and would cost approximately $250,000. Swift married Jane Eliza Tate on September 1, 1858, and they were the parents of three sons. (Courtesy the Sonoma County Library, Santa Rosa, California.)

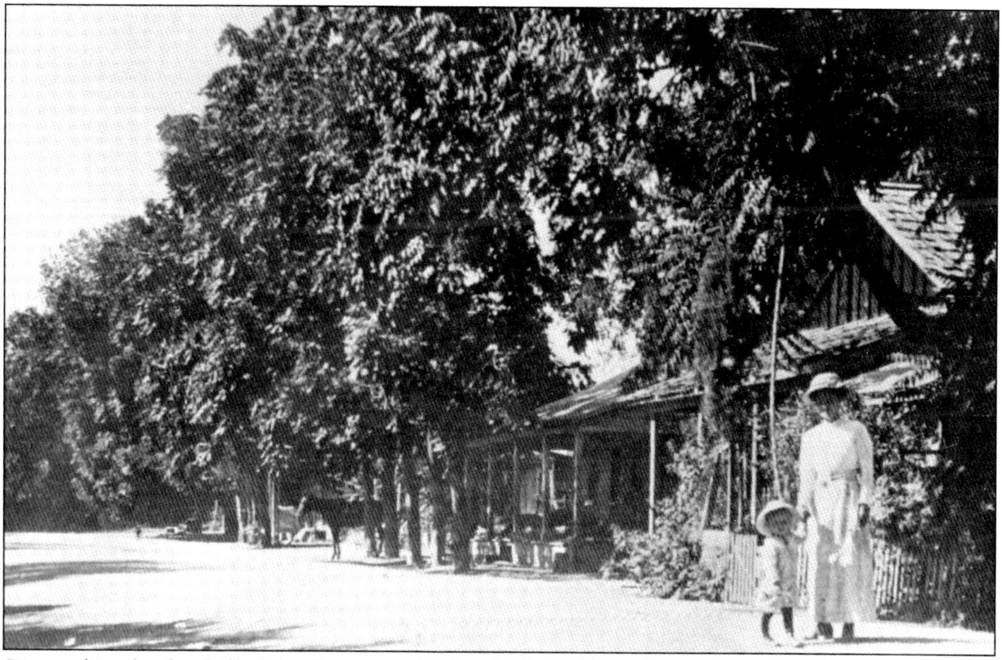

Situated in the foothills 22 miles west of Orland, Newville is Glenn County's oldest community. The first stockmen and settlers came in the mid-1850s because there was living water, lush grazing land, and no malaria-carrying mosquitoes, which abounded along the Sacramento River. The street scene above was photographed around 1914.

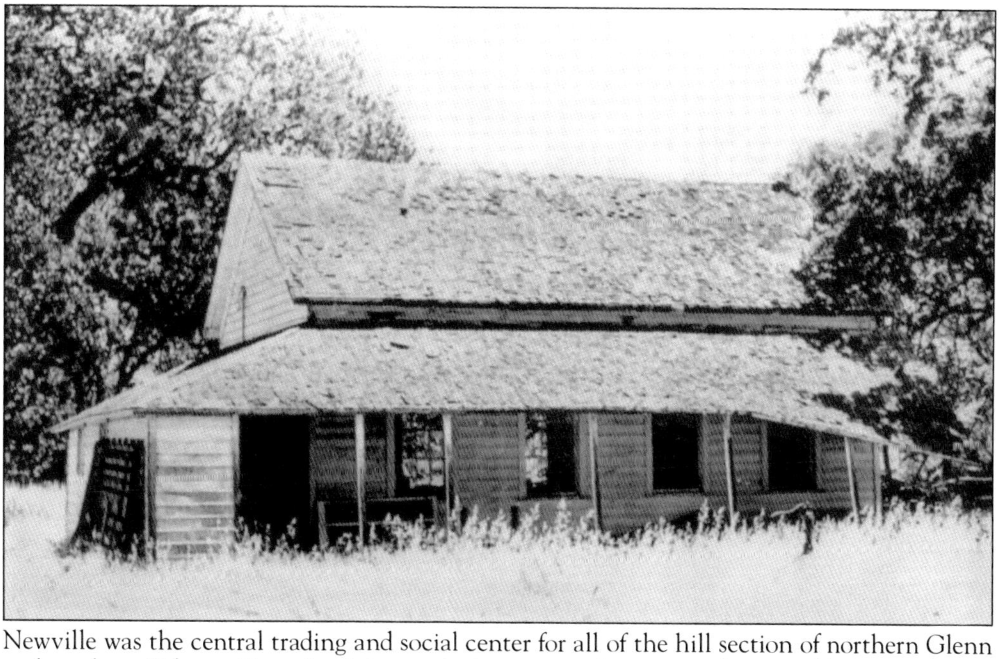

Newville was the central trading and social center for all of the hill section of northern Glenn and southern Tehama Counties. It boasted a large general store, two livery stables, two saloons, a blacksmith and tin shop, a racetrack, two hotels, and a U.S. Post Office (1868–1918). Pictured is the old Newville School that at one time had 60 pupils. (Courtesy Thelma White and Special Collections, Meriam Library, California State University, Chico.)

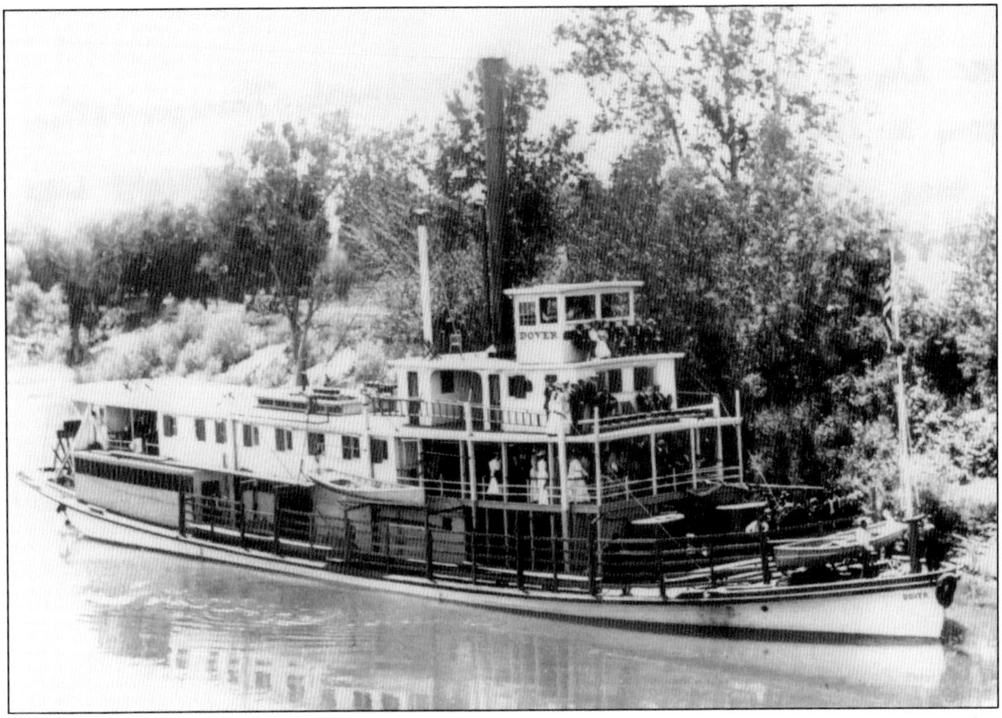

Stern-wheel steamboats traveled the upper Sacramento River from the early 1850s to 1936. Regular freight traffic was handled by river boat as far north as Monroeville until shortly before World War I. Gasoline to fuel the area's first automobiles, for example, was shipped from Sacramento by riverboat to Monroeville and then freighted to Orland. Barges, used principally for hauling grain to Sacramento, were a common sight on the Sacramento water highway. Red Bluff was the effective head of navigation on the river. (Above courtesy John Rankin and Special Collections, Meriam Library, California State University, Chico; below courtesy Glenn-Colusa Irrigation District and Special Collections, Meriam Library, California State University, Chico.)

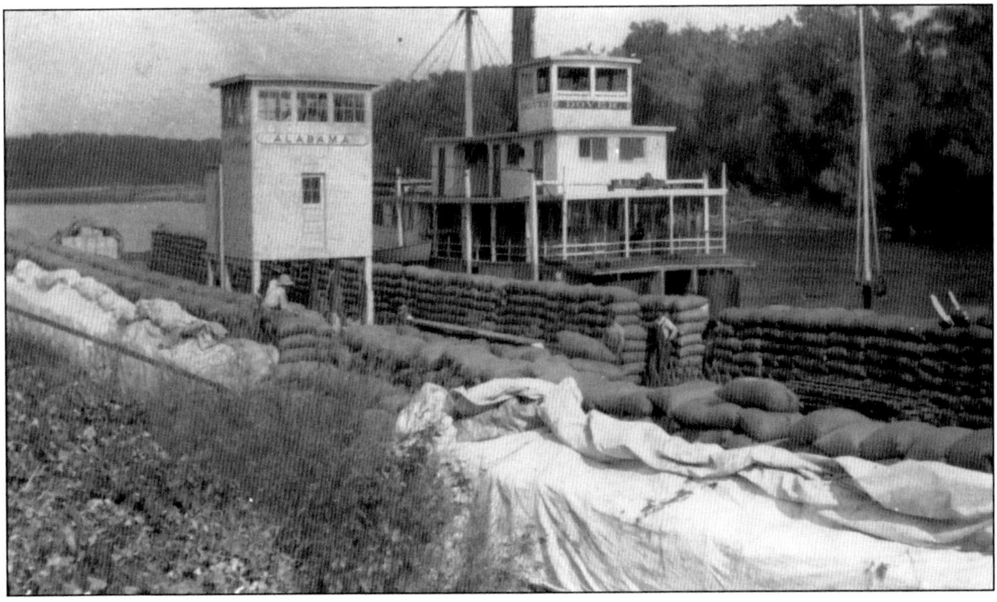

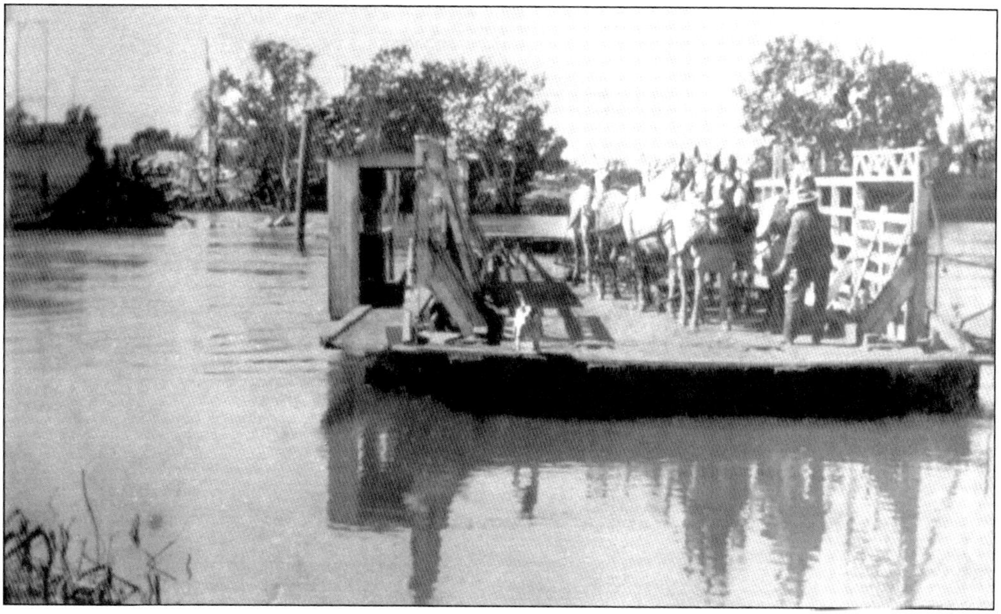

Ferries on the upper Sacramento River date from the 1850s. The Butte-Glenn ferry was located east of Hamilton City and began operation in 1903. Shown above is the river ferry boat carrying the Sacramento Valley Sugar Company's eight-mule team across the river before the construction of the Gianella Bridge in 1911. (Courtesy Sally Canfield Coupe and Special Collections, Meriam Library, California State University, Chico.)

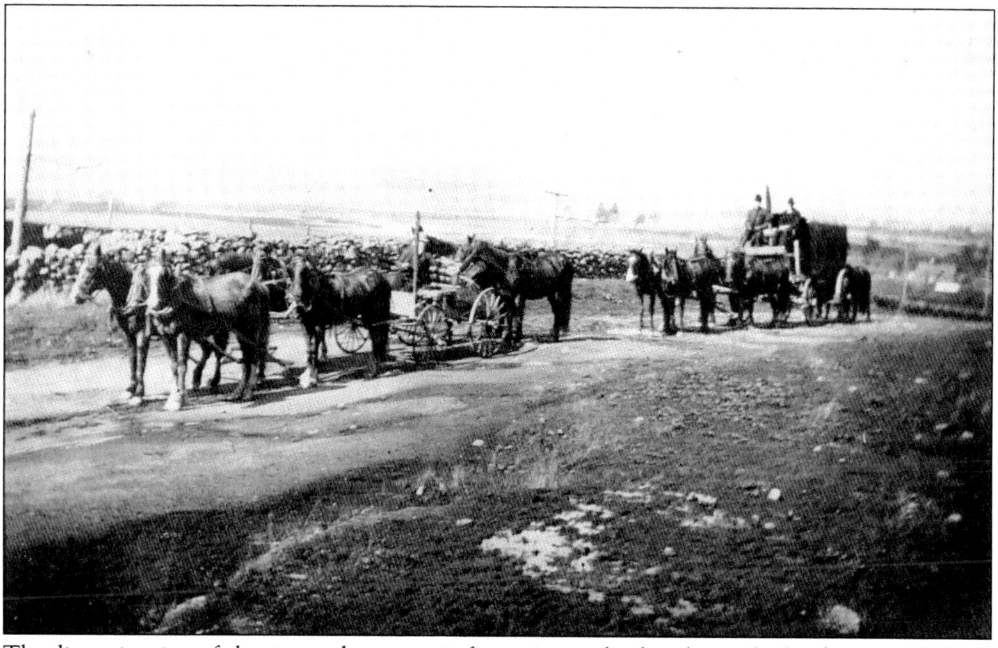

The dissemination of glowing and accurate information on husbandry in the lands around Orland was well received by the inquiring public. Orland had the right combination of sunshine, water, and good soil to convince ambitious men and women desirous of bettering their condition in life to come live in Orland. Horse-drawn wagons brought the household goods of many early families. (Courtesy Paula Crowell.)

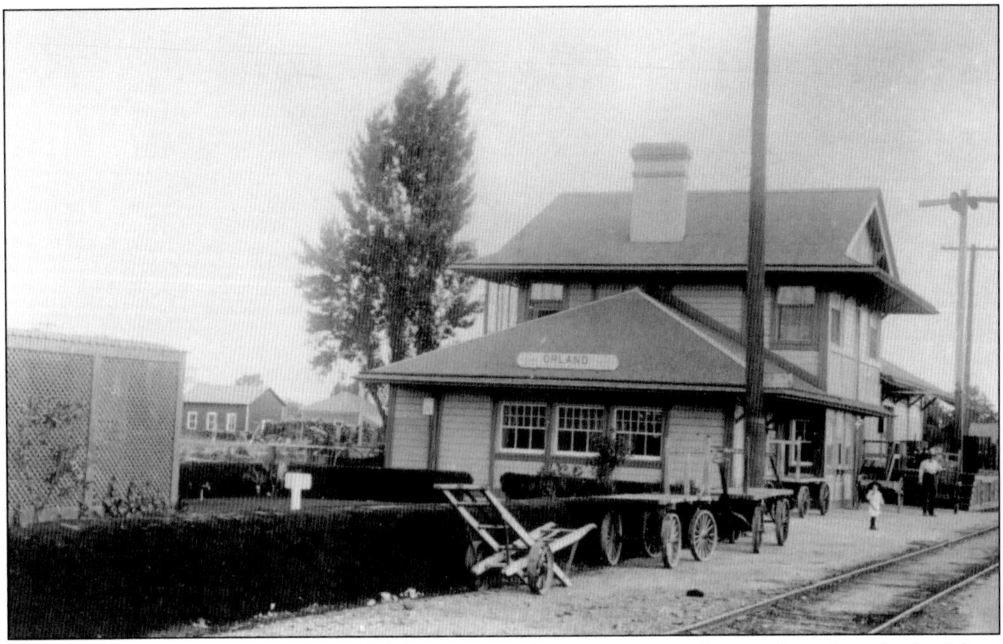

The initial decline of Newville and Olimpo as trading centers can be attributed to the building of the railroad up the west side of the valley, establishing the town of Orland in the mid-1870s. Construction of the line by the Northern Railway Company began in Woodland in August 1875. The communities of Arbuckle, Williams, Maxwell, Willows, Artois, Orland, and Corning were all established around this time as railroad towns. The railroad reached Willows by September 1878. After a lengthy delay, construction resumed, and the tracks reached Orland on July 31, 1882. The top photograph shows Orland's first park just north of the depot, which offered a welcomed respite for train passengers during a layover in Orland. The railroad water tank pictured below was built in 1908 and was removed in October 1952. The Southern Pacific depot was moved to the Glenn County Fairgrounds in 1980. (Below courtesy California State Railroad Museum, Sacramento.)

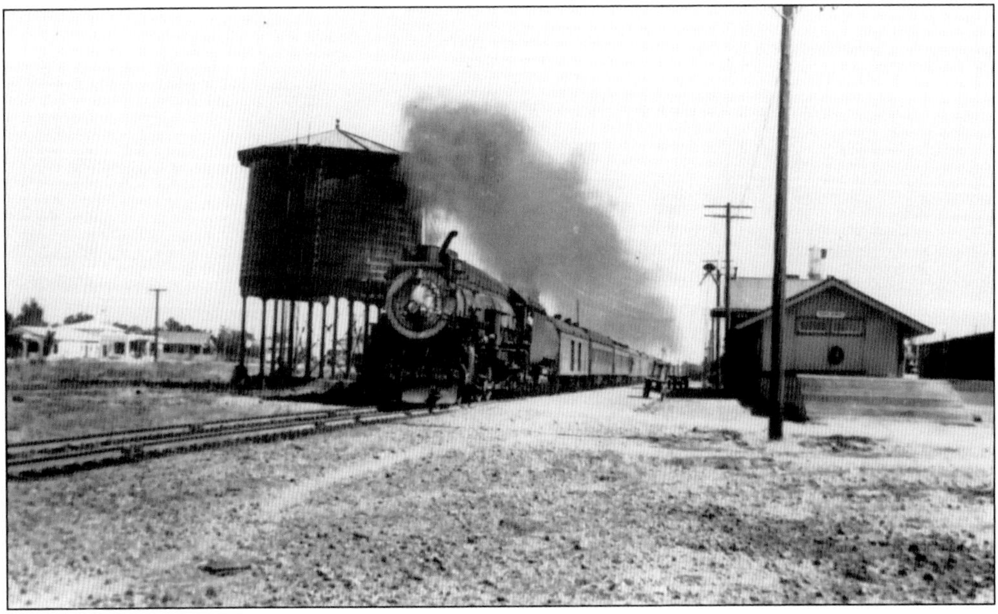

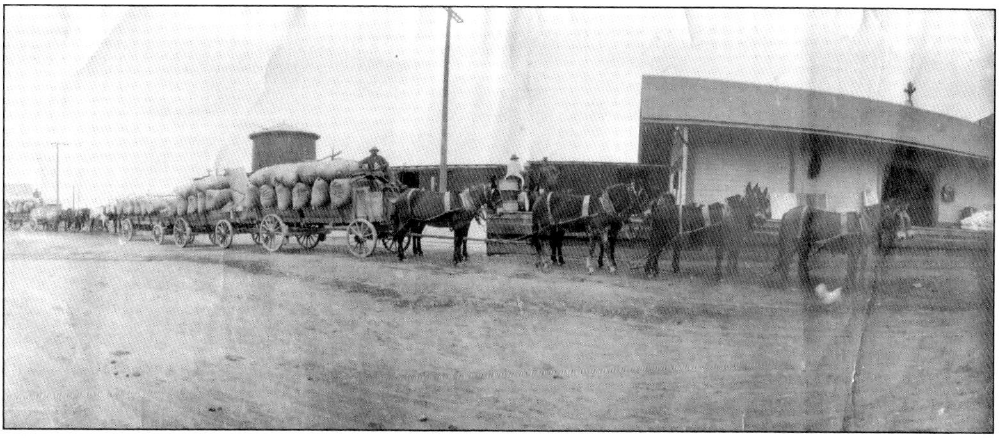

This image shows the delivery of wool to the Orland depot in the 1890s. Bill Green is on the lead wagon loaded with merino wool from the I. W. Brownell Ranch in the foothills west of Orland.

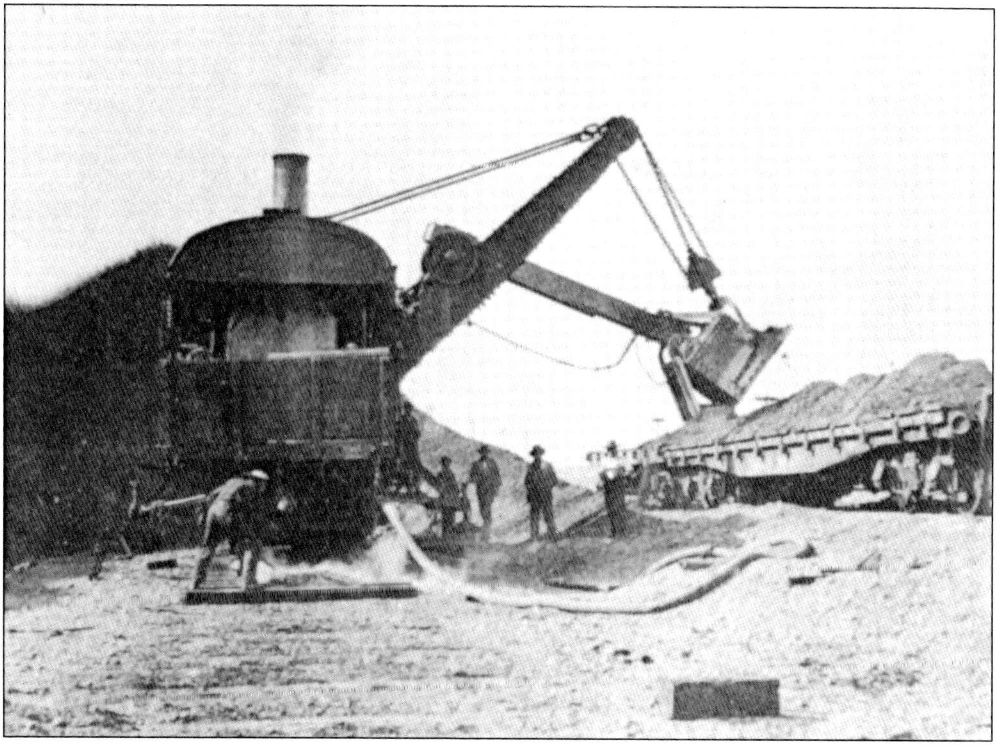

Gravel was an important export item from Stony Creek and the "Grapit" three miles south of town. In 1915, the Southern Pacific Company was taking an average of 1,200 cars of gravel from its pit each month. Each car held 40 tons, and the gravel was shipped all over the state and into Nevada. Pictured is a steam shovel at work in the "Grapit" in 1905. (Courtesy Mrs. Otto Rehse and the Colusi County Historical Society.)

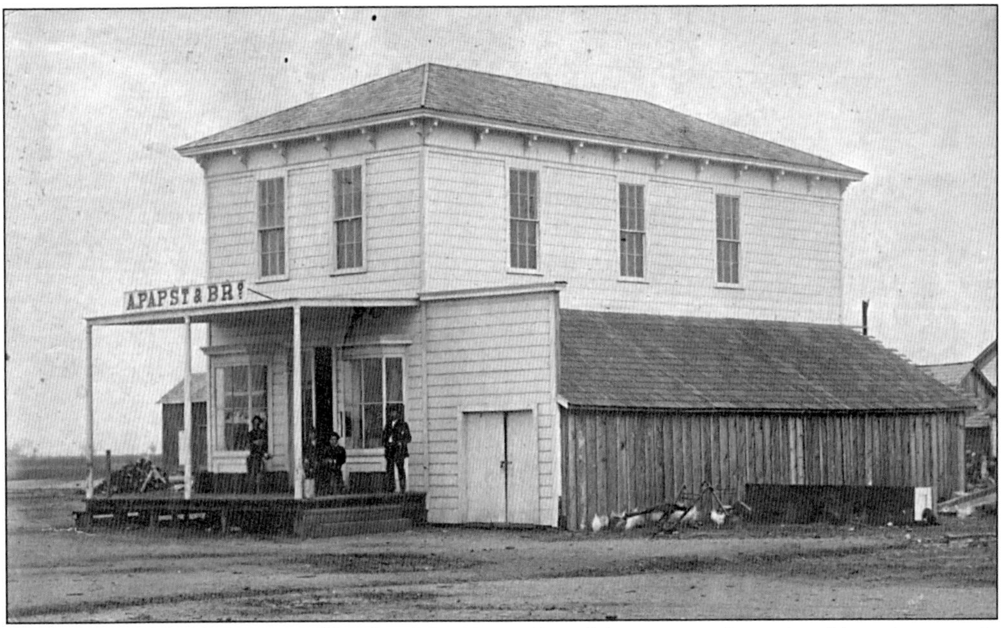

This picture of the A. Papst and Brother business on Fourth Street is perhaps the oldest photograph in this book. Albert Papst and his brother William were dealers in dry goods, groceries, clothing, shoes, and general merchandise in their popular store, known as the "White House," from 1880 to 1887. The Stony Creek IOOF lodge moved from its 16-acre site southeast of town to occupy the upper story of Albert's building. (Courtesy Jim Slyh.)

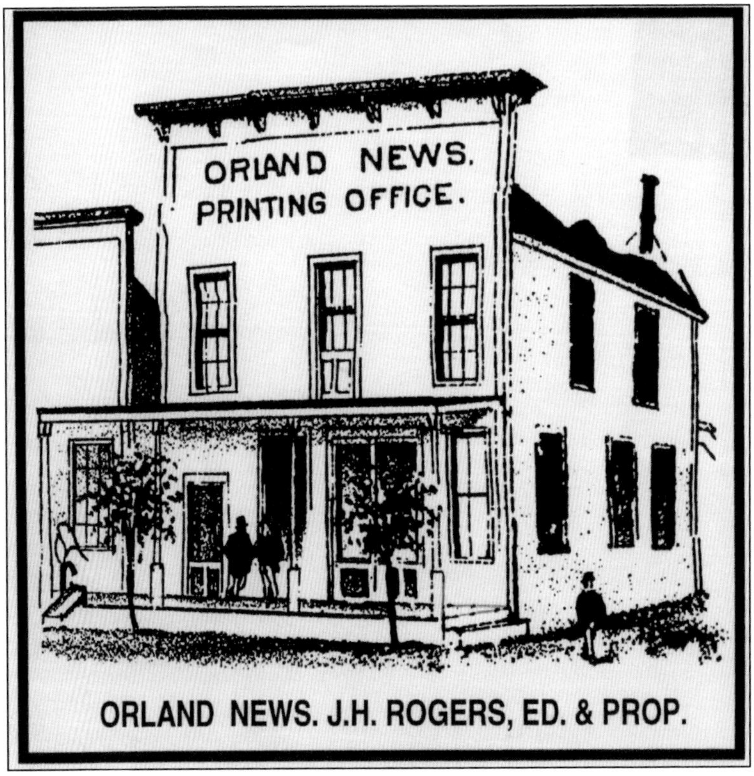

The *Orland News* was Orland's second newspaper when it first appeared on April 16, 1887. It was a four-page newspaper printed every Saturday in a Fifth Street shop by Justus H. Rogers. Coming from Colusa, he purchased the defunct *Orland Times* to start his own printing office in Orland. Rogers sold the *News* to Thomas H. Dodson on October 2, 1890. He also published *Colusa County: Its History and Resources* in 1891.

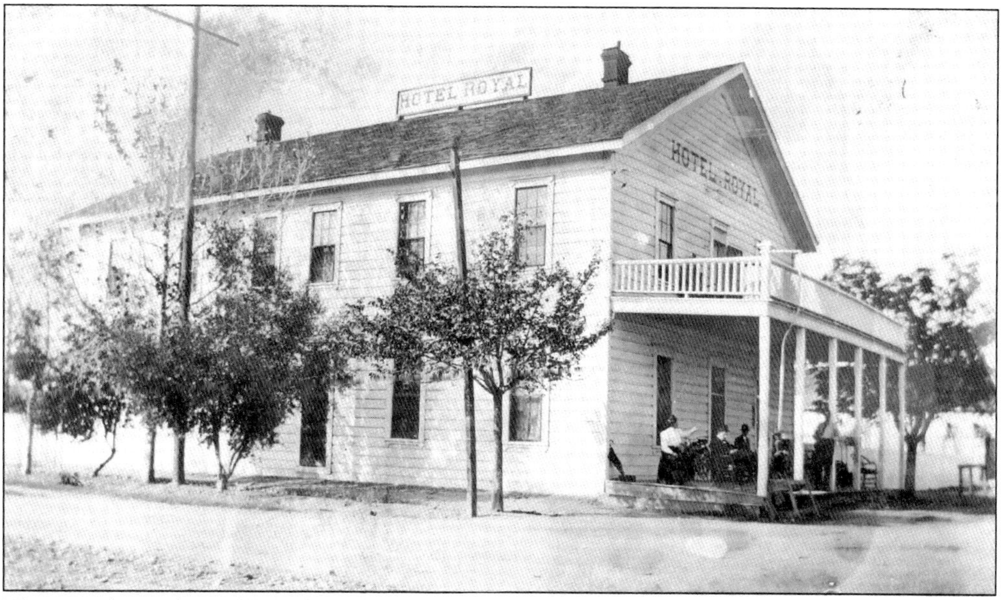

The Hotel Royal, established in the early 1890s, originally used this frame building at Fourth and Colusa Streets. It had been used as the dormitory at the Orland College in the 1880s. The building was torn down after the three-story concrete hotel just west of it was completed. The photograph was taken about 1914.

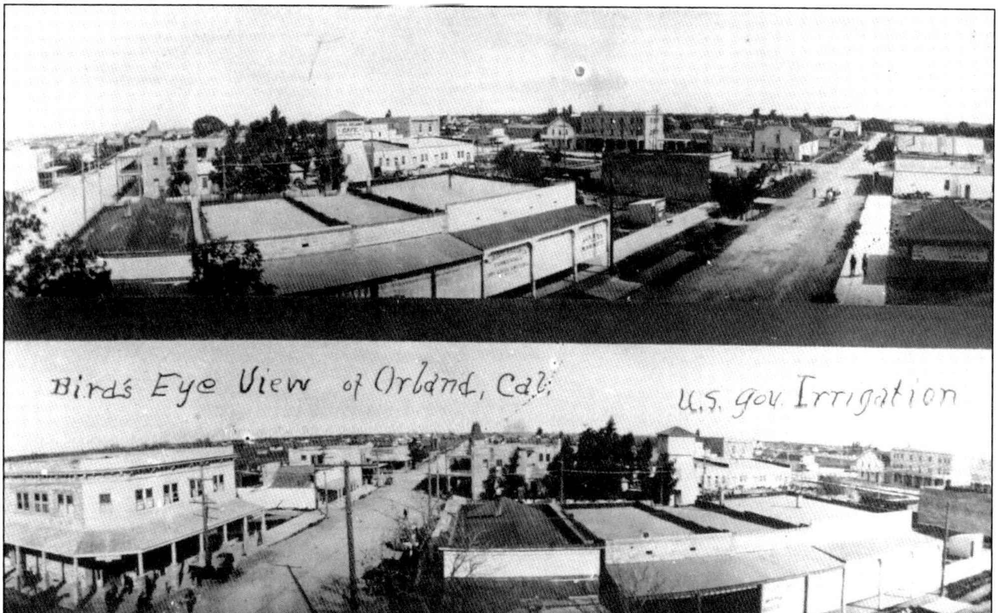

Taking pictures from the roofs of tall buildings was a popular technique used by early Orland photographers. The "bird's-eye view" photographs shown above were taken around 1912 from the top of the Bank of Orland building with the camera facing east.

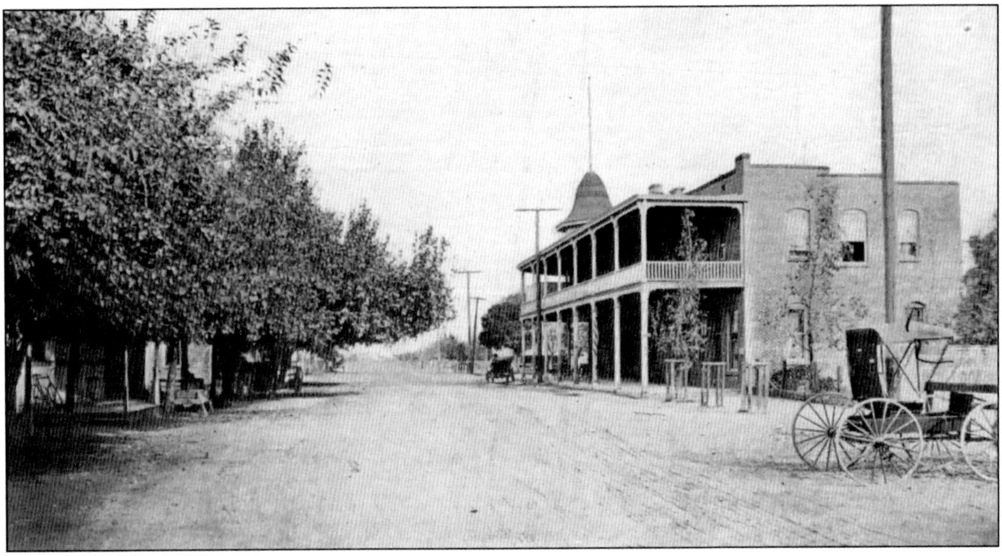

Walker Street has always been the major east-west thoroughfare through Orland. On the right is the Hotel Orland with copula. Across the street to the north and behind the trees is the Barceloux-Iglick Building.

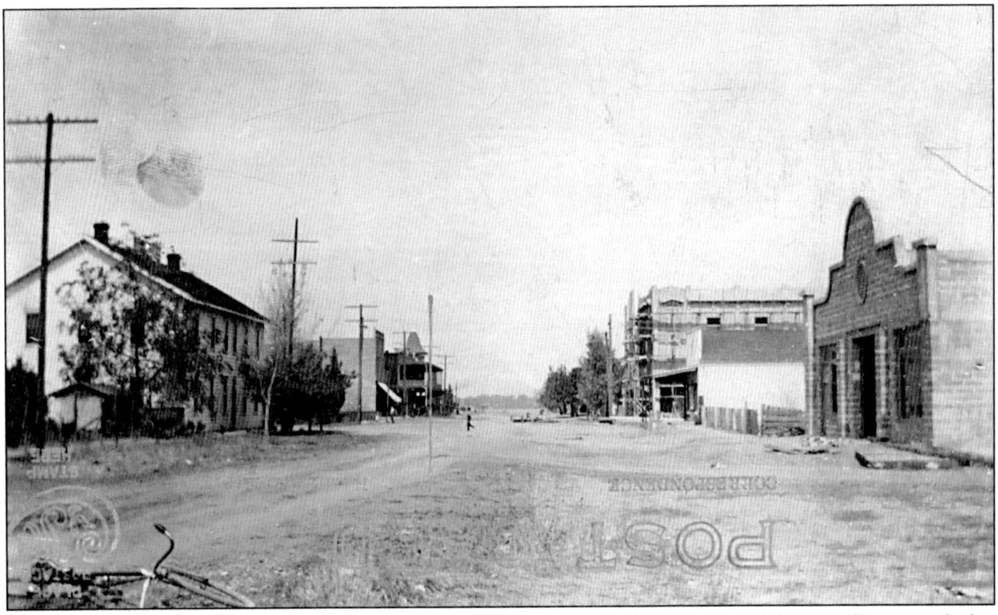

This picture of Fourth Street was taken in 1910–1911 with the scaffolding still around the unfinished Odd Fellows building at the corner of Colusa Street. The original Royal Hotel is on the left. Orland's population in 1910 was 510.

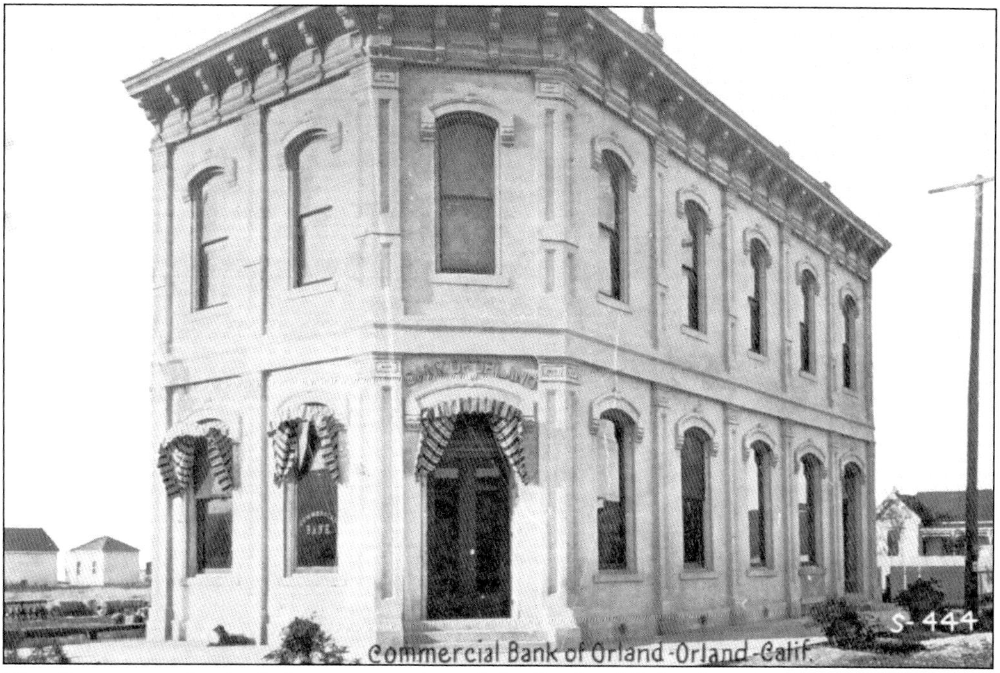

The directors authorized the construction of the Bank of Orland in the spring of 1887. The bricks were produced in a brickyard in the Plaza District. The building at the corner of Fifth and Walker Streets became the core around which Orland's early business section grew. Purchased by the City of Orland, the structure was modernized and used as the city hall from June 1943 through March 1986.

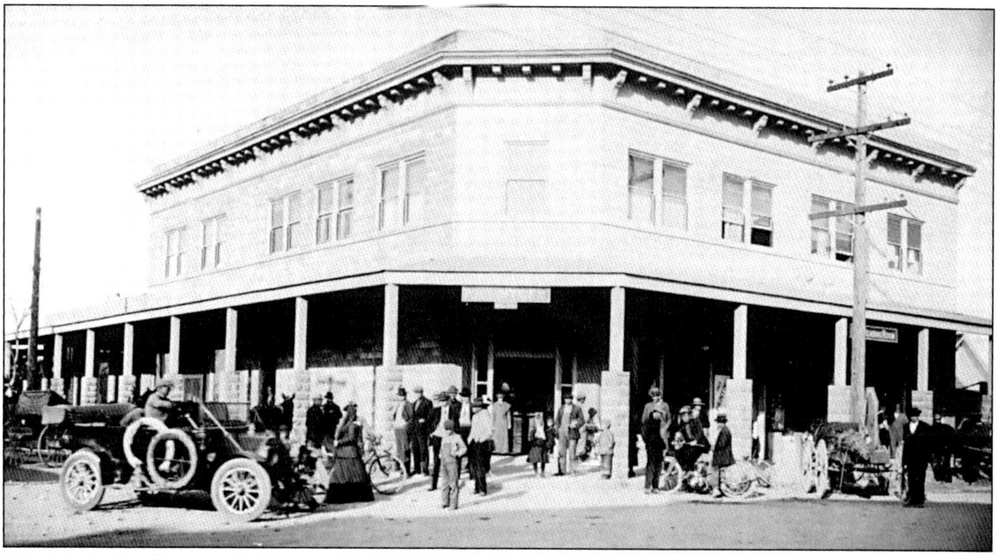

The Hicks Building at Fifth and Walker Streets was built in 1910 of concrete blocks made locally. Proctor Knott Hicks and William Chaney had a hardware store in the room at the right. The Rochdale Store was in the corner room, which was later occupied for a number of years by the post office. The *Orland Unit* had its first newspaper office upstairs, as was the reading room maintained by the Orland Women's Improvement Club. (Courtesy Special Collections, Meriam Library, California State University, Chico.)

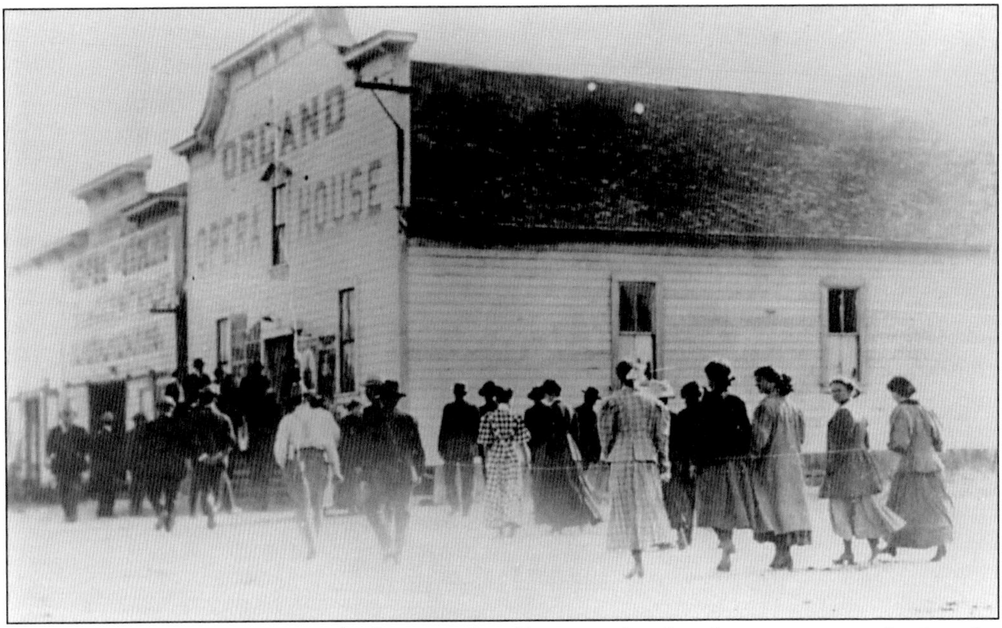

The Orland Opera House was the location for all major school and community gatherings for over a quarter of a century. Events held here included political and patriotic meetings, stage plays, dances, high school basketball games, and the first Firemen's Ball. The building was located at the southeast corner of Fifth and Colusa Streets and was torn down in March 1920. (Courtesy Special Collections, Meriam Library, California State University, Chico.)

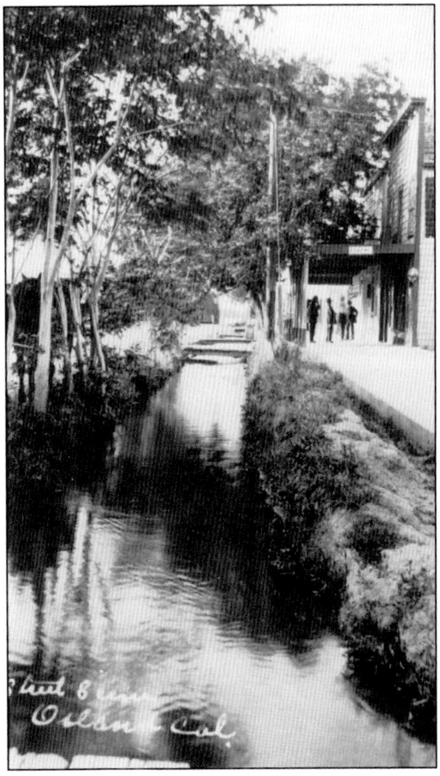

This photograph of Fifth Street was taken in the late 1890s when the old Southside Irrigation District's canal ran through the main business section of town and Fifth Street was given the title of "the waterfront." Water from the canal irrigated the farms in the southern and eastern parts of what is now a residential section of Orland. The irrigation district had been formed in 1887, and the canal was covered over in 1915. (Courtesy Thelma White and Special Collections, Meriam Library, California State University, Chico.)

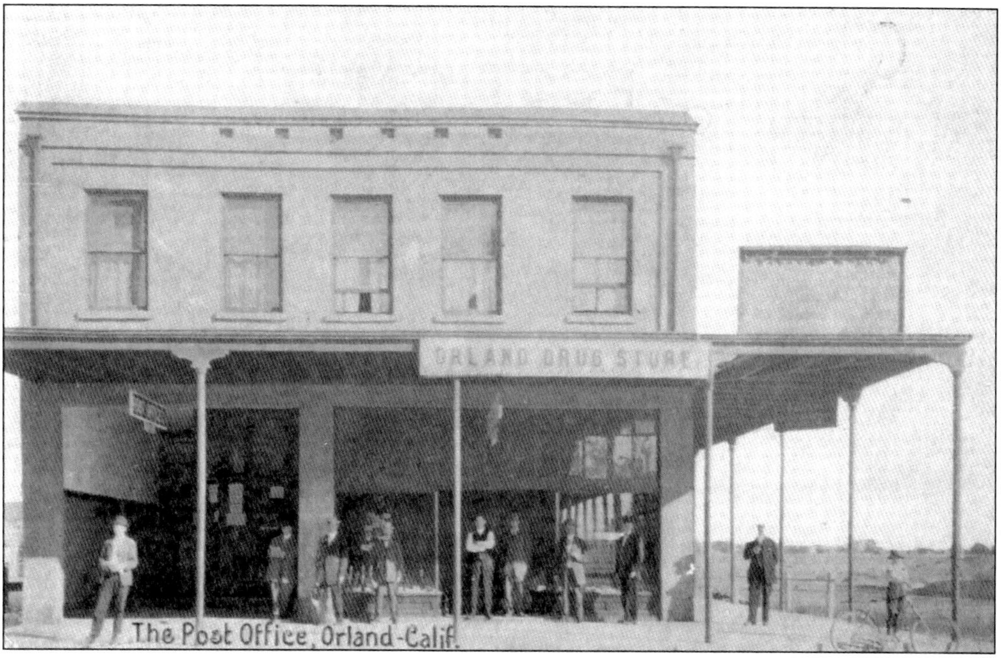

The Barceloux-Iglick Building, constructed in 1909, was at the northwest corner of Fourth and Walker Streets and housed important early Orland businesses. On the ground floor, the Orland Drug Store was operated by Michael T. Harrington when he first moved to Orland from Willows. The U.S. Post Office was in the west half, and Dr. George Rawlins had his dental office upstairs.

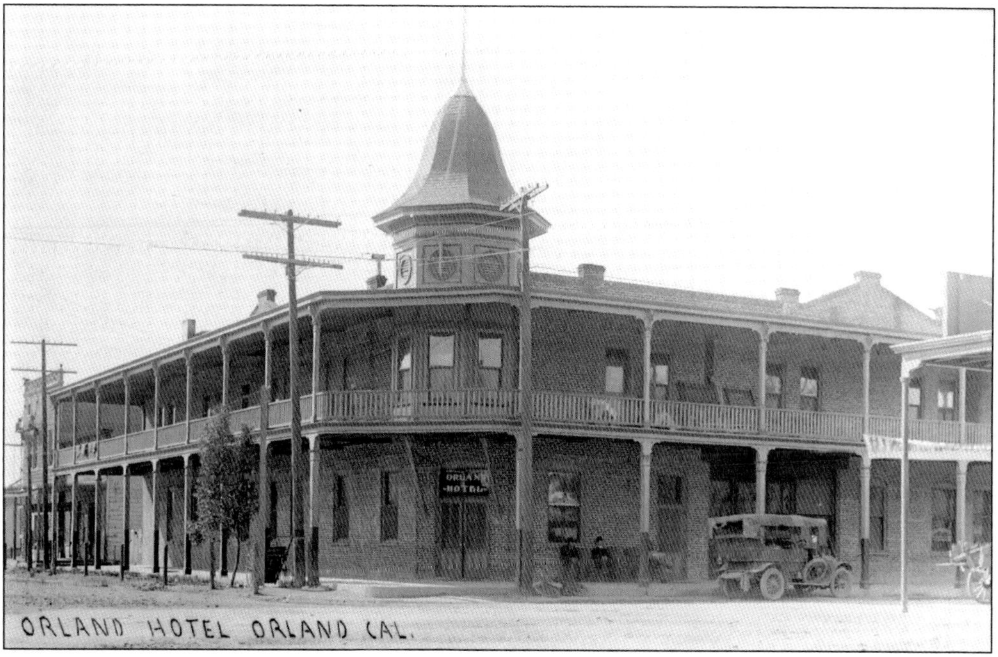

Construction of the Orland Hotel, located at the corner of Fourth and Walker Streets, was started January 20, 1902. The building contained a dining room, kitchen, large office, barbershop, and 27 sleeping rooms. Projections estimated the two-story structure would contain 400,000 bricks and cost $20,000.

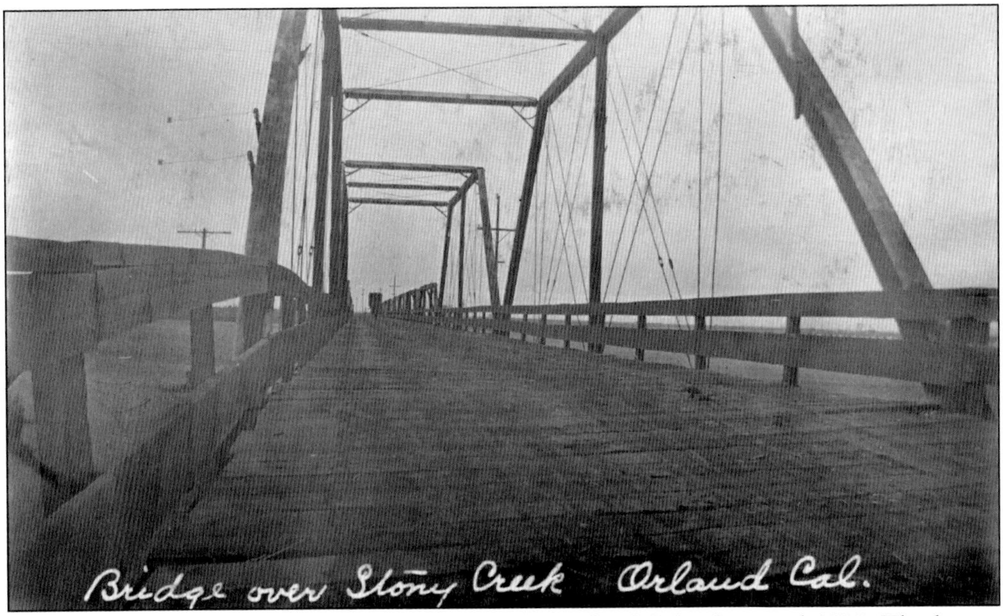

This is the early truss bridge across Stony Creek north of Orland around 1900. The horse-and-buggy on the wooden planked bridge is traveling in a northerly direction away from the photographer. This bridge was removed after the completion of the concrete bridge built to the left of this structure in 1913–1914.

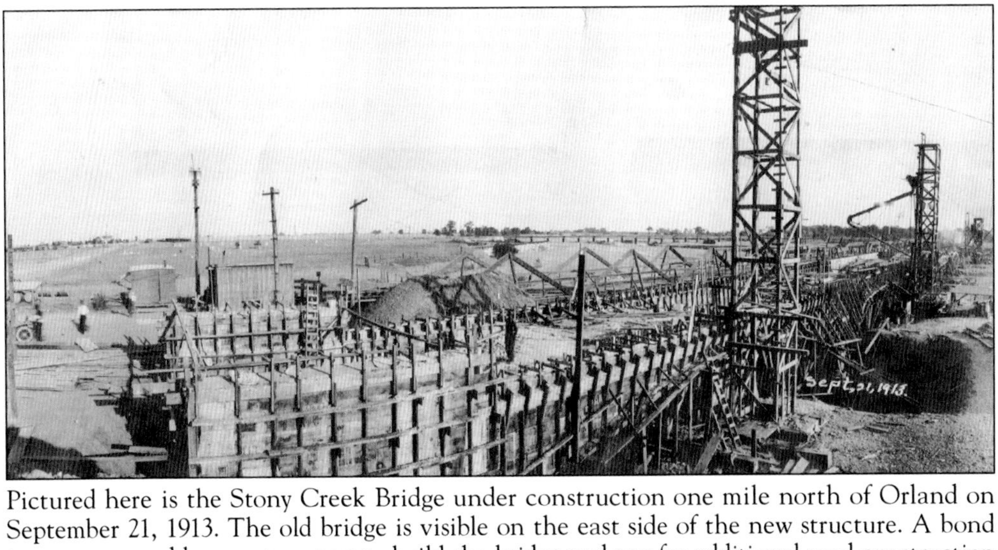

Pictured here is the Stony Creek Bridge under construction one mile north of Orland on September 21, 1913. The old bridge is visible on the east side of the new structure. A bond issue was passed by county voters to build the bridge and pay for additional road construction in other parts of Glenn County. The Masonic Cemetery and the railroad bridge can be seen in the background.

Two

Orland Irrigation Project

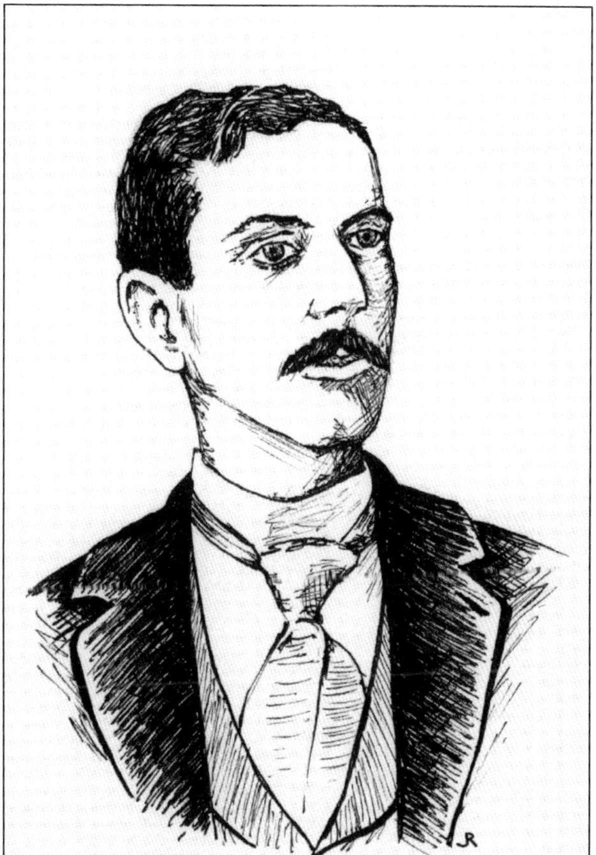

William Semple Green, the state's pioneer irrigationist and "The Father of Irrigation on the Westside," was the first to suggest that Stony Creek water should be captured for use as irrigation on the dry lands in the Orland area. As a "disciple" of Green, Frank S. Reager (right) became an early advocate for bringing a dependable and steady supply of water to Orland farmers and is generally credited with being the prime mover for the organization of the Orland Irrigation Project. He traveled throughout the local area signing up landowners to take the water and made several cross-country trips to Washington, D.C., to secure Congressional appropriations for construction of the first federally funded irrigation project on the West Coast. Besides being an irrigationist, Reager was a respected educator, banker, merchant, farmer, and historian.

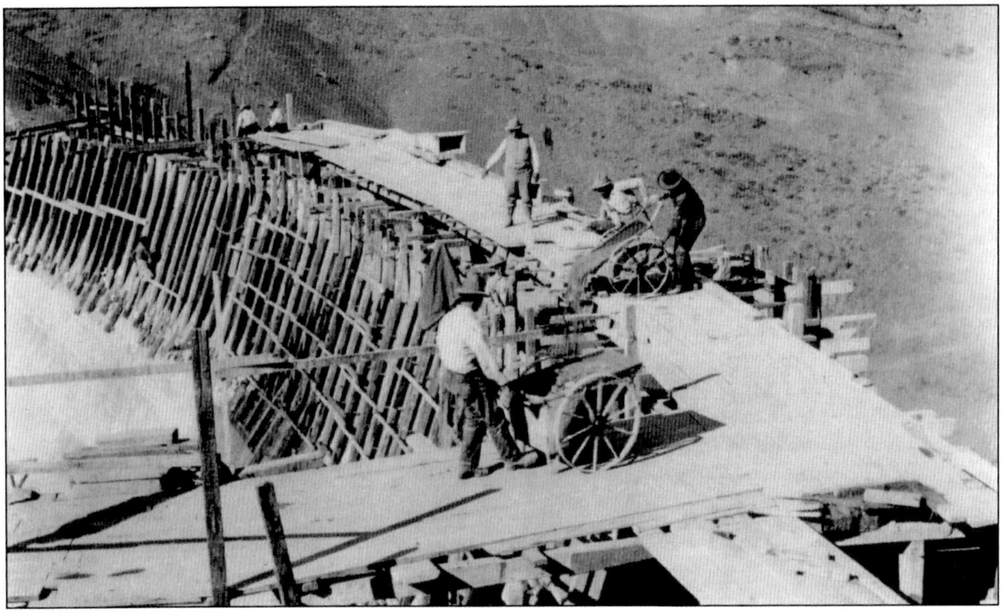

The Orland Irrigation Project, one of the oldest federal reclamation projects in the country, was authorized by Secretary of the Interior James R. Garfield on October 5, 1907. The U.S. Reclamation Service announced on October 5, 1908, that the Stanley Contracting Company of San Francisco had submitted the winning bid for the construction of East Park Dam, a spillway, and dikes. Preliminary work had started at the dam site by August 1908, and materials had to be hauled in wagons drawn by six-horse teams over 18 miles of winding road. Equipment included donkey engines, gasoline engines, pile drivers, scrapers, wheelbarrows, and construction supplies. Stanley's men began actual work on June 11, 1909. In September, they hit bedrock 50 feet below the bed of Little Stony Creek. No one was killed during construction of the dam, and only three workers were reported injured from 1908 to 1910. (Both courtesy Orland Unit Water Users' Association.)

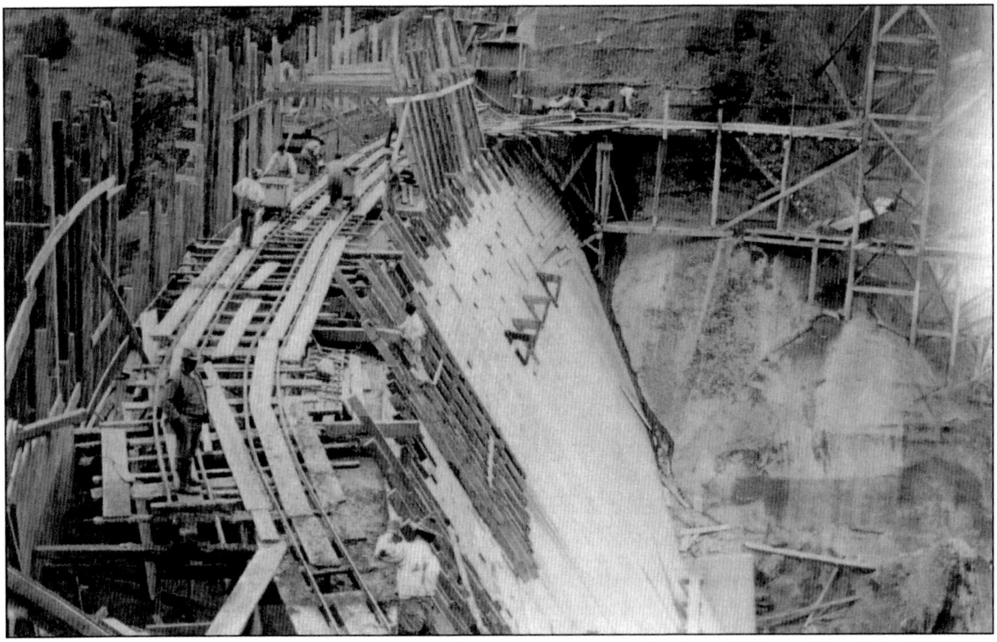

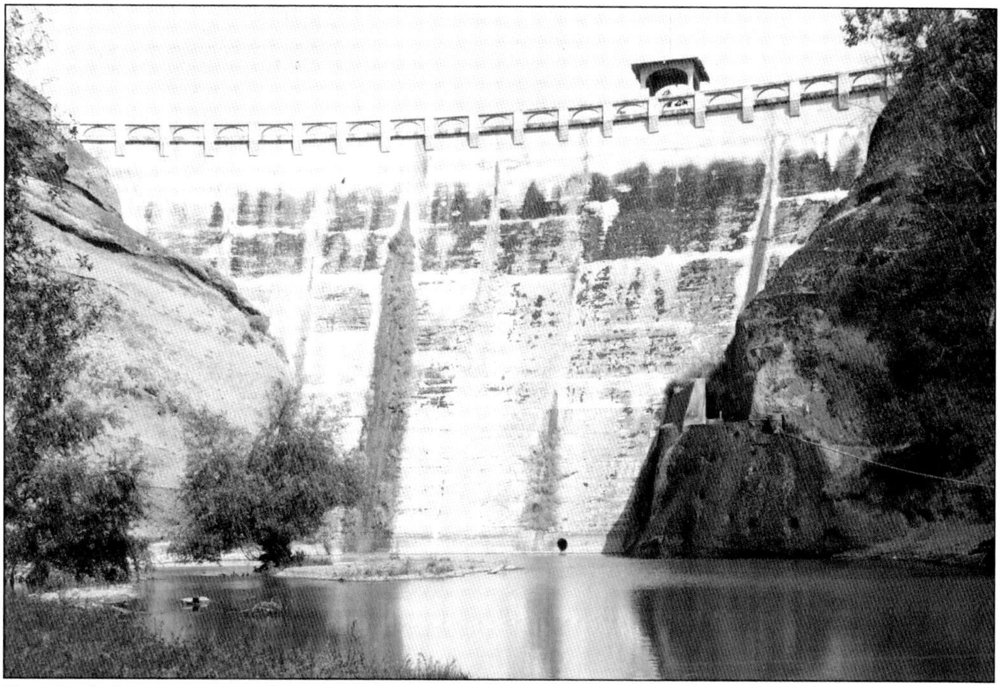

East Park Dam is situated 60 miles southwest of Orland near the town of Stonyford. Because of the narrow opening between the two bluffs, the site was the perfect location for a dam. The Stanley Contracting Company bid had been the third lowest at $79,881.65. The concrete-arch, gravity-type dam is 139 feet in height and 250 feet in width. The dam is 10 feet thick at the top and 86 feet thick at the bottom. The completed dam contains 12,200 cubic yards of concrete and impounds a reservoir of 51,000 acre-feet when full. Much of the land now at the bottom of the reservoir was owned by J. F. Easton, and a grove of oak trees there was known to area residents as Easton Park, later abbreviated "East Park."

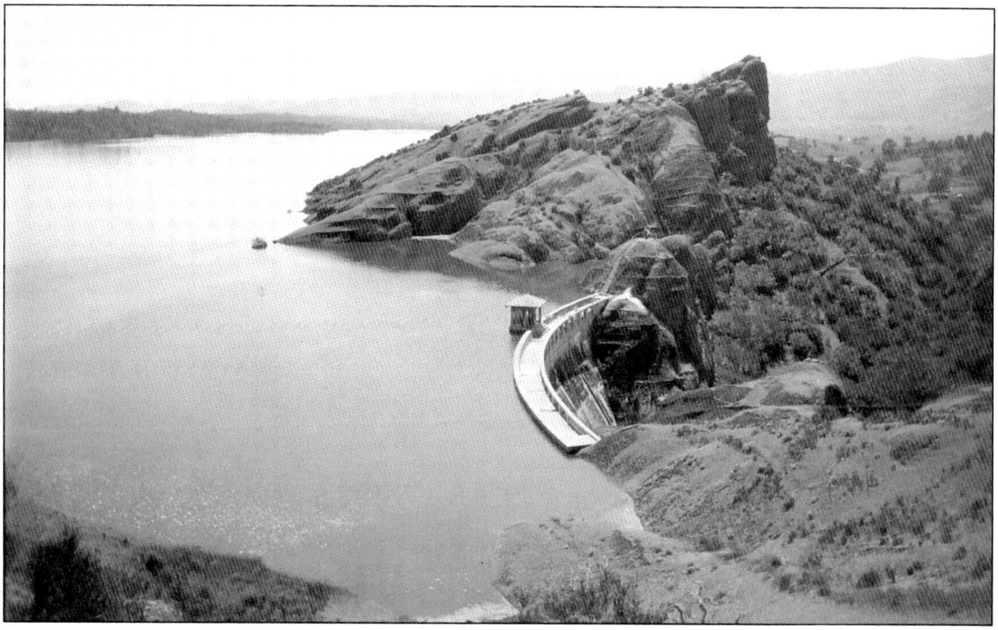

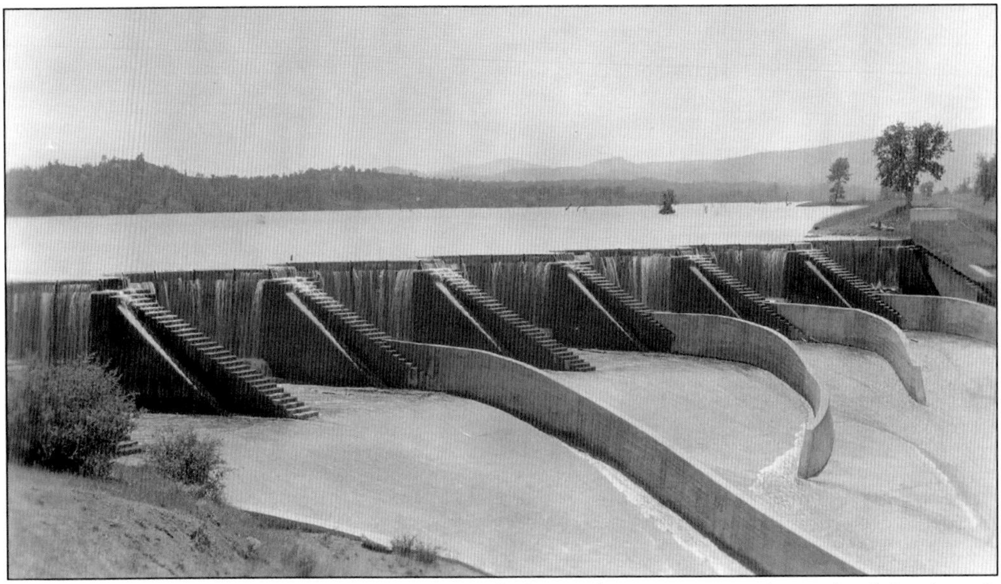

The unique spillway at East Park Dam is actually located one-quarter mile south of the dam. It has a length of 460 feet and a height of 12 feet. The spillway is 85 feet above the Little Stony Creek bed and is of multiple-arch section construction.

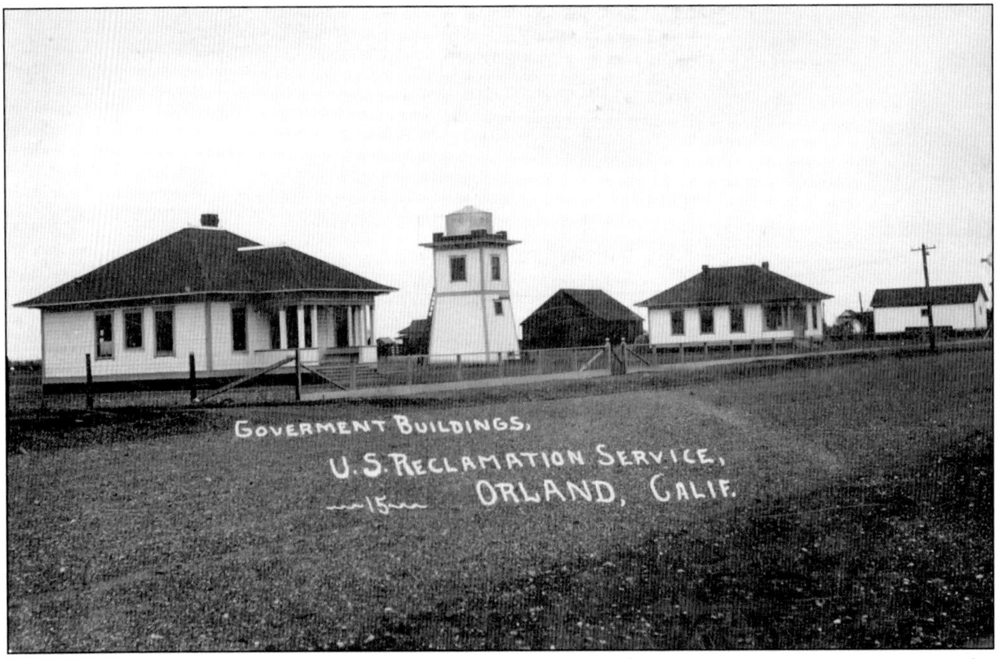

A 10-acre tract of land on Eighth Street was purchased at $37.50 per acre in January 1908 for Orland Project buildings. By summer, offices and headquarters for the engineers, two wells, a shed, and a storeroom were under construction by local contractor A. J. Harelson. Five or six acres were to be set aside for a small experimental farm under the supervision of the U.S. Department of Agriculture.

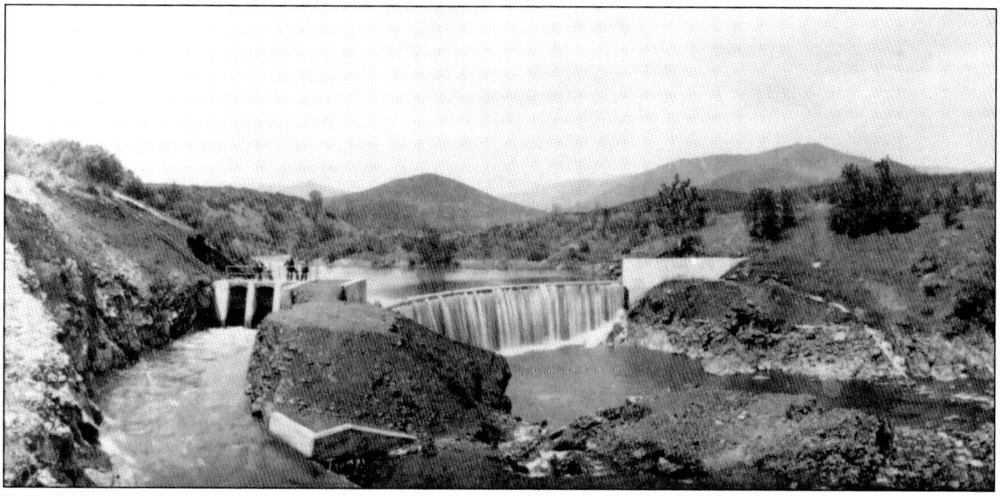

Rainbow Dam is a 25-foot dam that diverts water from Big Stony Creek to East Park Reservoir. The contract to build the diverting dam was awarded in the spring of 1914. Frank Reager named the dam for the rainbow colors often seen at the waterfall. (Courtesy Special Collections, Meriam Library, California State University, Chico.)

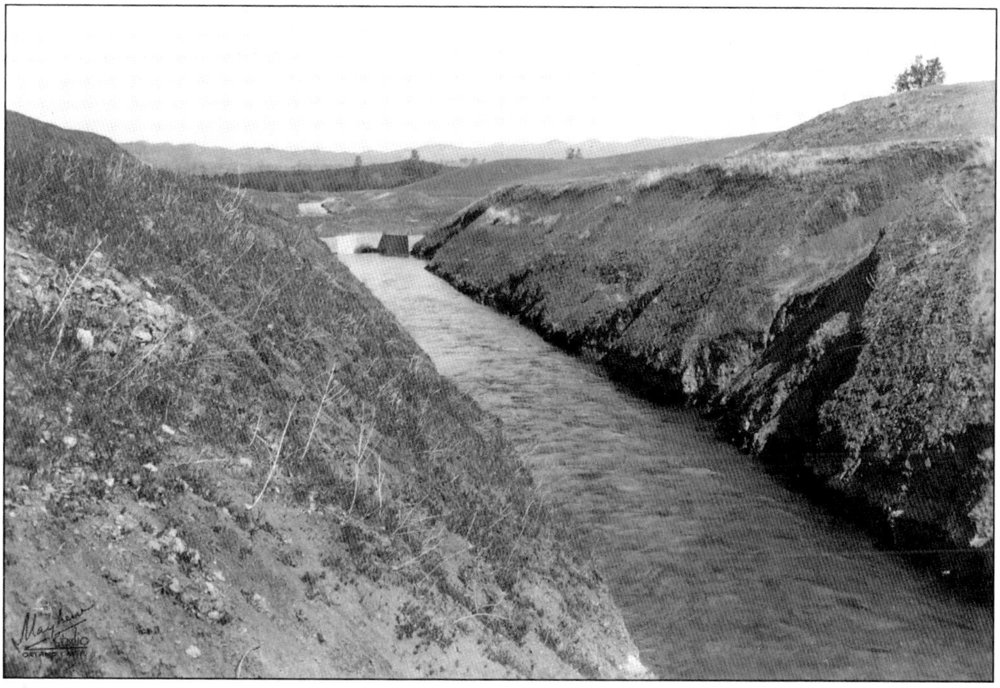

The Big Stony Creek feed canal was a separate project from the construction of the diversion dam. The contract to build the six-and-one-half-mile canal to East Park Reservoir was awarded to P. Schuyler of Oakland for $53,130 in the fall of 1913.

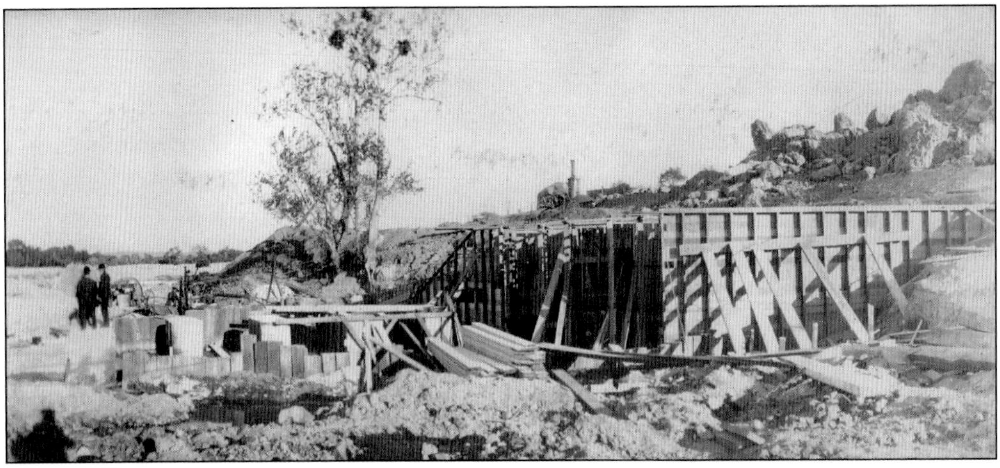

Stony Creek exits the foothills at a point known as the Miller Buttes. Located 10 miles west of Orland, this was the site for the first of two diversion dams to divert water into the irrigation project's south canal. The first load of materials left Orland in July 1908 and included tents, lumber, and materials to be used in establishing a camp for the work crew to construct the 800-foot-long dam. Engineers had to design the structure to withstand a heavy volume of water during flood times flowing over the diversion dam, as well as the strain of diverting water into the canal. That summer and fall of 1908, about 30 men and a number of six-horse teams were working on the dam, head gate, and canal.

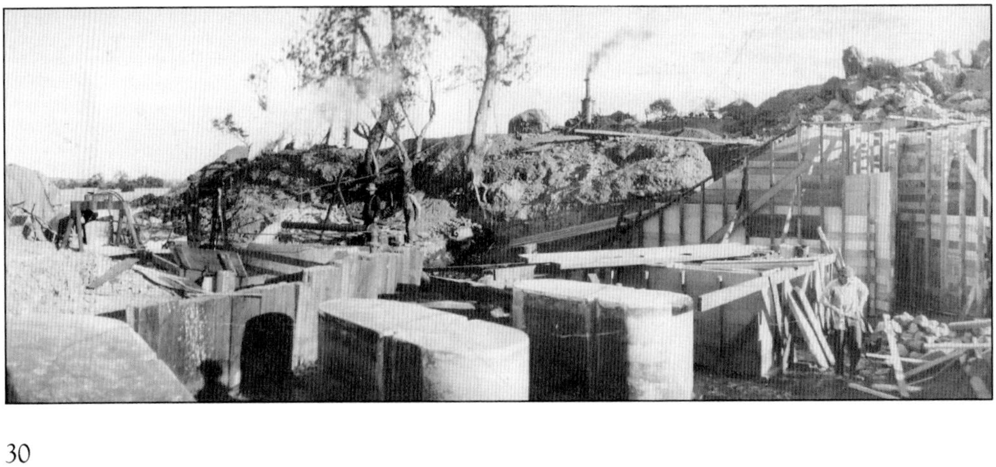

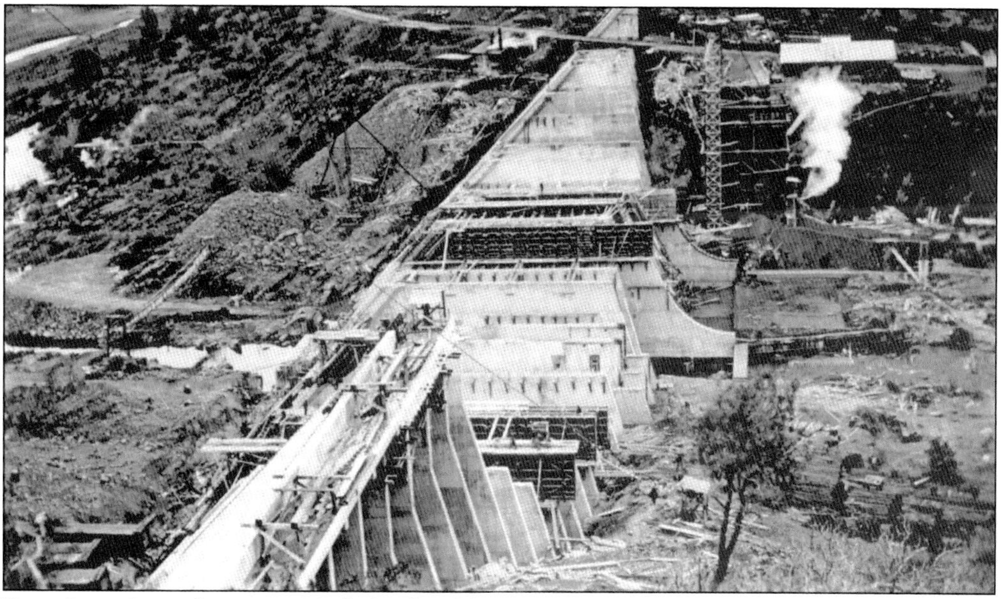

Drought and crop losses in 1924 led to local farmers and water users to agitate for an additional dam and reservoir on Stony Creek. Appropriations were approved by Congress and signed by President Coolidge in May 1926. The $1,100,000 contract was awarded to Ambersen Construction Company of New York City. Hundreds joined the car caravan on May 3, 1927, to travel to the concrete pouring ceremony at the dam site near Elk Creek. (Courtesy Orland Unit Water Users' Association.)

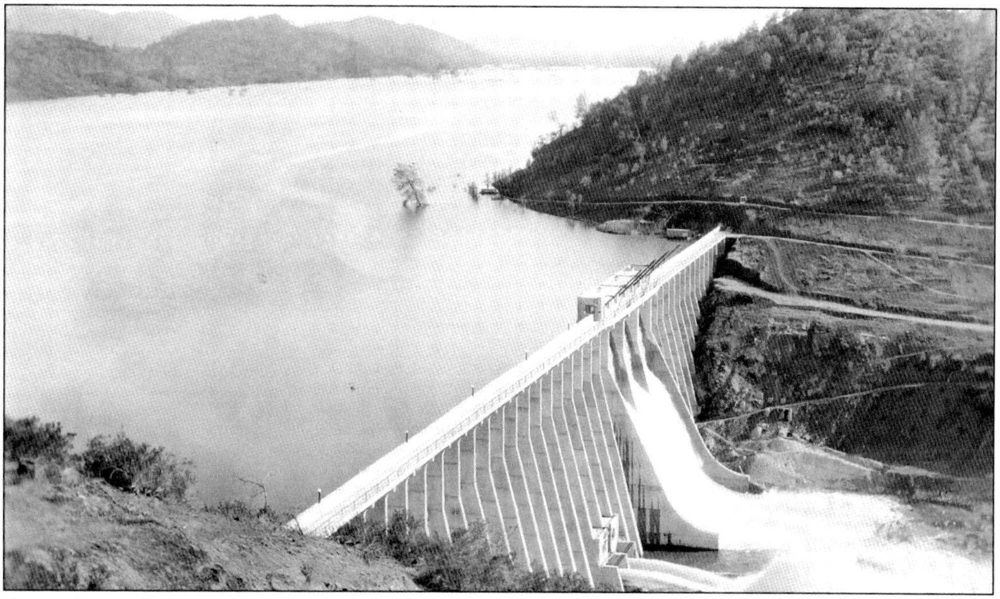

Stony Gorge Dam is 40 miles from Orland and was completed in October 1928. The height of the dam is 142.5 feet, and it has a length of 868 feet. Stony Gorge Reservoir is one-half mile wide and five miles in length. To mark the completion of the dam, special celebrations were held, first at the dam and then at the Glenn County Fairgrounds. Three thousand people were in attendance to hear special music, listen to featured speakers, and partake in one of the community's biggest barbeques.

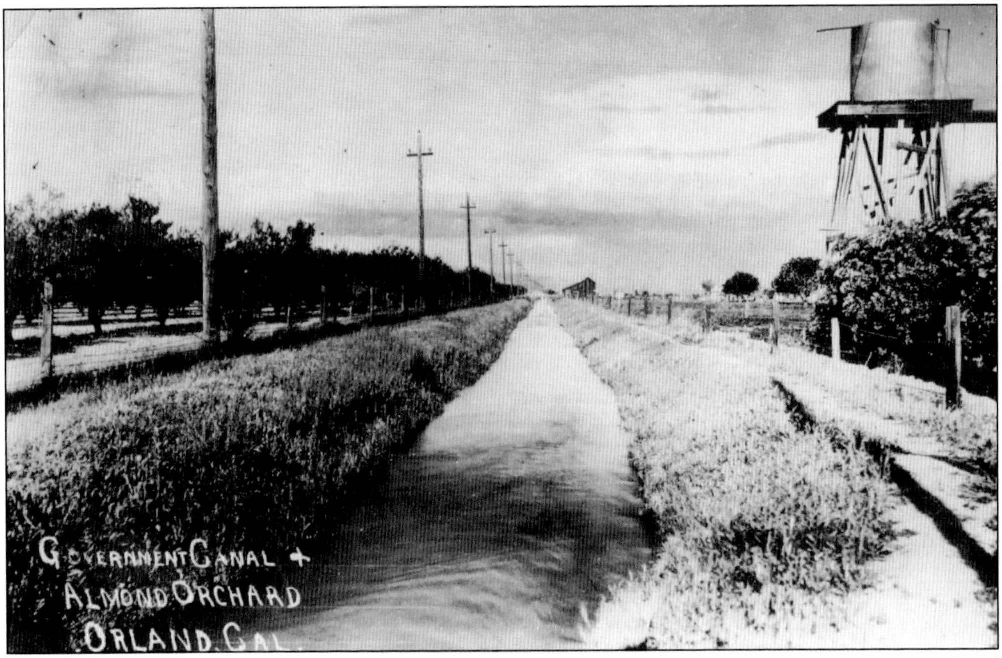

There are approximately 146 miles of canals and laterals in the distribution system of the Orland Irrigation Project. Most are now lined with concrete, but that was not the case in the early years of the project when this c. 1930 real-photo postcard was prepared.

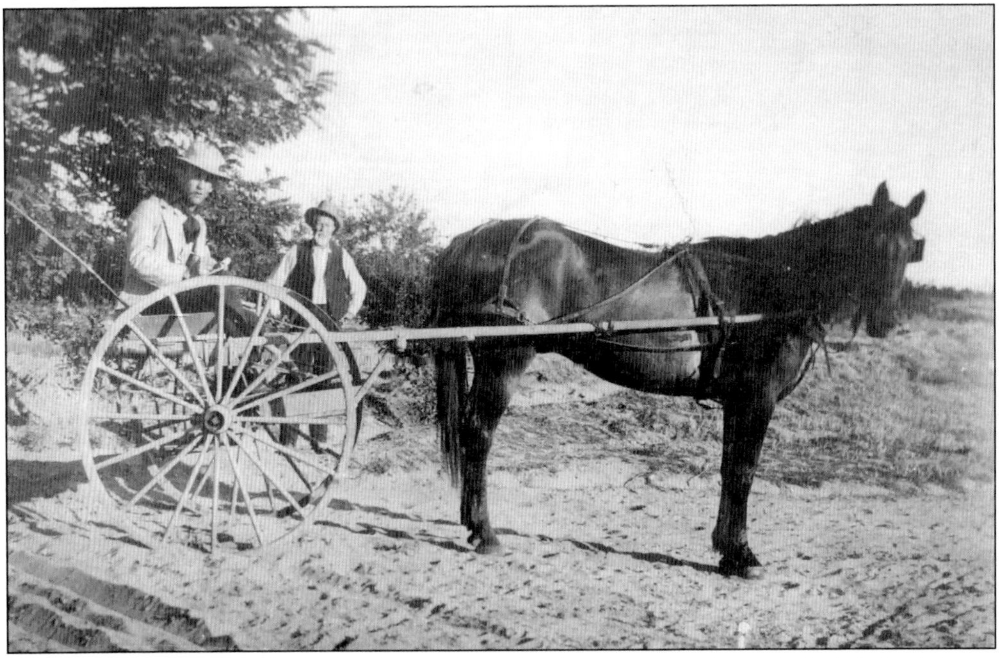
Phil Bollinger was an early ditch rider on the Orland Project. His duties included checking to make sure there was a good head of water flowing in the main ditch and notifying irrigators the day, hour, and length of time they would have the water. Documentation would have been kept in a journal for the water master and office workers. He probably had to provide his own means of transportation.

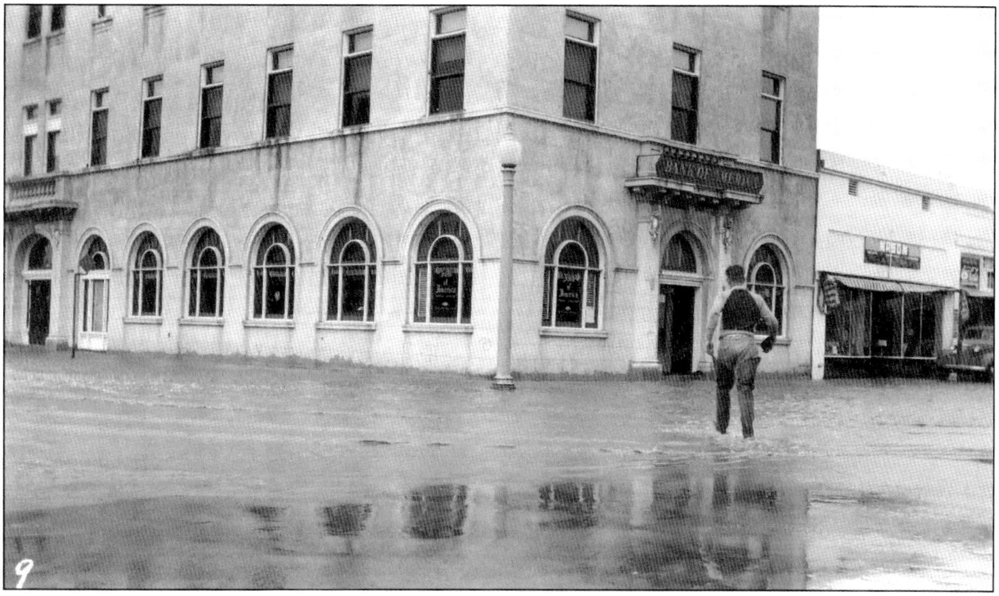

There have been a number of floods in the land of Orland since its founding in 1875–1876. Record rainfalls in 1878, 1909, 1915, and 1940 have resulted in the loss of livestock, damage to personal property, and the inundation of the downtown business district. On the evening of February 27, 1940, Stony Creek burst its bank and spread over a large territory. Floodwaters were increased by the overflow from both East Park and Stony Gorge Reservoirs. The general alarm was sounded the next morning at 6:30 a.m. as water began pouring southward down Highway 99 West through the arch toward Orland. Sandbag barriers were able to divert much of the water away from the business section. At 10:00 a.m., water was within two inches of entering the Bank of America at the corner of Fourth and Colusa Streets. The flood peaked shortly after 1:00 p.m., and waters rapidly receded during the afternoon. (Below courtesy Jack Bucke.)

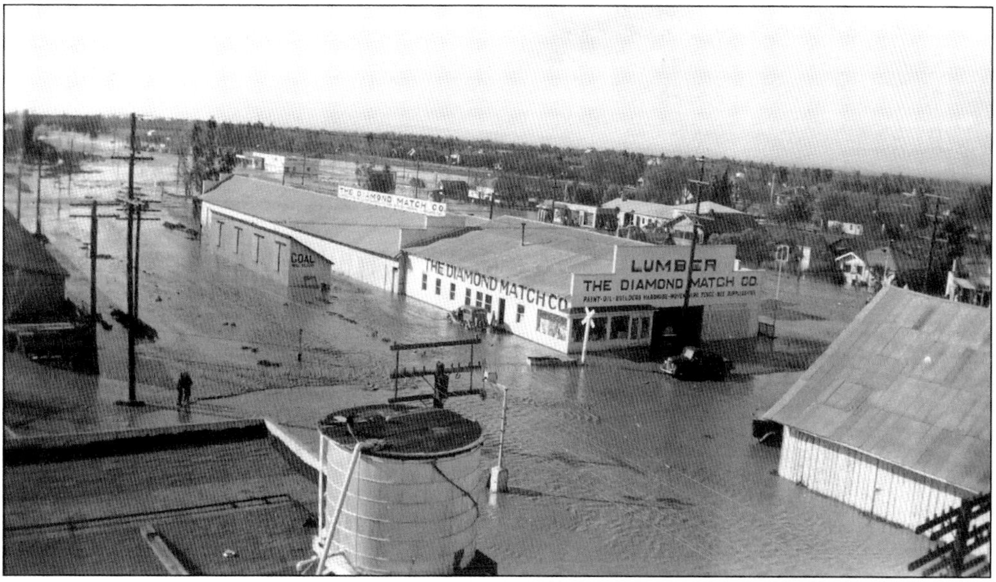

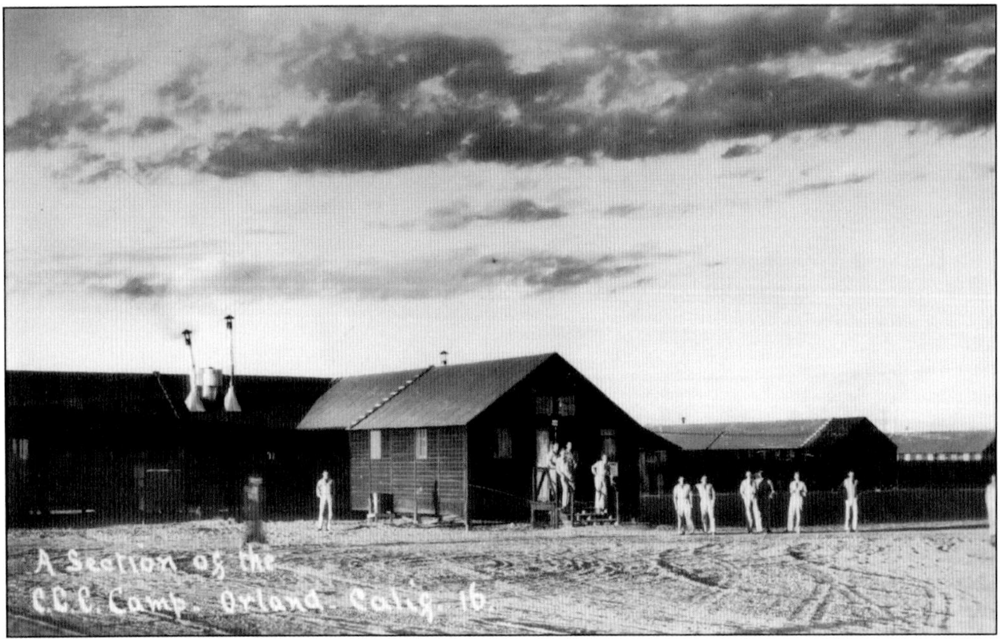

A Civilian Conservation Camp (CCC) for Orland was authorized on March 7, 1938, after a two-year effort by the Orland Unit Water Users' Association. Camp Orland was designated Camp Big Creek No. 1578 and was situated on a 10-acre site one half mile west of town. The CCC enrollees, many from Kentucky, Mississippi, North Carolina, and southern Ohio, were used in enlarging ditches, raising banks, cleaning canals, eradicating weeds, and lining canals with concrete. Camp Orland enrollees lived in barracks (shown above) and participated in a full range of academic, athletic, and social activities. Camp Orland closed in November 1941, and the enrollees entrained to Camp Newlands, a Reclamation Bureau camp, at Fallon, Nevada, to continue the same sort of work done so well in the Orland Project.

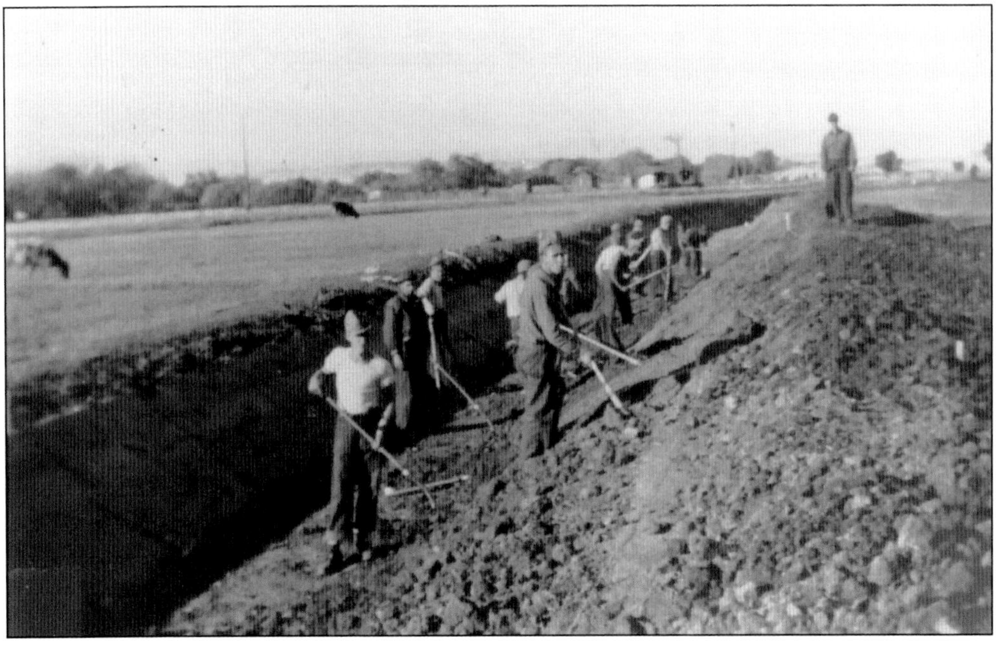

Three

THE FRUITFUL LAND

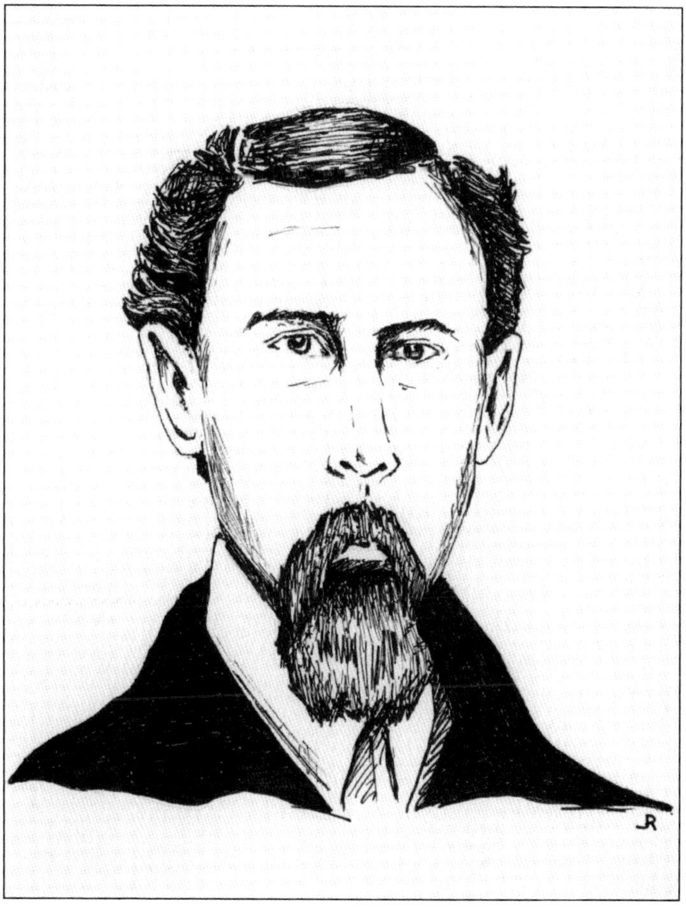

Samuel Crawford Cleek brought his bride, Elizabeth Gillet, to Orland in 1877 from Virginia. As one of Orland's earliest settlers, Cleek established his one-acre farm and within two decades brought national attention to Orland's agricultural potential. "Uncle Sammy" was scoffed at when he planted his first orange and lemon trees in the early 1880s. However, many local farmers soon planted their own orange orchards when it was determined that the area's soil was suited for citrus fruit. Orland's pioneer orange grower and first horticulturalist passed away on November 30, 1903.

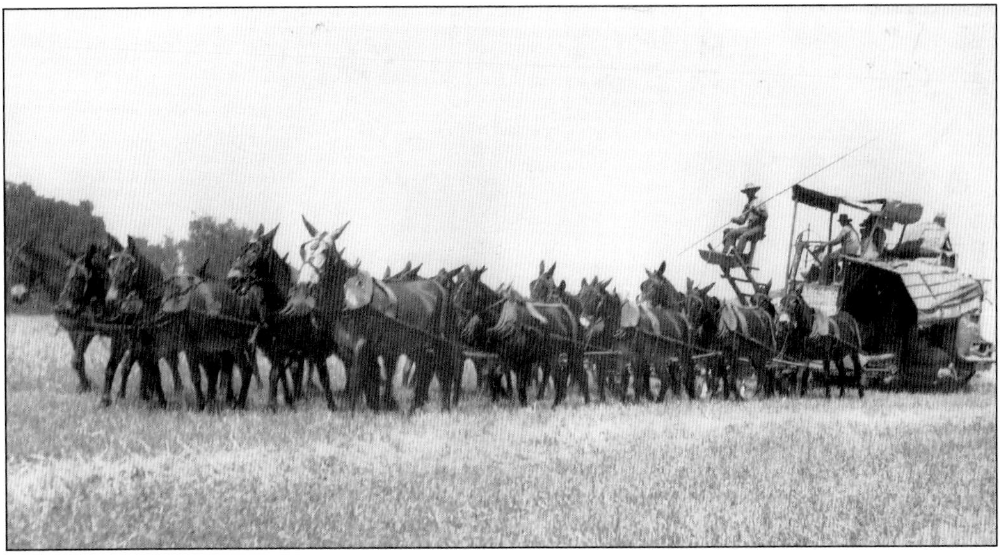

Mules were excellent draft animals, as seen in this typical harvest scene around 1900. Mules required less care than horses, were steadier workers, were healthier, ate less, and were less affected by the area's hot weather. A fair-sized part of the ranch, however, had to be devoted to growing the feed for these surprisingly intelligent animals.

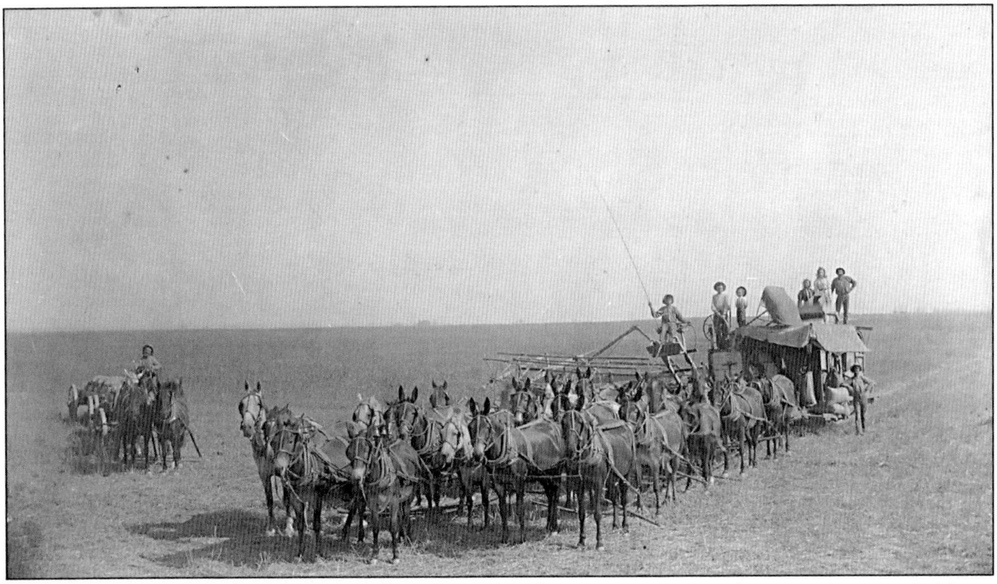

Commercial photographer George Collom from San Francisco took this photograph of the Schluter and Mordhorst harvester around 1890. Grain and barley were early crops grown on the Colusa Plains. The harvesting crew are, from left to right, Gus Mezenberger (driving wagon), Gus Schluter (driving harvester), Henry Jasper (header tender), Howe Schluter, Emma Schluter, Alma Schluter, John Mordhorst (machine boss), and unidentified (sack sewer). (Courtesy Ruth Reimers.)

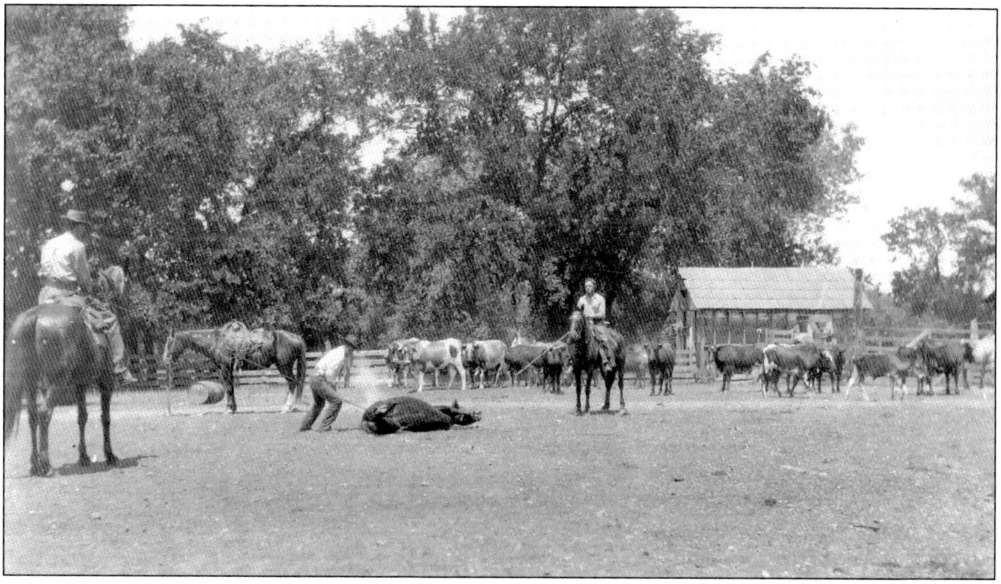

Granville Swift was an "open range" rancher, meaning he never actually owned any land but controlled strategic watering places. In 1850, Swift bought Thomas O. Larkin's cattle and brand, and grazed his vast herd over this part of the valley. In 1852, he was assessed for 2,000 cattle at $12 per head. Branding is shown in this postcard cancelled in Orland on May 29, 1914.

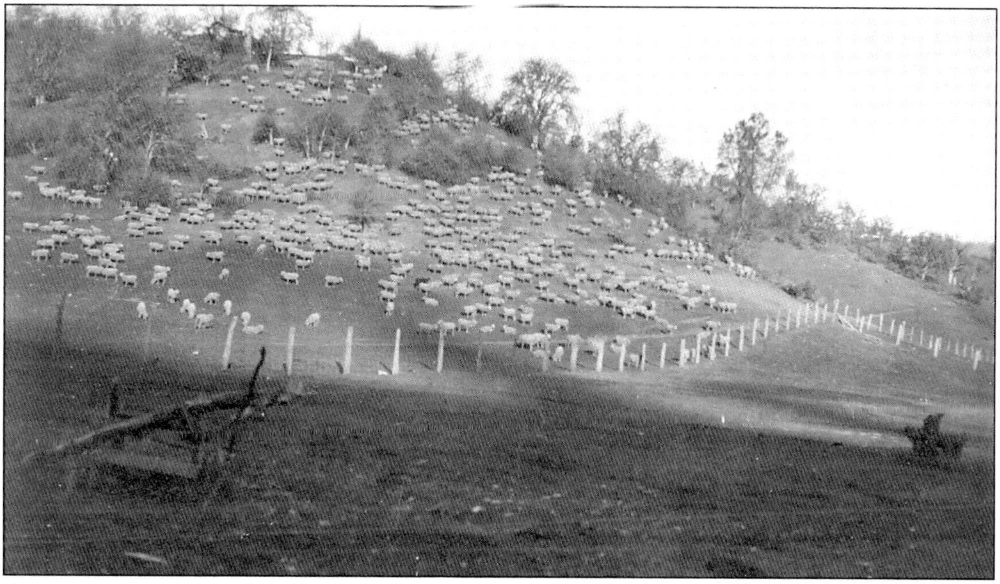

Sheep were an early and profitable industry in the Orland area, especially in the foothill country to the west. Early sheep ranchers had flocks numbering in the thousands, and many bands were driven from valley fields to Coast Range (even Sierra) meadows for summer grazing. Lambing takes place in December and January, with most animals being kept out in the open year-round. Wool was clipped twice a year by itinerant crews.

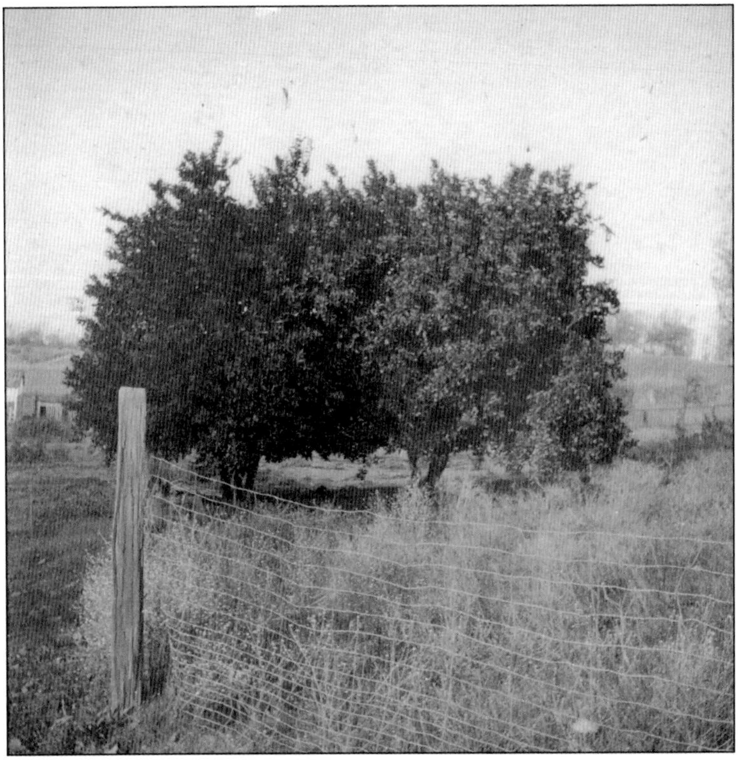

The first orange trees in the land of Orland were planted in 1863 by Lois (Mrs. I. W.) Brownell from oranges given to her son Harry, who was ill with scarlet fever. A compassionate stranger took three oranges from his saddle bags and gave them to Harry. Lois Brownell planted the seeds that were inside the oranges, and two trees grew. These original orange trees, shown above, were destroyed about 1950. Harry died a few days after receiving the oranges.

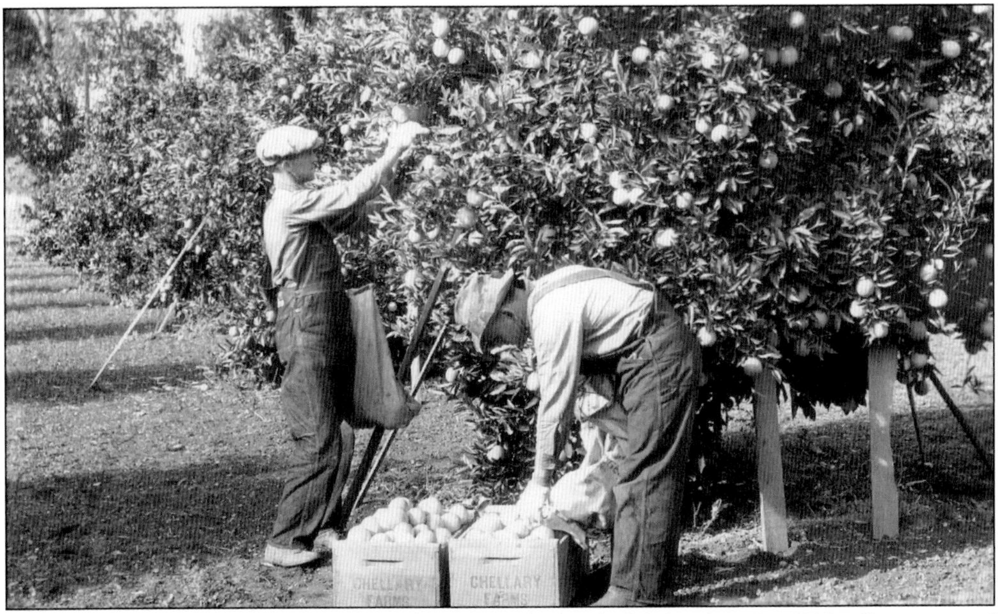

Orland orchards were plentiful and productive in the land of Orland in the 1920s. Organizers of the Orland Orange Growers Association, Inc., had hopes of signing 50 local growers to adopt the constitution and bylaws in August 1923. Plans called for having a 50-by-60-foot packinghouse with railroad siding ready to serve members for picking and packing the navel crop that November. The large, dark blue, orange crate label depicting East Park Dam inside the letter "O" was created at this same time.

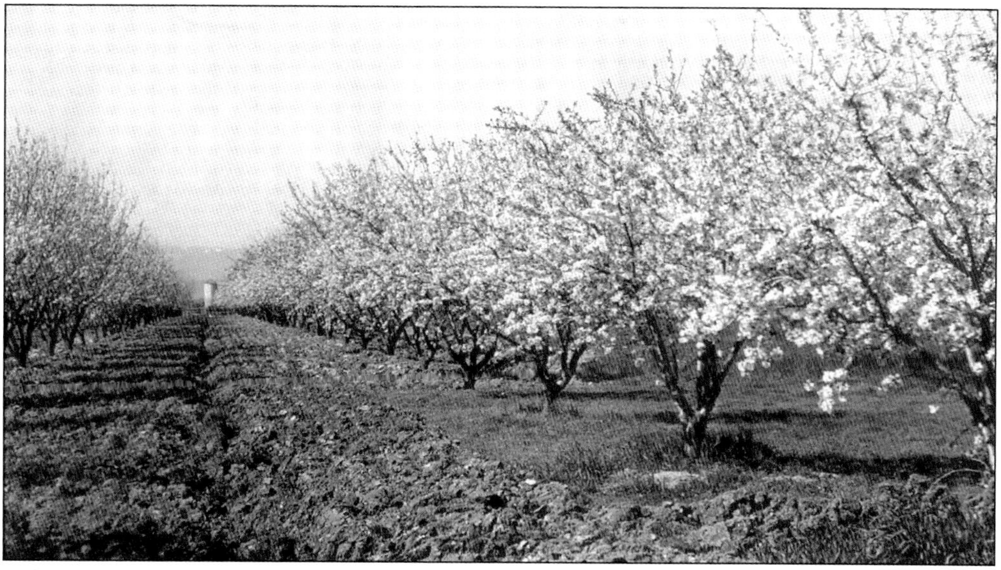

Orland almond orchards are in full bloom in February and are mature by late August or September. P. D. Bane planted the first almond orchard in the area around 1900 and brought home blue ribbons from exhibiting his Orland-grown almonds at the 1904 World's Fair and Louisiana Purchase Exposition in St. Louis, Missouri. The photograph of the blooming Orland almond trees was taken in the late 1930s.

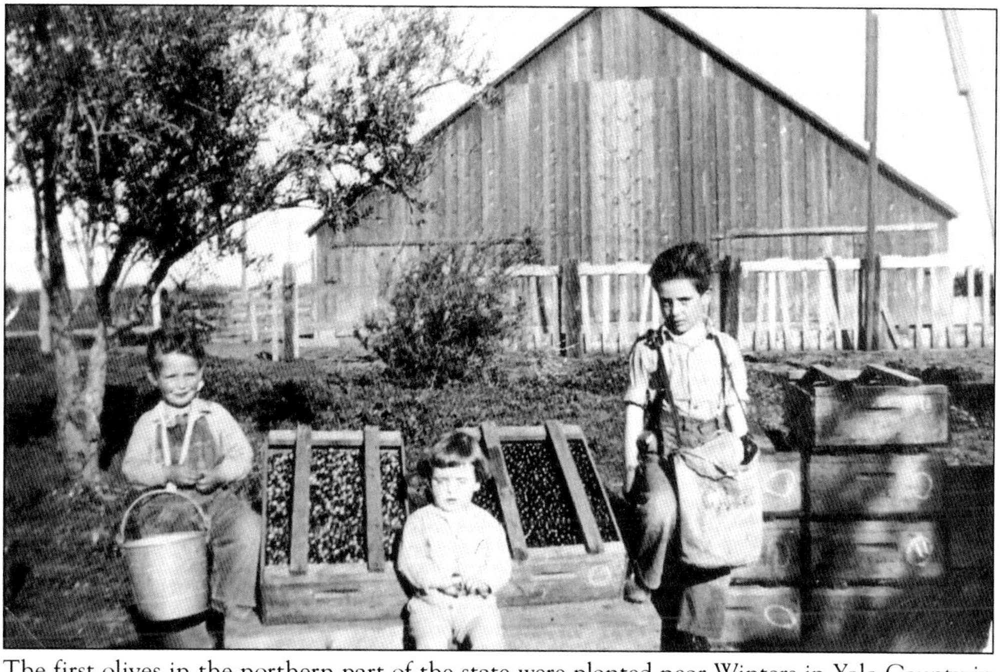

The first olives in the northern part of the state were planted near Winters in Yolo County in 1865. Cuttings from these mission olive trees were planted all over the Sacramento Valley. Acreage was sufficient by 1927 for the formation of the Orland Olive Growers Association. Frank Aguiar came from the Azores in the 1920s and started planting olives on his property west of Orland. Pictured from left to right are Frank's sons George, Louis, and Lawrence Aguiar helping with the olive harvest in the mid-1930s. (Courtesy Aguiar Ranch.)

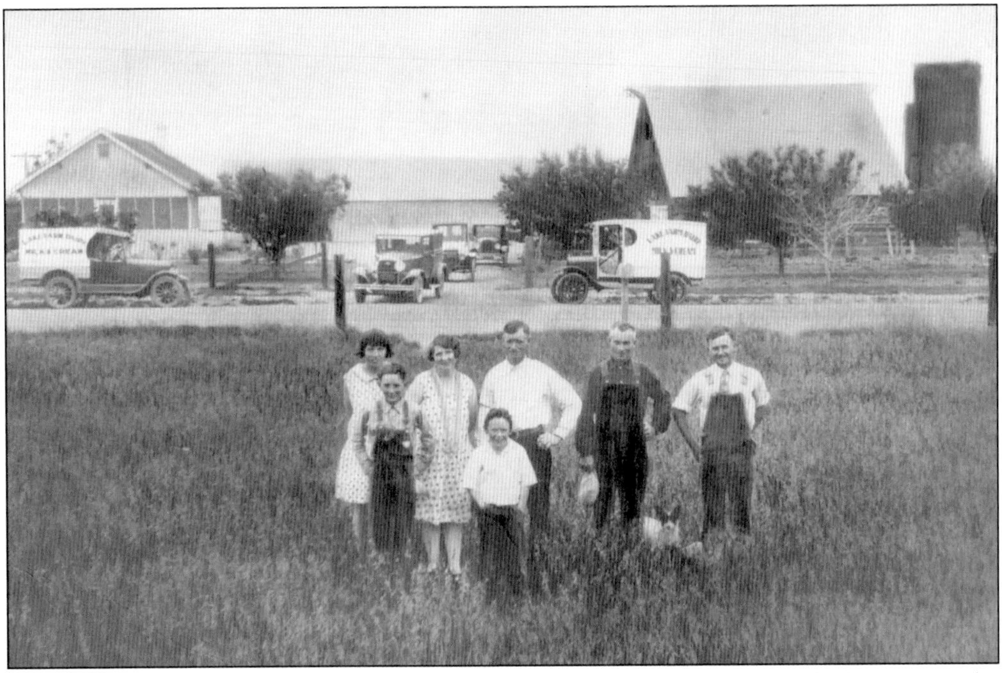

Orland was recognized as one of the principal dairying sections of the state in the late 1910s. The Lake Farm Dairy had a herd of 30–35 cows in 1928 when the owners posed for this photograph. Standing in their alfalfa field, from left to right, are (first row) Bob Gilmore and Joseph "Buzz" Gilmore; (second row) Mildred Gilmore, Isabelle "Bella" Gilmore, Robert Gilmore, Isaac Kernahan, and Bill McCaughey. (Courtesy Bruce Gilmore.)

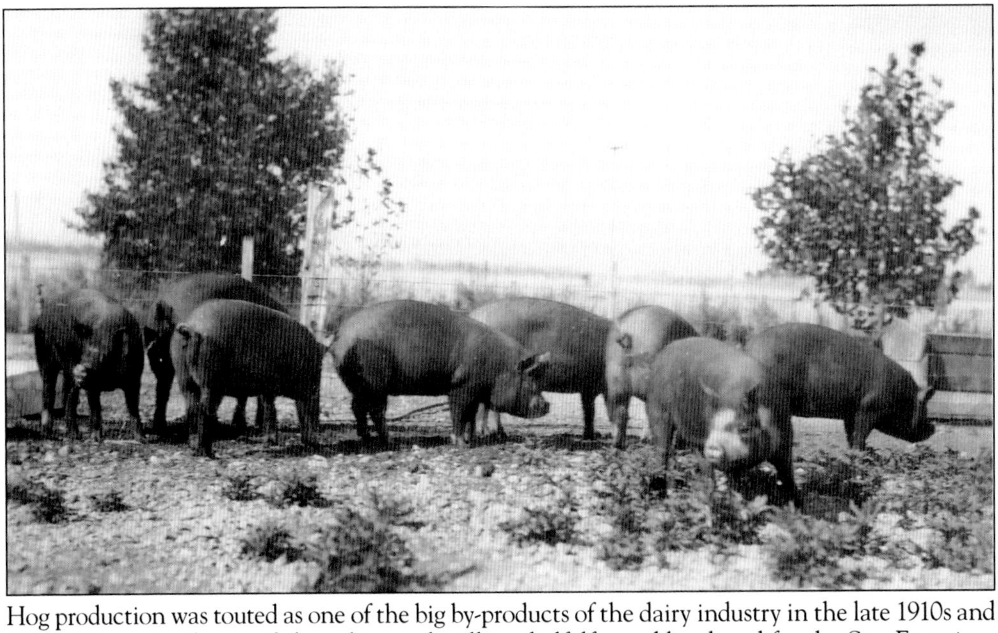

Hog production was touted as one of the big by-products of the dairy industry in the late 1910s and 1920s. The animals were fed on skimmed milk and alfalfa, and hardened for the San Francisco markets on corn.

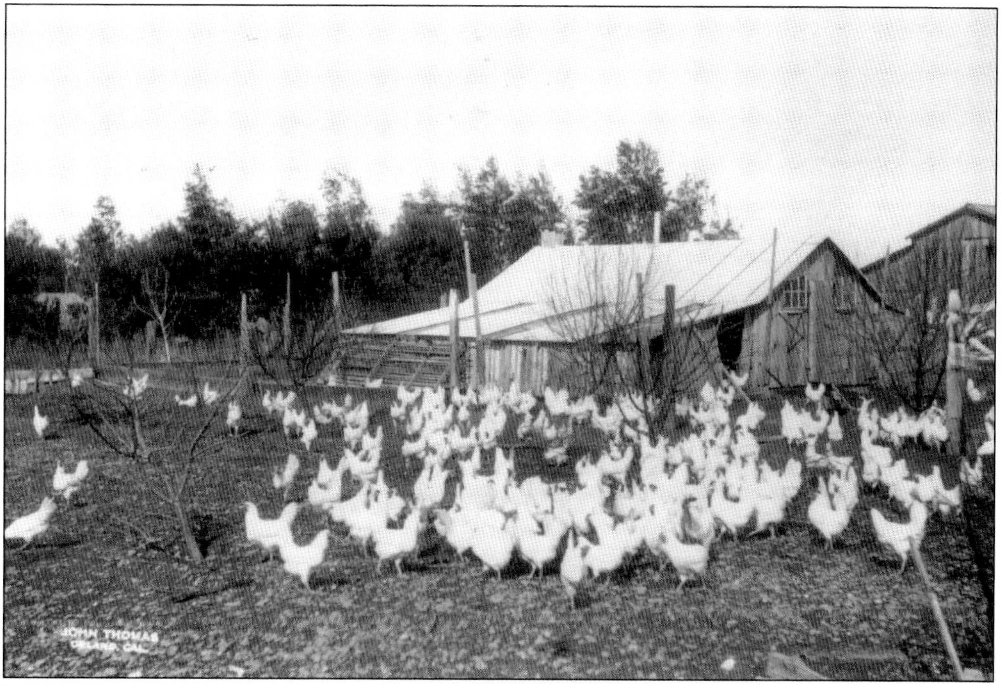

Poultry was once a major industry in the Orland area with chickens being shipped to the San Francisco and Los Angeles markets, and millions of eggs were processed by the poultry cooperative. White leghorns were the favorite breed. Shown is W. H. Macy's chicken ranch east of Orland. Macy had success raising his birds in a young orchard before the trees came into bearing. (Courtesy California History Room, California State Library, Sacramento, California.)

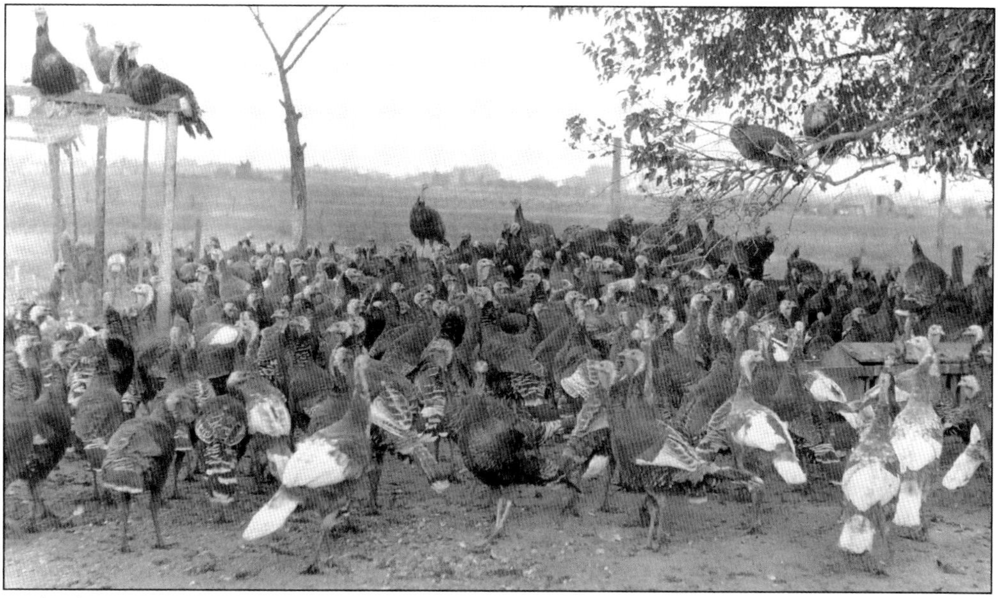

In the late 1930s, Orland turkeys were shipped all over the West Coast for the holiday markets. Most of the turkeys were handled through the California Turkey Growers Association. Some of the local flocks numbered 10,000 birds and were herded in much the same manner as are sheep, with a small shepherd dog being used by the herders.

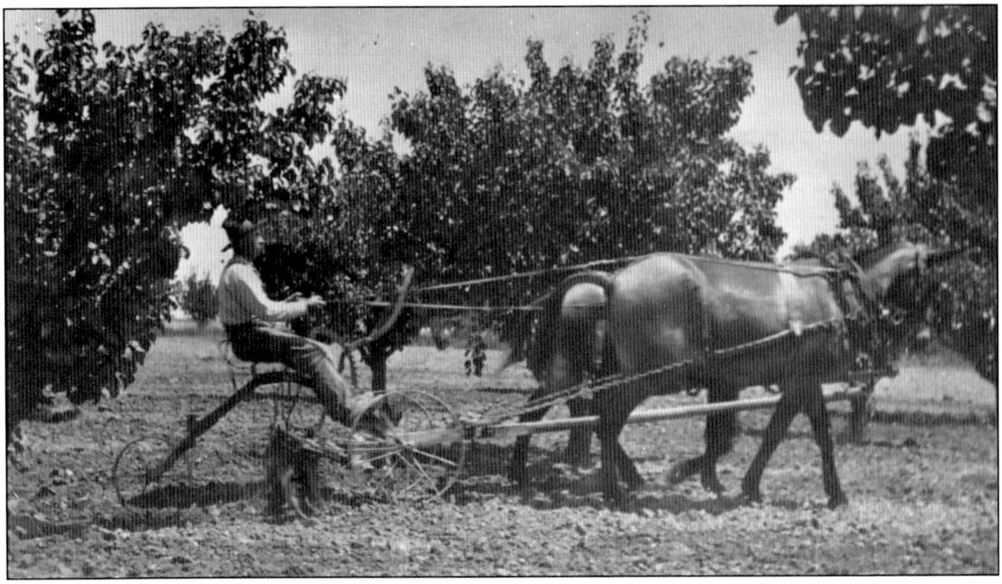

Adelbert "Del" Harelson is shown cultivating his orchard using a steel two-horse cultivator. The orchard was bounded by Yolo, Marin, Central, and East Streets, and later became the Harelson Addition to the city of Orland.

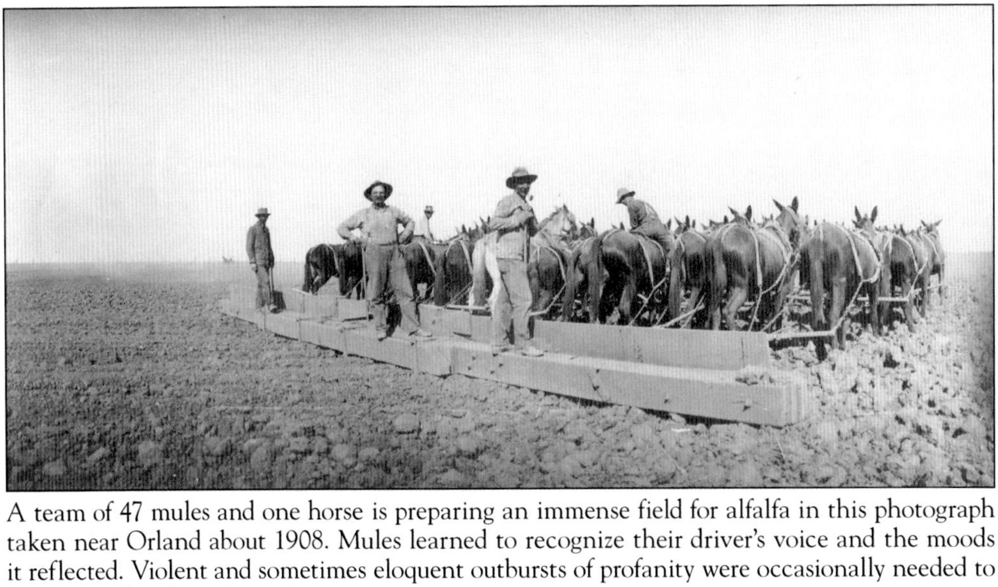

A team of 47 mules and one horse is preparing an immense field for alfalfa in this photograph taken near Orland about 1908. Mules learned to recognize their driver's voice and the moods it reflected. Violent and sometimes eloquent outbursts of profanity were occasionally needed to get more effort from the mules.

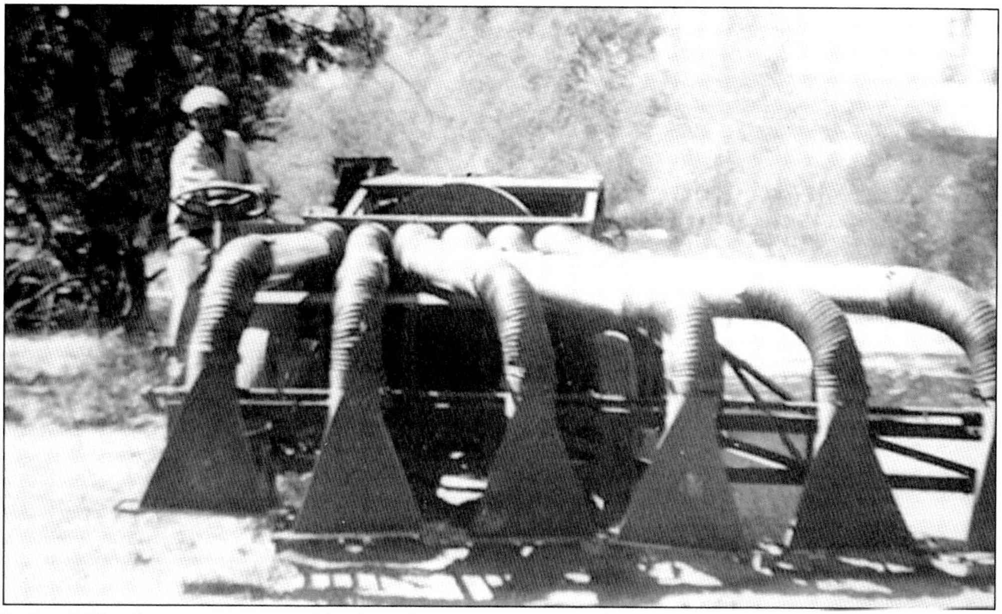

Ruland Hardy was 18 years old when he came to Orland in 1912. He invented and built this machine to pick up nuts that had been knocked from the Hardy and Anchorage Farms almond orchards. The usual driver was Carl Lowery, who was a foreman on the Hardy Ranch. This photograph was taken about 1935. (Courtesy Landy Hardy.)

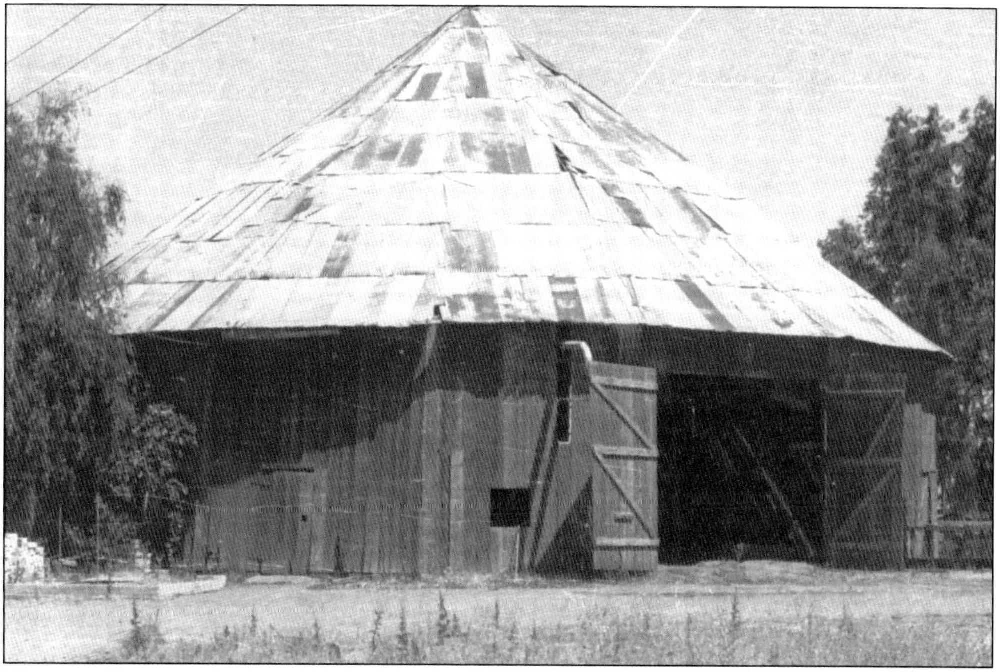

The round barn was built in 1914 by John Berlinger Sr. and was located in the Norwegian Colony where County Roads 7 and 3 intersect. Jim Wolcott, who ordered the building of the barn, came to Orland from Minnesota, where round barns were common. A round structure covers more area with less lumber. The round barn held 120 tons of loose hay, and 80 cows could be around the edge. The barn was torn down in the 1960s.

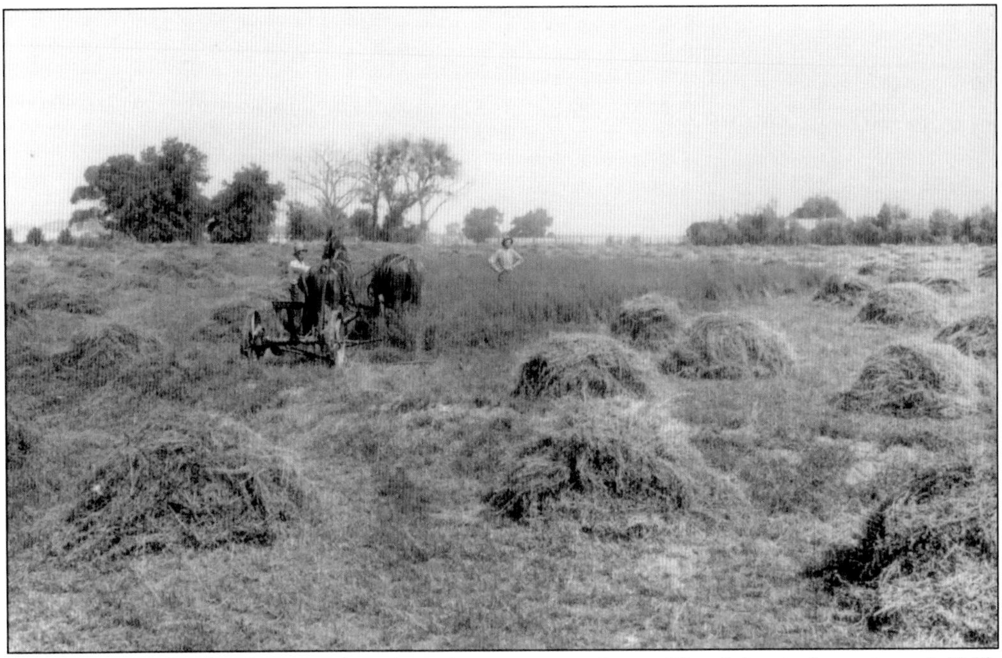

Taking a break for the photographer, these farmers are in the middle of the sixth cutting of alfalfa on the Wilkins ranch east of Orland. Alfalfa was considered the most stable crop in the newly formed Orland Project. The annual yield was approximately 10 tons with five to seven cuttings per season. (Courtesy California History Room, California State Library, Sacramento, California.)

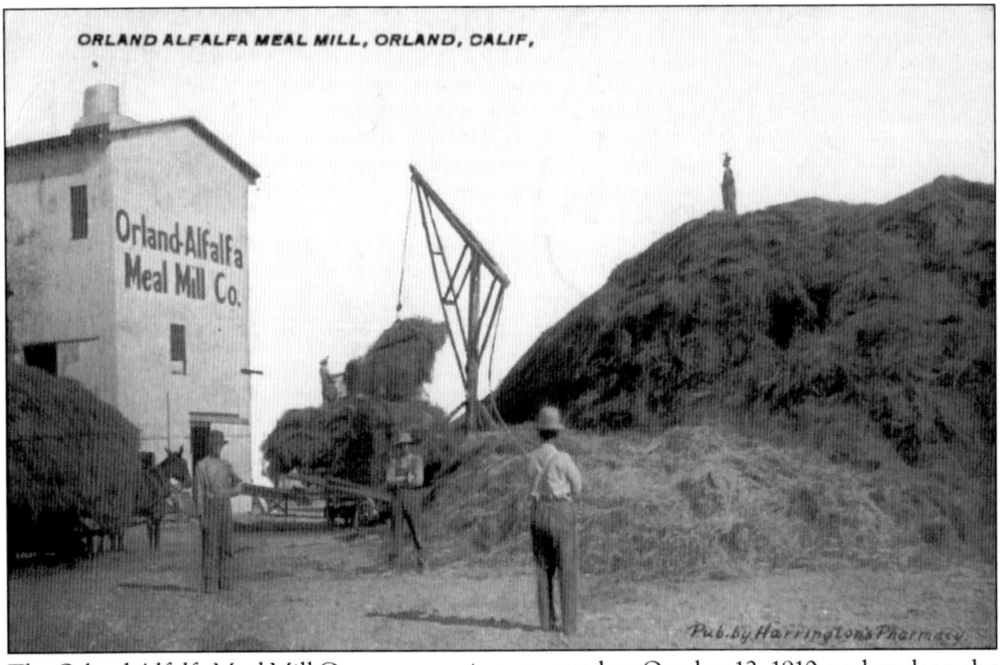

The Orland Alfalfa Meal Mill Company was incorporated on October 12, 1910, and work on the mill house began on April 10, 1911. Inside the mill were grinders, mill bins, dust collectors, and a 500-gallon water tank. The mill started operation on September 9, 1911, with a net capacity of 1,000 tons per month while running 10 hours per day.

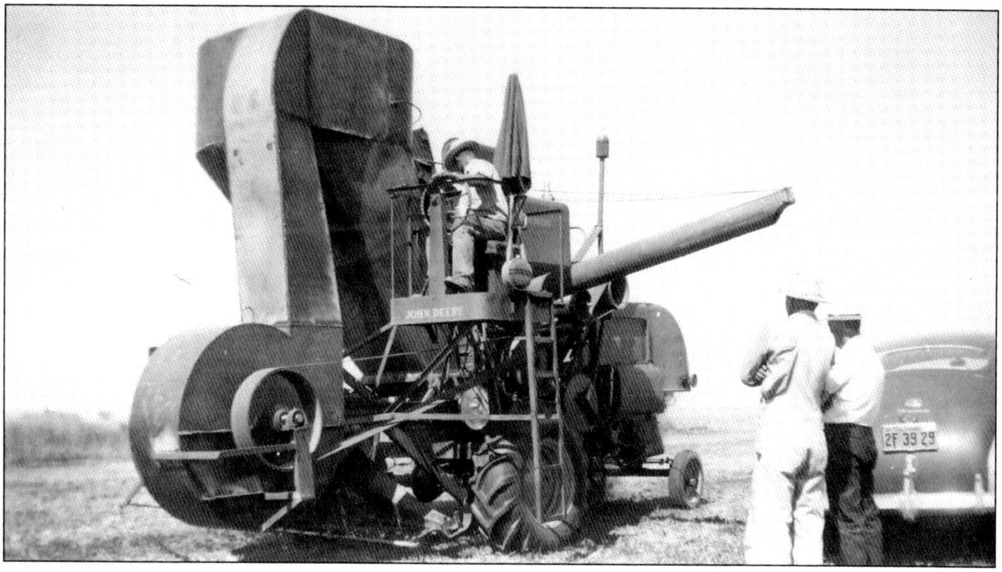

Ladino clover seed was a very valuable and profitable crop in Glenn County during the 1950s. Large acreages were leveled specifically for the crop. After the hay had been cut and picked up, the clover vacuum harvester went over the field to collect the loose seed. The machine shown in the top photograph, with Harold Mathews as driver, was fabricated locally by Wim Lely, Ben Ponci, and Elmer Ponci. Between 400 and 600 pounds of seed were usually collected per acre. Placed in 100- to 125-pound bags, the seed was trucked to a mill, such as the Sacramento Valley Milling Company in Ord Bend, for cleaning. The clover seed was sold after cleaning. Overproduction and federal government price support forced local farmers to stop growing the clover. These photographs were taken about 1950 on the Irvin Gee ranch in the Lake District. (Courtesy Charles Gee.)

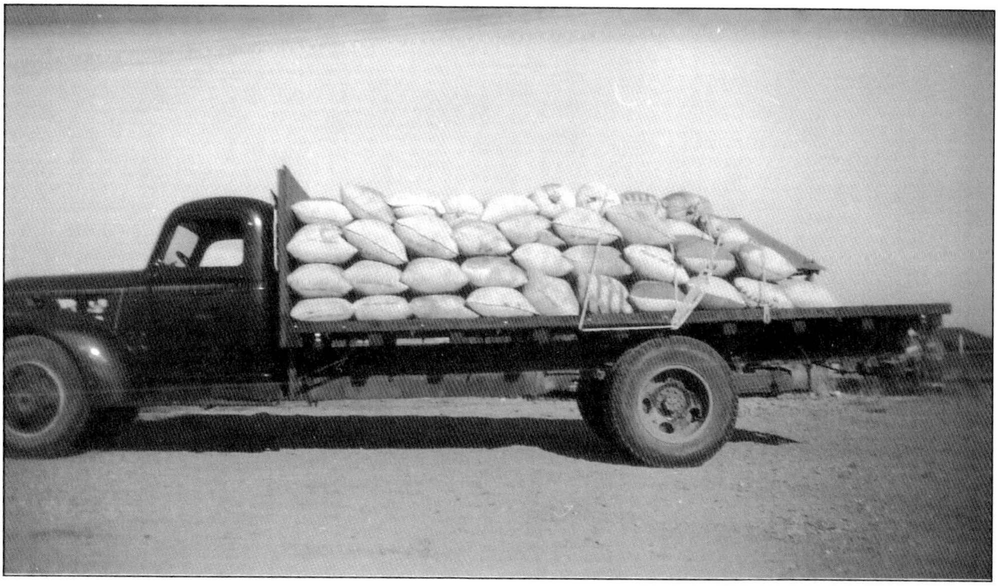

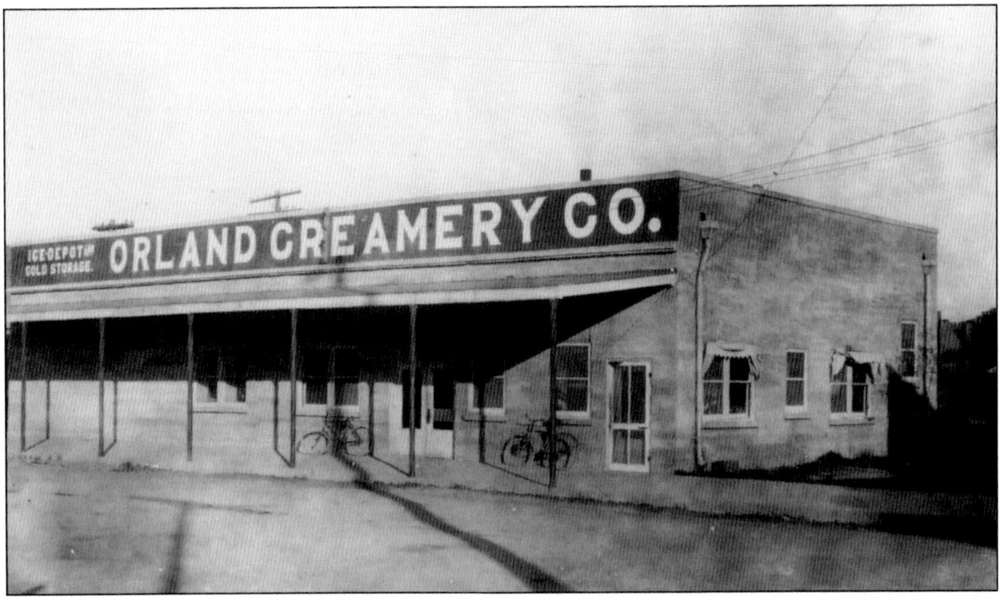

The Orland Creamery was established in 1902 by Ed F. Hale. The good yields of alfalfa in the area made dairying a profitable enterprise for local farmers. The creamery, a dealer in milk and cream, manufactured Orland Creamery Butter for the local consumers. Hale was also a dealer of ice, wholesale and retail, and delivered it to all parts of the town. Shown is Hale's second creamery building about 1912. (Courtesy California History Room, California State Library, Sacramento, California.)

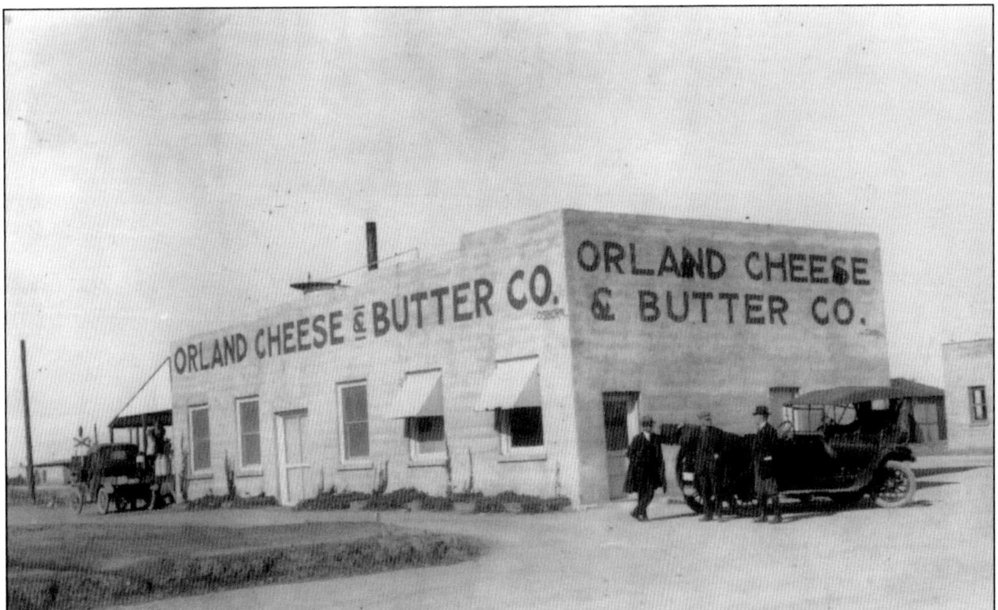

The Orland Cheese and Butter Company opened for business on April 10, 1915. It was owned and operated by the farmers and dairymen of the Orland Project. Chris Myhre, from Junction City, Oregon, was hired to manage the operation of the modern creamery located on the southwest corner of Fifth and Tehama Streets. (Courtesy California History Room, California State Library, Sacramento, California.)

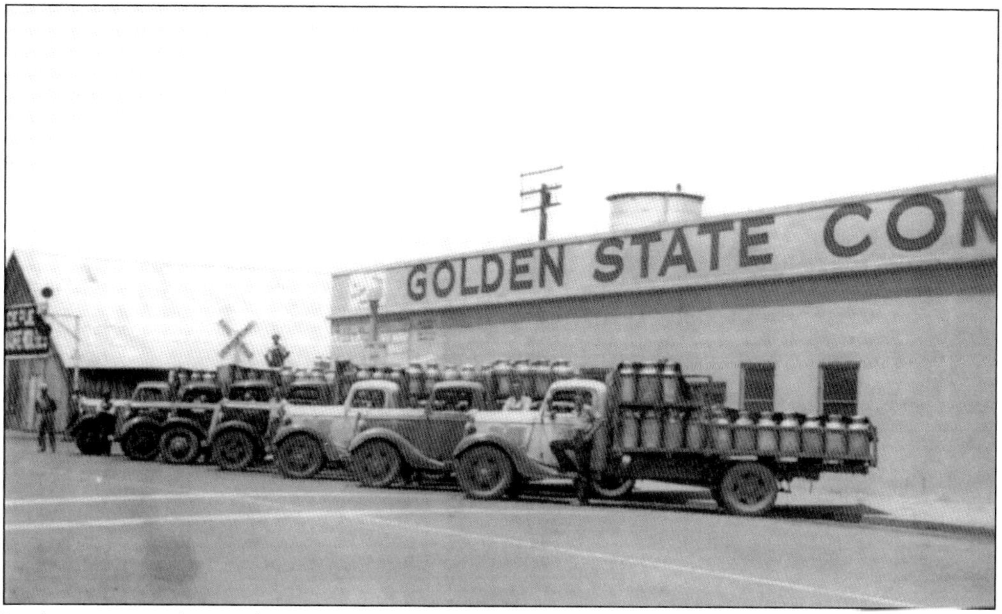

In the summer of 1935, the Golden State Company built a $30,000 three-story building to house a new powdered or dried milk plant. With a capacity of 100,000 pounds of whole milk per day, the new plant made Orland the dairy center of the valley. Pictured is the fleet of trucks used to deliver the sterilized milk cans to the ranches and return with whole milk for processing. (Courtesy Bruce Gilmore.)

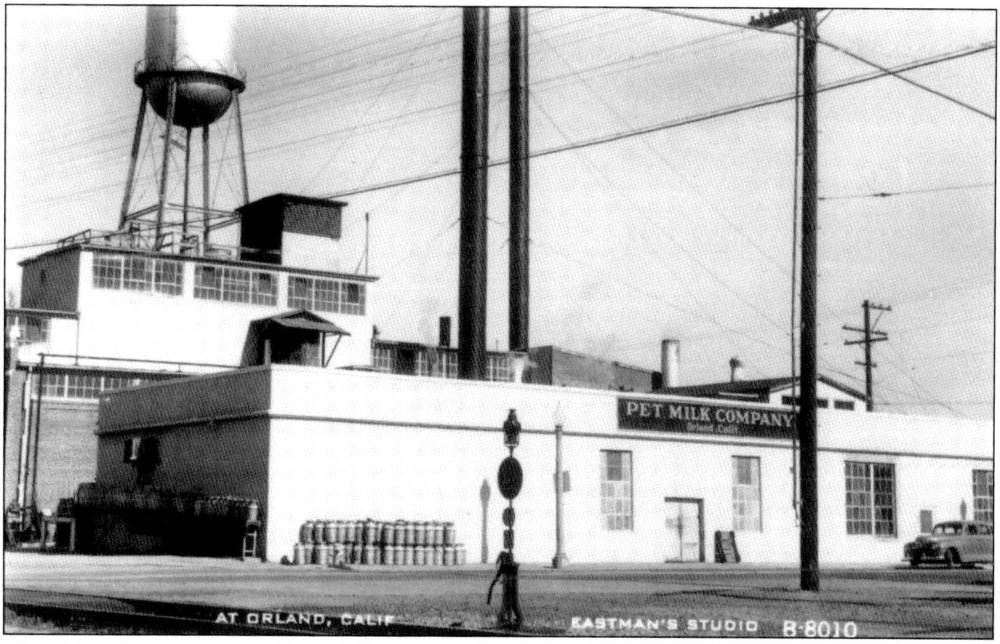

The Orland evaporated milk plant of the Pet Milk Company was in operation for 15 years. Rapid changes in the milk industry to increase efficiency were given as reasons that the Orland plant was no longer economically sound. The ice cream mix business was sold to a Modesto buyer. The end of production at the plant was on April 8, 1965. (Courtesy California History Room, California State Library, Sacramento, California.)

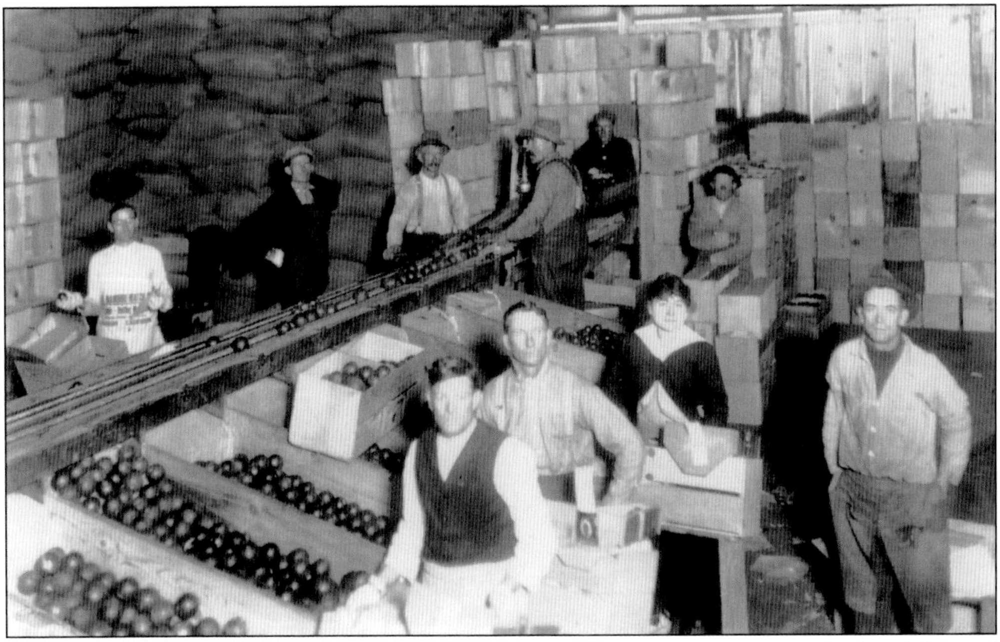

Pictured is the orange packinghouse in full operation. These oranges were packed and shipped from Orland to Eastern cities and were pronounced *par excellence* by Eastern customers. Note the bags of almonds in the background piled to the roof and ready for shipment to Sacramento. (Courtesy California History Room, California State Library, Sacramento, California.)

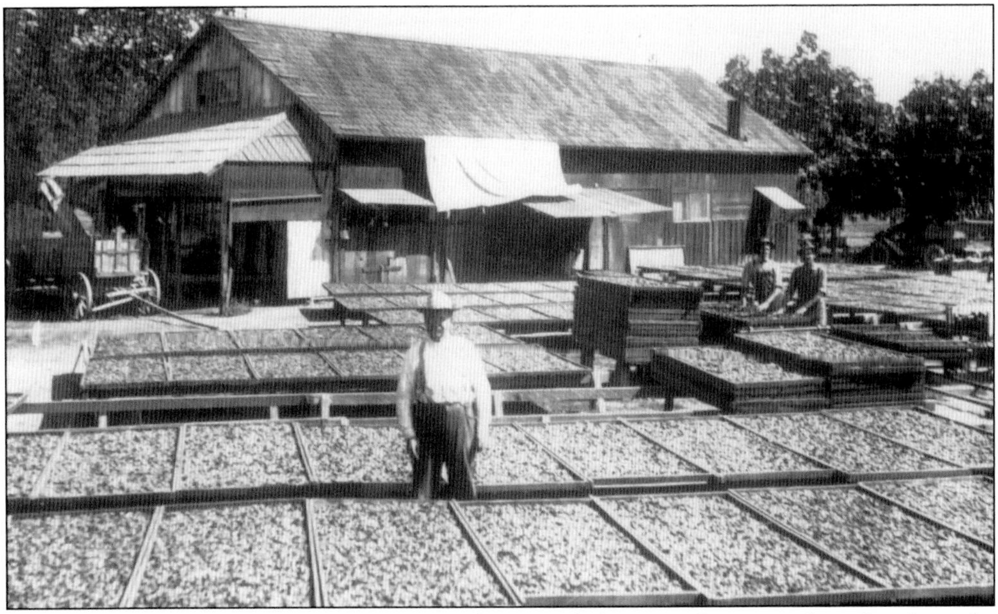

Paul "P. D." Bane came to Orland in 1890 to be a ranch foreman. Two years later, he planted a 66-acre almond orchard and was criticized by his neighbors, who believed the trees would not grow without irrigation. Bane became the area's pioneer almond grower and is pictured in the drying yard at his ranch east of Orland about 1910. At that time, his orchard was bringing him an annual income of $100 per acre, net. (Courtesy California History Room, California State Library, Sacramento, California.)

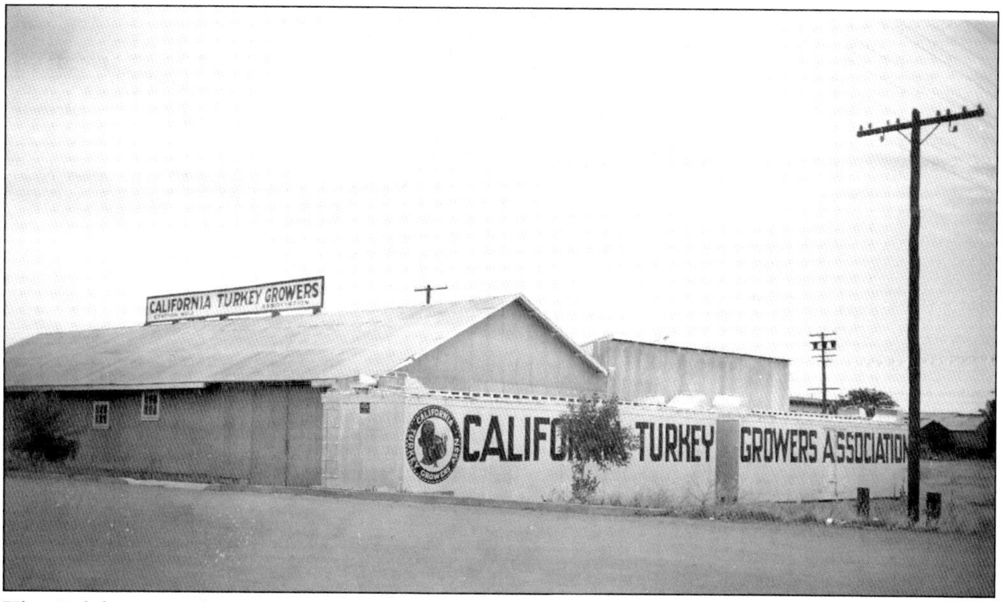

The California Turkey Growers Association was a cooperative with plants throughout the state. Pictured in 1939 is the Orland facility, which consisted of the killing plant, picking plant, and shipping center. During the peak season, carload lots of dressed turkeys packed in large wooden boxes, 6 to 12 turkeys in a box, were shipped daily from the land of Orland.

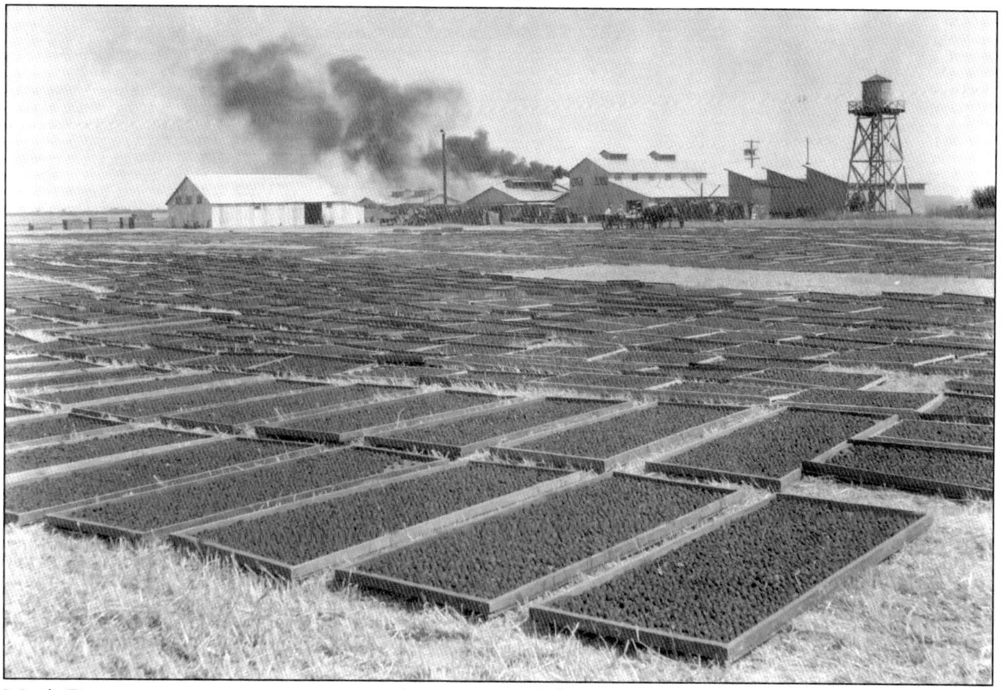

Mark Requa was a mining engineer, financier, and friend of Herbert Hoover. In 1912, Requa purchased 1,100 acres two miles southeast of Orland and started the Loam Ridge Tract and Anchorage Farms. He brought in purebred livestock and planted alfalfa and fruit trees. In the 1930s, the Anchorage Farms company had large orchards at Chico, Monroeville, and Orland, and was one of the largest fruit operators in the state.

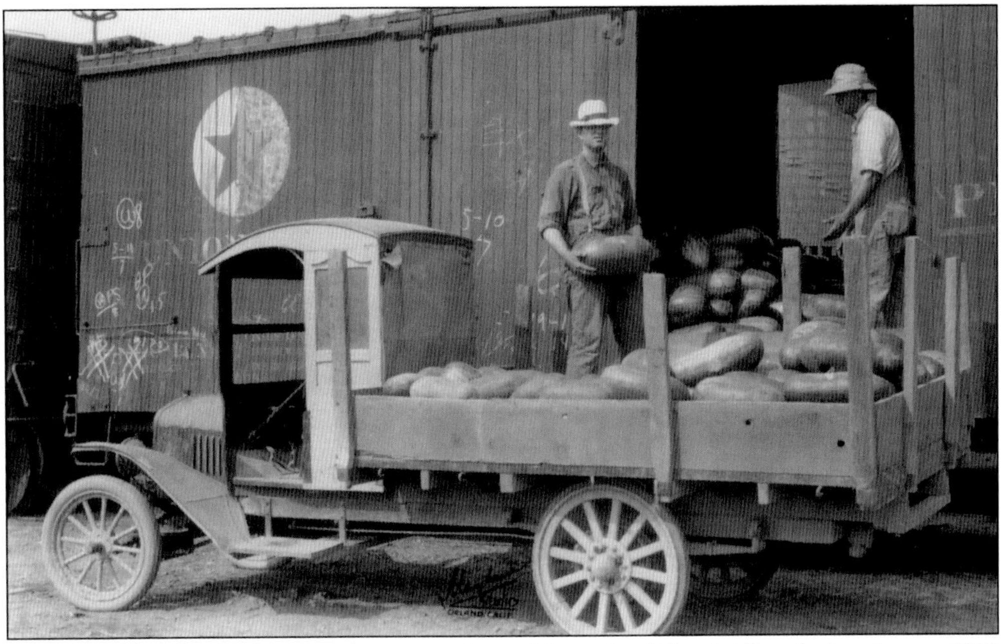

Two railroad carloads of watermelons were shipped from the Orland siding during August 1920 to markets in Portland, Oregon. Each weighing between 30 to 40 pounds, the melons had been raised by Carl S. Tout on his ranch west of Orland. It was estimated that each boxcar was filled with between 1,500 and 1,600 melons. (Courtesy California History Room, California State Library, Sacramento, California.)

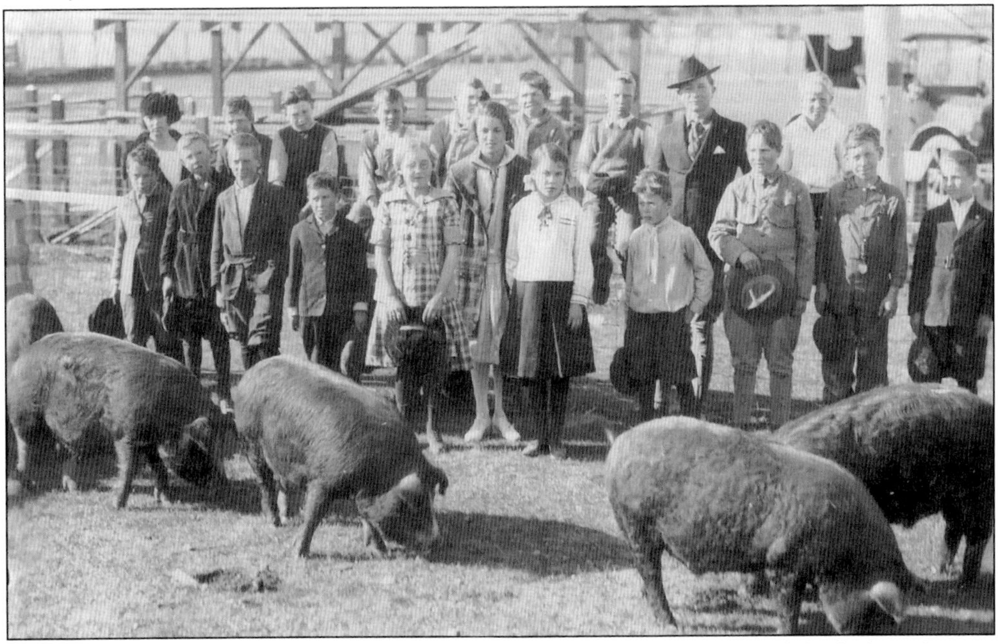

Any local boy or girl under the age of 21 could participate in the Fat Barrow Club of Glenn County under the direction of the club leader and the farm advisor. Pigs were fed under supervision for 110 days before being judged and sold at auction. Pig and calf clubs were popular in rural areas during the 1920s.

Four

BUSINESS ENTERPRISES

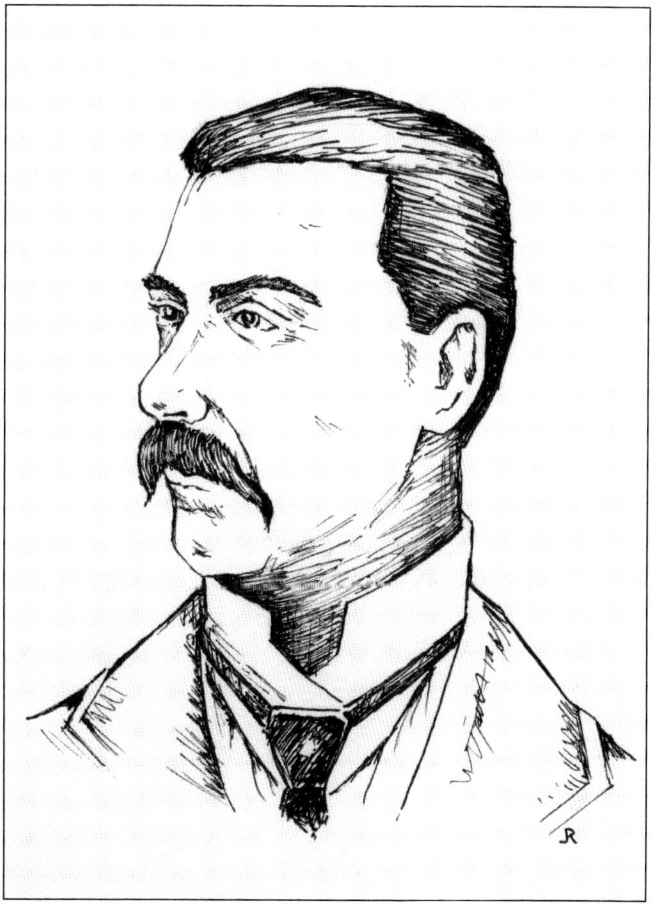

Frank Freeman came to Orland in 1879 and opened the village's first hardware store with partner Louis Behrens. It was while in the hardware business that he saw the need to divide Colusa County and form a new county with Orland as the county seat. In late 1881, Freeman sold his interest in the hardware store and purchased the *Orland Times* newspaper to advocate county division. When the community did not support his cause, he suspended the *Times* and moved to Willows to start the *Willows Daily Journal*. Freeman's persistence paid off with the formation of Glenn County in 1891 with Willows as the county seat. He became a respected Willows lawyer but kept an interest in the Orland Irrigation Project and the Glenn County Fair. He passed away on April 13, 1924.

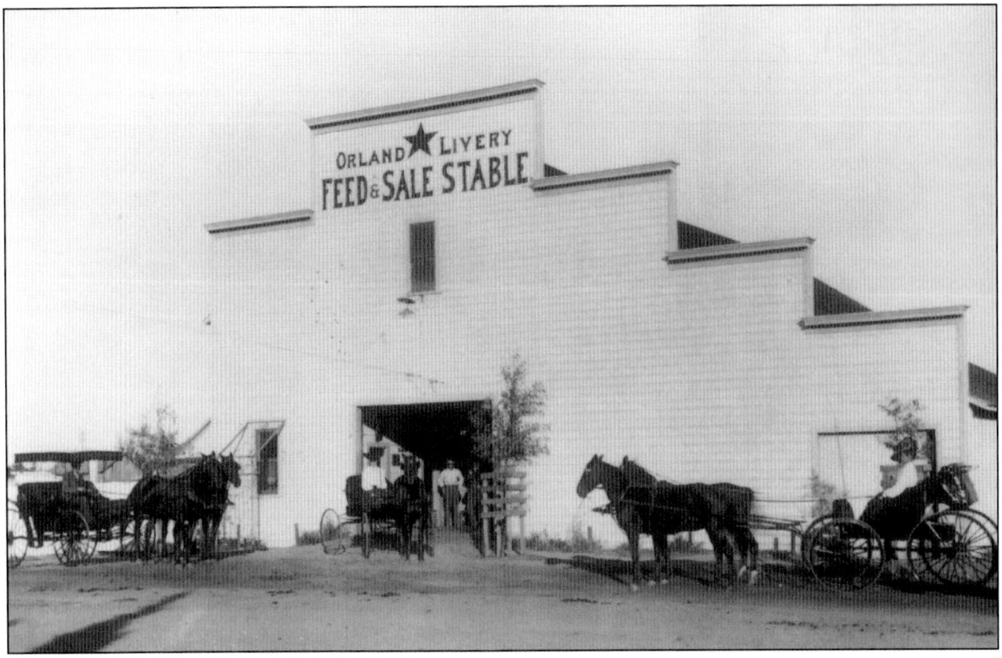

The Star Stable was located on the east side of Fourth Street extending from the old Odd Fellows Hall to the site of the new Odd Fellows Building. The stable was started by Henry S. McBain and his son in 1903. The top photograph was taken before the days of paved streets and sidewalks, when the eucalyptus trees were carefully protected from the horses. Orland had several different livery stables, the last one being at the southwest corner of Fifth and Colusa Streets. The lower photograph shows the interior of an Orland livery stable ready to accommodate traveling patrons and their animals. About 1913, the large Star Stable building became a popular spot for the young people in the community when it was converted to a roller skating rink. (Courtesy California History Room, California State Library, Sacramento, California.)

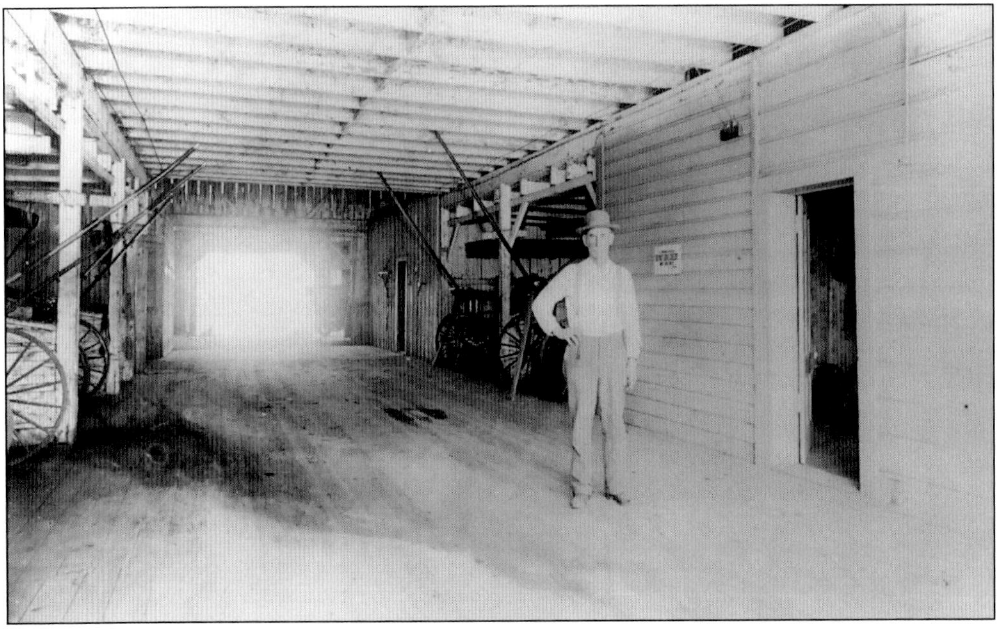

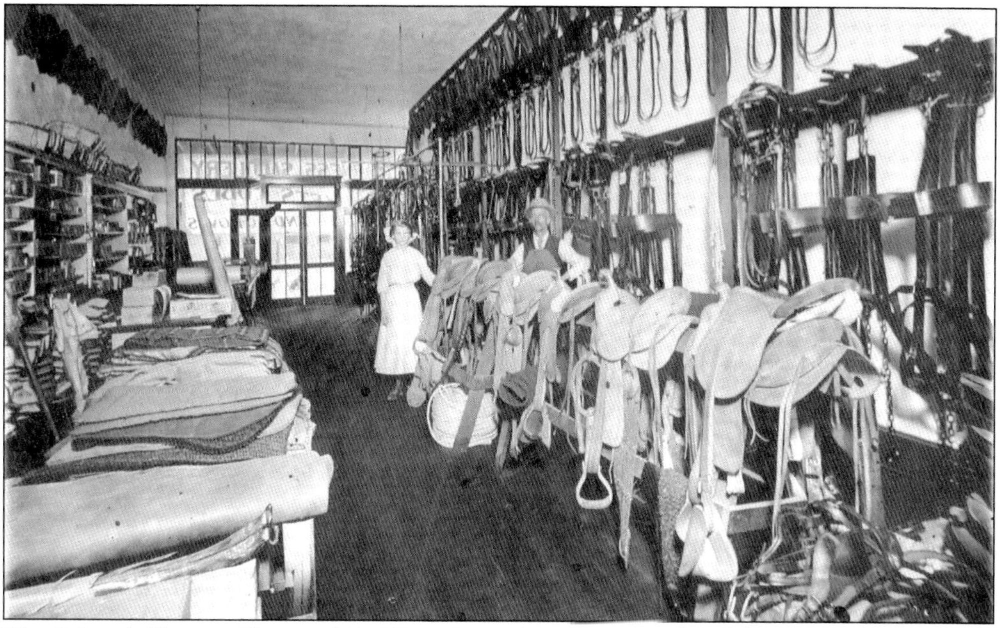

The Schmidt Harness Shop and Saddlery, located on the east side of Fourth Street, was one of Orland's pioneer businesses. Seen in the photograph are C. F. Schmidt, the proprietor, and his daughter Edna. After Schmidt's death in 1916, the business was carried on by his son Everett Schmidt. Everett took the business through several transitions, from harnesses to cloth tops and tires for automobiles, to electric appliances and television sets, keeping up with the times.

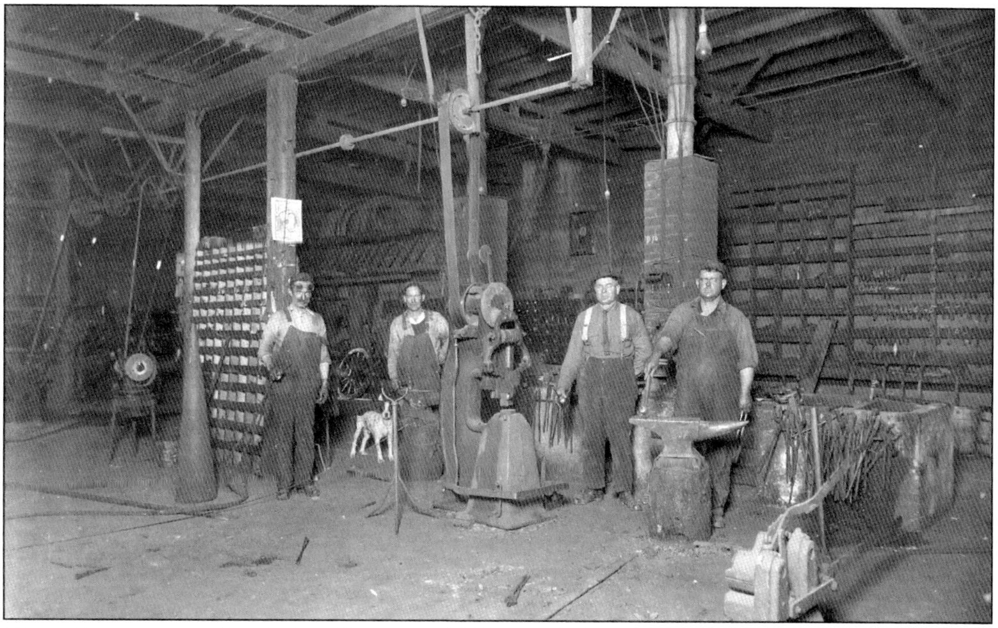

Harry Strawn arrived in Orland between 1907 and 1910. He found work in a butcher shop but soon met George Wright, one of Orland's earliest blacksmiths. Strawn went to work at Wright's Fifth and Colusa Streets shop where he learned the blacksmith's art. In 1919, Strawn—the "Village Blacksmith"—built his own shop on Fifth Street. Pictured from left to right are John Lake, Fred Strawn, Bill Barnum, and Harry Strawn.

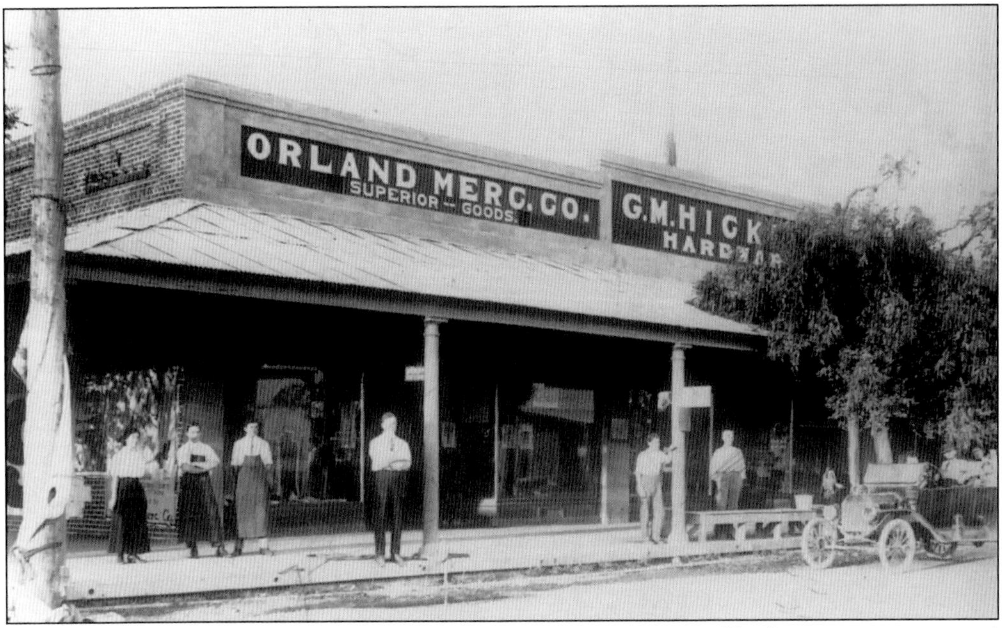

George M. Hickman came to Orland from San Francisco in 1912 and built up a pioneer general store into one that was known all over the valley for its large and complete stock. Hickman ran the store at the corner of Fourth and Walker Streets until his death in the late 1940s. Walter and John Berlinger Jr. bought the store in July 1950. (Courtesy California History Room, California State Library, Sacramento, California.)

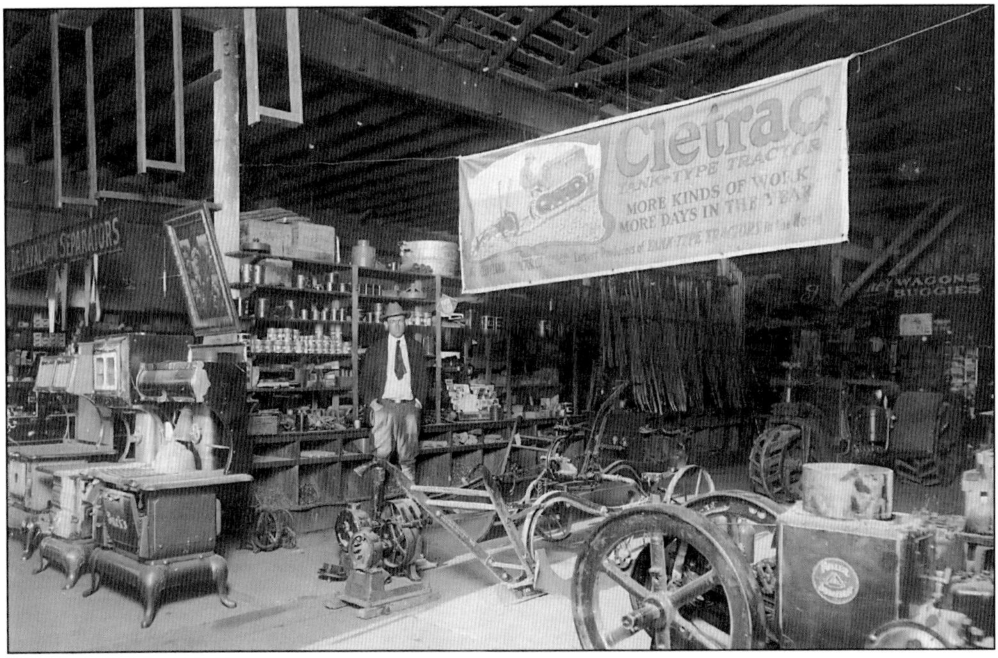

John Wright was a salesman for his father in George Wright's Hardware Store on Fifth Street. In this late-1920s photograph, the farm equipment is displayed on the right while the dishes, glassware, and kitchen utensils are in the left half of the store. The office, shop, and restroom were in the back portion of the building.

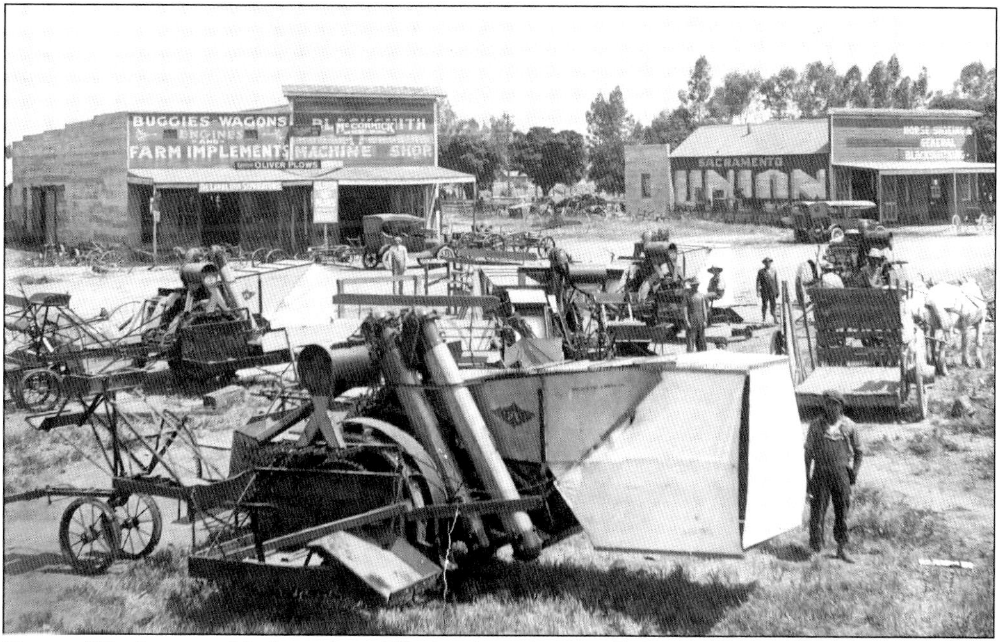

George Wright was a blacksmith in Elk Creek and Newville before coming to Orland in 1893. After several partnerships, Wright purchased property on both sides of Fifth Street and built his own blacksmith shop and showroom near the northeast corner of Mill Street. In August 1917, Wright sold his wagon-making and blacksmith shop to concentrate on his hardware and implement business. Wright is standing in the top photograph across Fifth Street from his original Orland Hardware store and is between the car and the farm machinery. In the lower photograph from the early 1930s, John Wright, George's eldest son, is shown wearing light-colored pants and standing beside the display of farm tractors. The Wrights were dealers in International Harvester, McCormick-Deering, and Oliver farm equipment. George Wright retired in 1939 and sold his store to the partnership of Joseph Baugher and Paul Blacet.

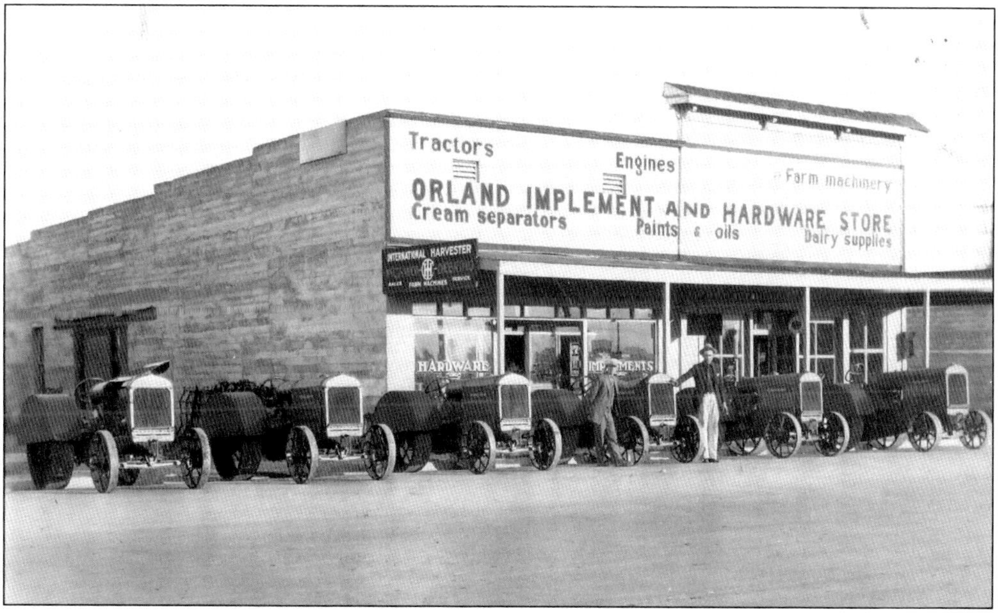

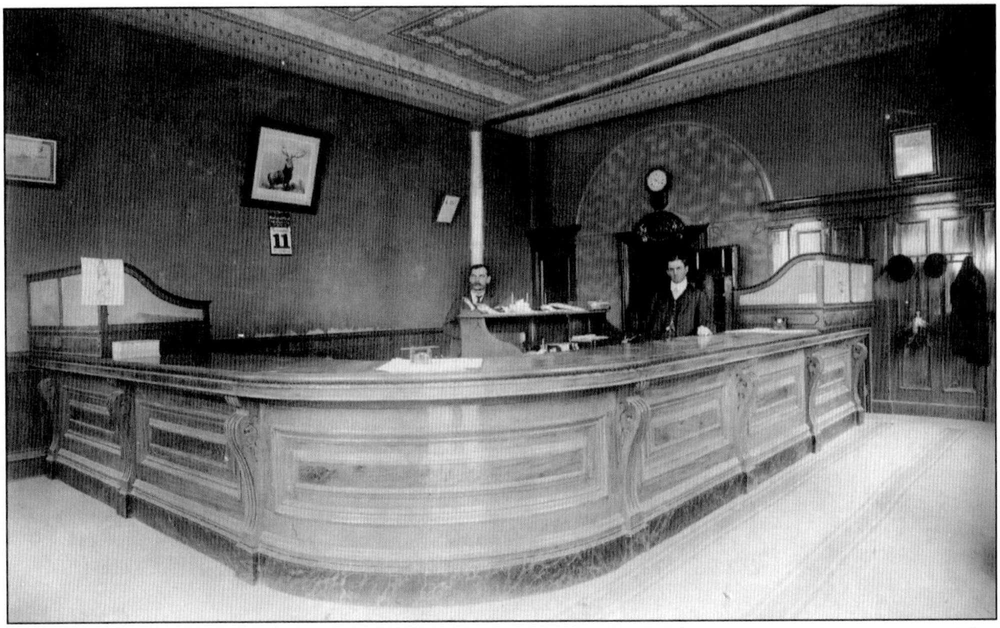

The Bank of Orland was the town's leading financial institution for 40 years. The interior of the bank is pictured in 1902–1903. The Bank of Orland was sold in late 1927, and the new name became Security Bank and Trust Company, Orland Branch on January 23, 1928. All officers and employees continued in their positions with the new organization. The only change was on the front window and on the stationery.

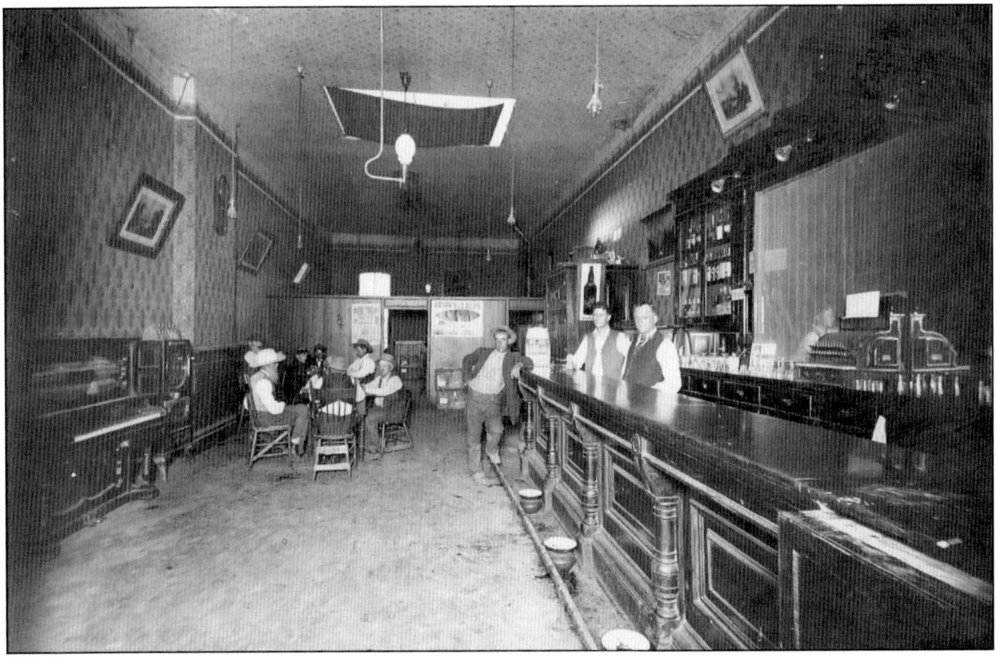

Bartender Albert Papst Jr. (left) and an unidentified helper are behind the bar of this Fifth Street saloon. Papst descendants believe that Albert Papst Sr. had a financial interest in the tavern and that the photograph dates from about 1900. Over the years, a number of saloons were on both sides of what was commonly known as "Canal Street." (Courtesy Shirley Hodge.)

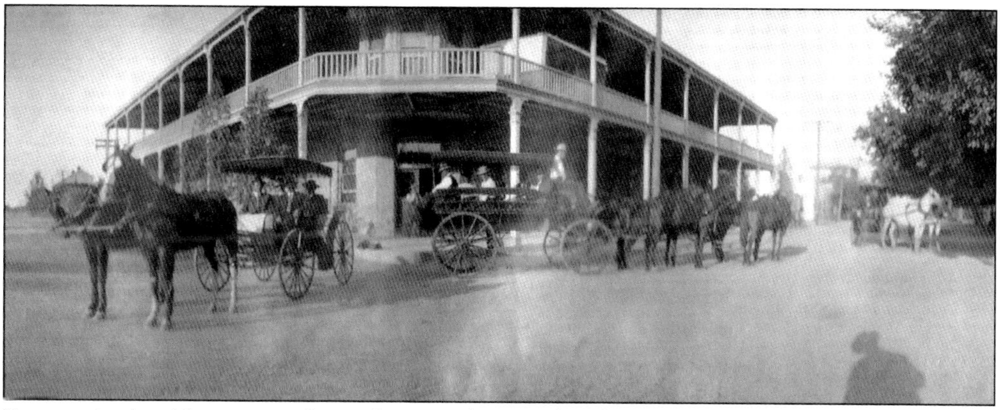

Prospective land buyers are shown leaving the Hotel Orland for an early-morning tour of the farms around the community. The photograph was taken about 1905 when the Orland Land Colony was sponsoring these buggy trips as an effective method to showcase the agricultural potential of the area.

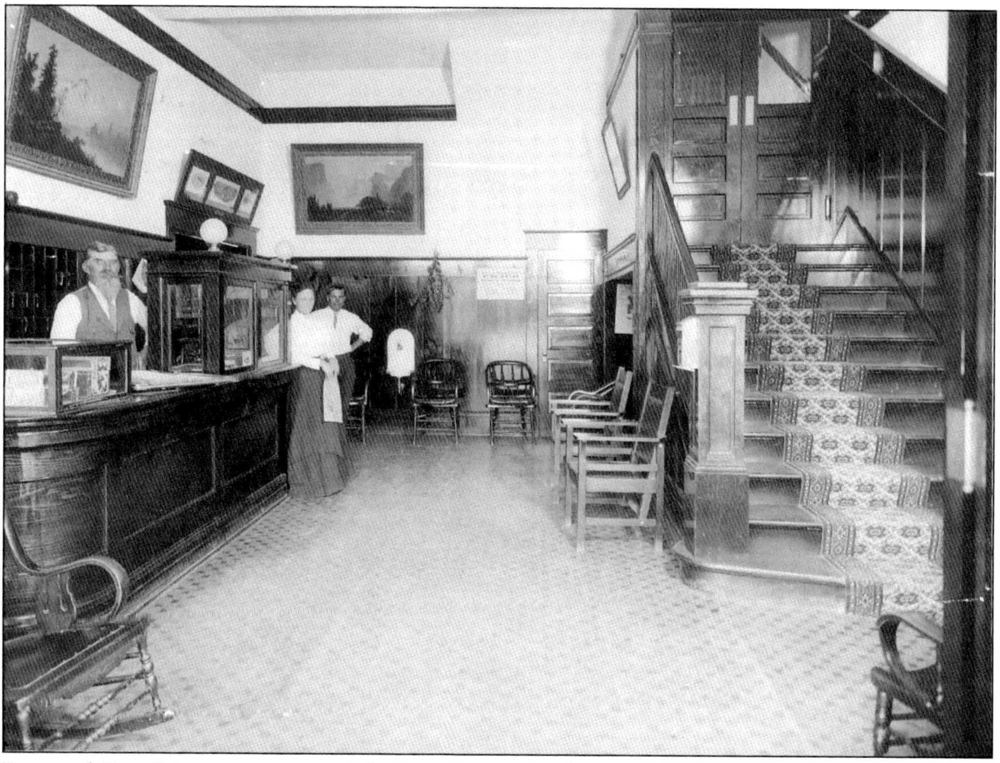

Emanuel Kesselring was a successful wheat farmer, but he entered the hotel business in 1893 and later was responsible for the construction of the new Hotel Royal on Colusa Street. "Mr. K," behind the hotel's counter, met new arrivals to Orland at the train depot with his pushcart, greeting the people and taking their luggage to the hotel. Anna Kesselring, Emanuel's wife, is at the end of the counter in this c. 1915 photograph.

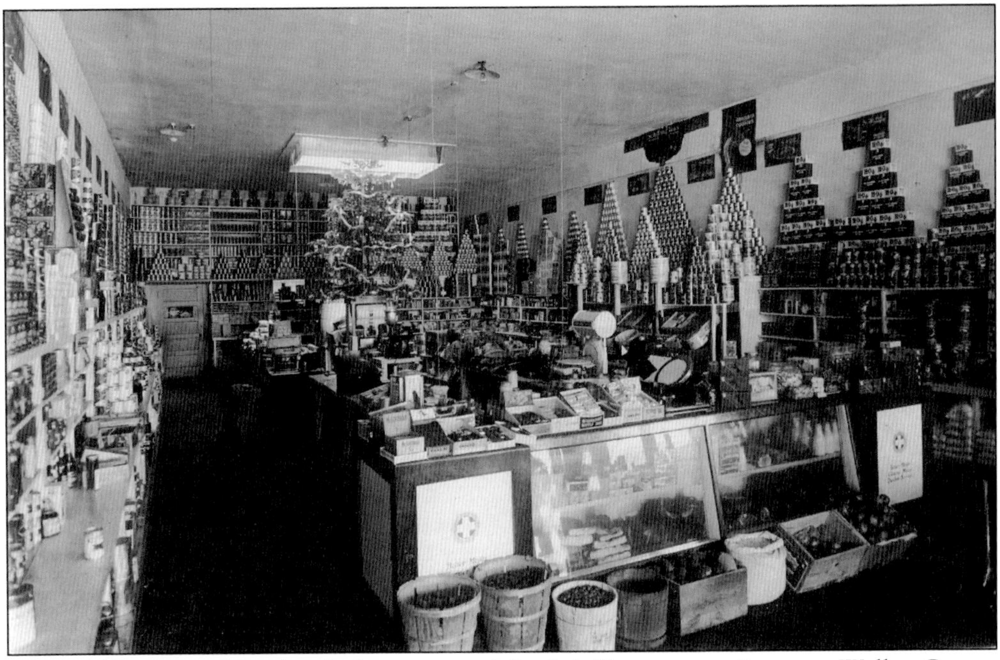

Reinhold Bucke and his family first operated Bucke's Department Store on Walker Street. Groceries were in the basement until they opened Bucke's Grocery Store, pictured here, next to the Orland Variety Store on Fifth Street. Later they moved across the street to the vacant "Hap" Holt Chevrolet building. (Courtesy Jack Bucke.)

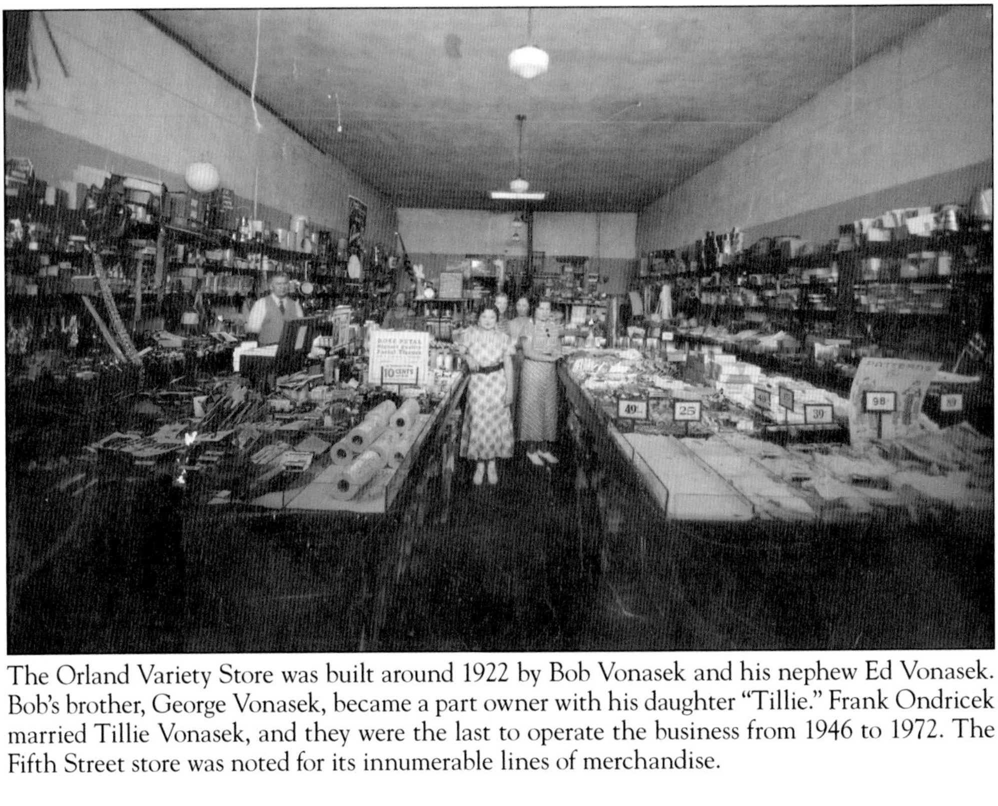

The Orland Variety Store was built around 1922 by Bob Vonasek and his nephew Ed Vonasek. Bob's brother, George Vonasek, became a part owner with his daughter "Tillie." Frank Ondricek married Tillie Vonasek, and they were the last to operate the business from 1946 to 1972. The Fifth Street store was noted for its innumerable lines of merchandise.

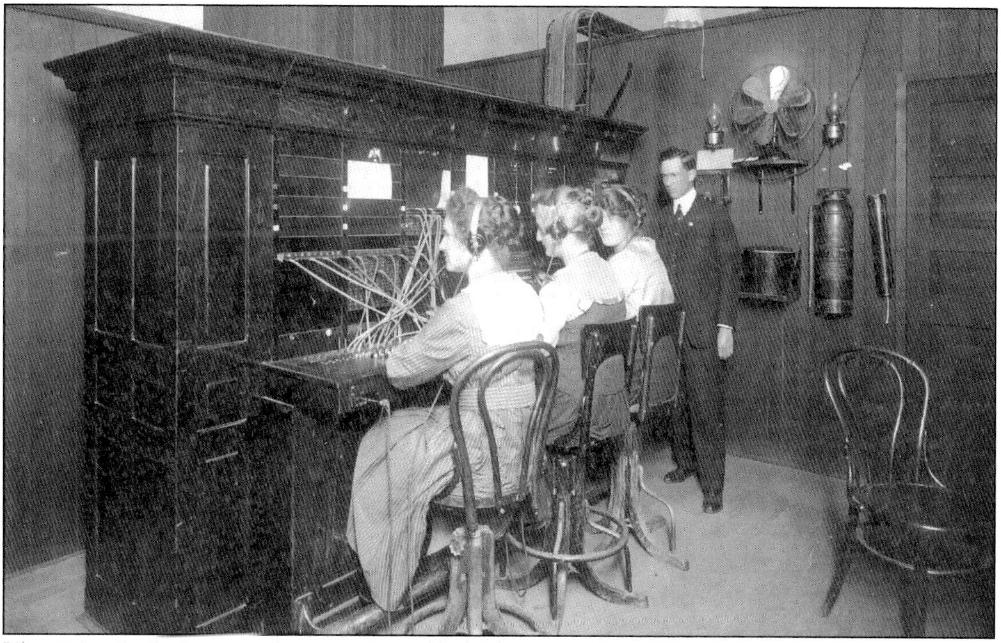

The Orland telephone exchange was established in 1895 through the efforts of I. E. Mecum. The first switchboard was installed in Mecum's store and connected 25 telephones. Winnie Brown was the first operator, and she also attended to the duties of postmaster and clerk. The Pacific Telephone Company and the Glenn County Telephone Company both had switchboards in Orland in the early 1910s, forcing merchants to maintain two telephones.

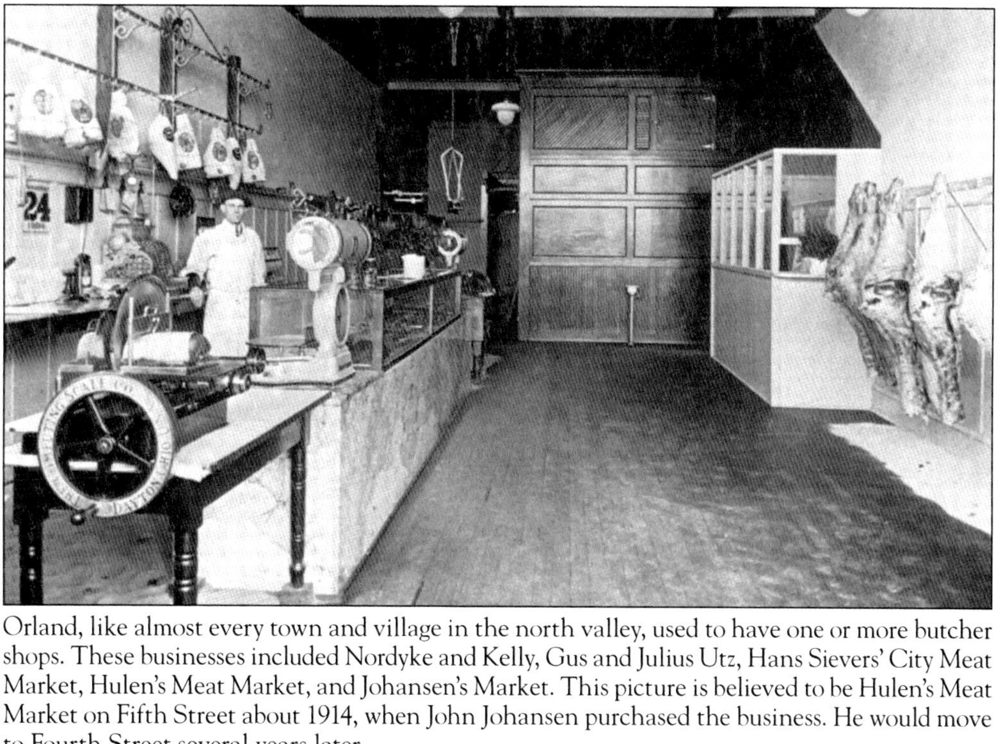

Orland, like almost every town and village in the north valley, used to have one or more butcher shops. These businesses included Nordyke and Kelly, Gus and Julius Utz, Hans Sievers' City Meat Market, Hulen's Meat Market, and Johansen's Market. This picture is believed to be Hulen's Meat Market on Fifth Street about 1914, when John Johansen purchased the business. He would move to Fourth Street several years later.

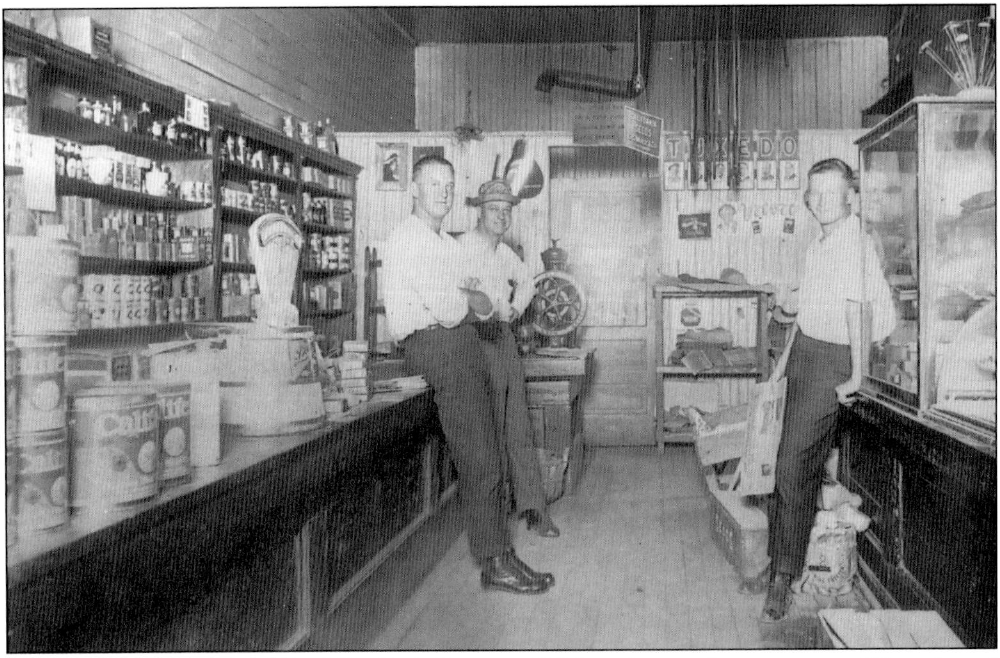

William De Fries opened the IXL Cash Store in 1908 at the southeast corner of Fourth and Colusa Streets. He carried a line of general merchandise and was also a news agent for all the leading daily newspapers and periodicals. The photograph was taken about 1914 and shows John De Fries, Herman De Fries, and Frank De Fries.

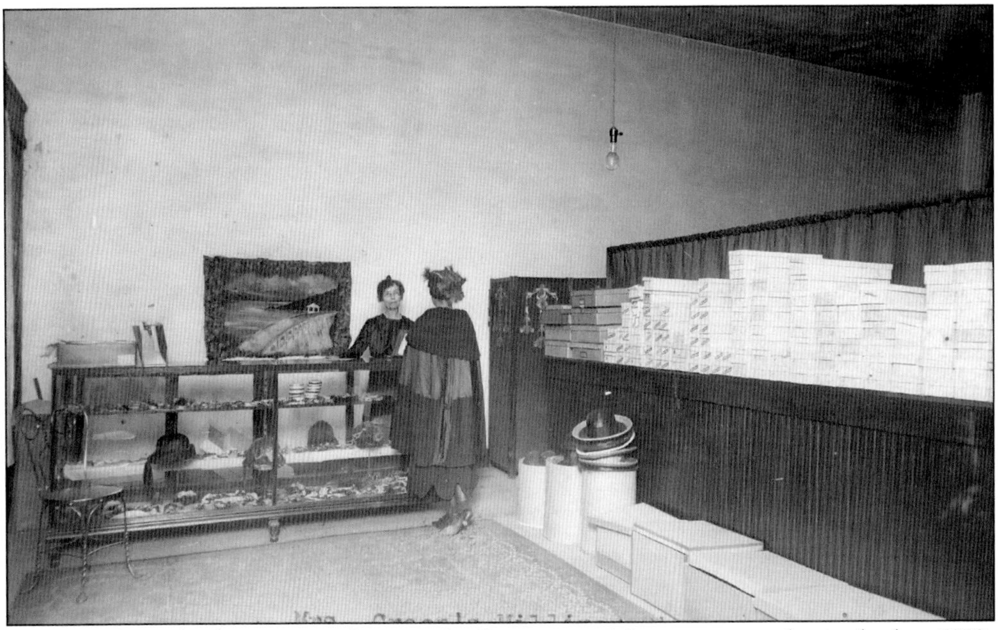

Millinery shops for designing, making, and selling women's hats were popular in the late 1910s and 1920s as women demonstrated their newly found freedoms and responsibilities. Hats were used for decoration and protection against the elements, and were designed specifically for the individual. Large hats with masses of floral trim were in style at the time Mrs. Green's millinery shop was photographed about 1920.

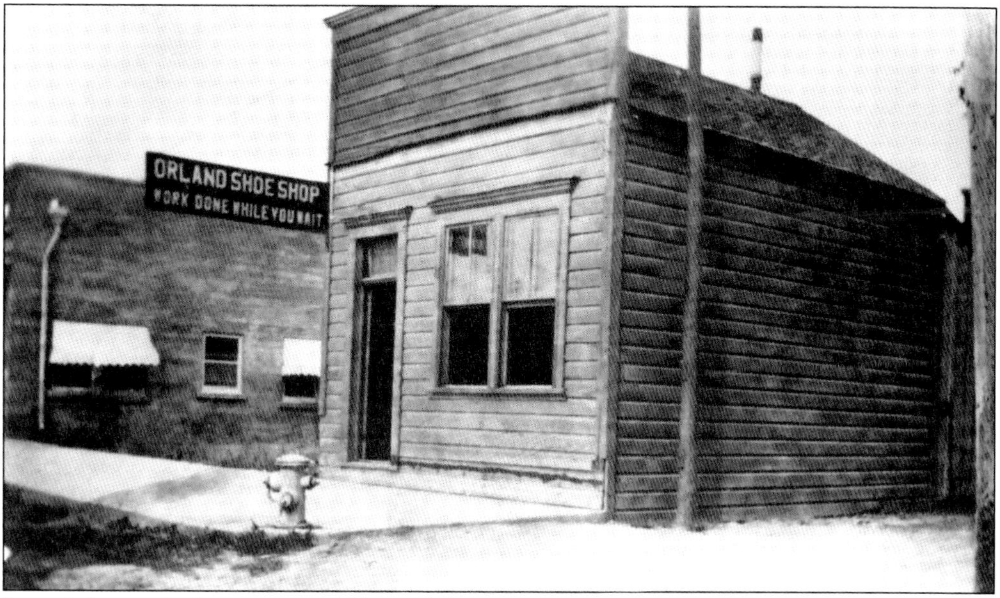

Louie Johnson Sr. began as a cobbler and shoe repair operator in this shop on Walker Street in March 1914. The rent was $6 per month. The following year, he moved to a shop near the newly completed Masonic Temple and added a line of ready-to-wear shoes. After stints as a railroad brakeman and military service in France during World War I, Johnson returned to Fourth Street to start a shoe and men's clothing business. Johnson was an Orland businessman for six decades. (Courtesy Louie Johnson Jr.)

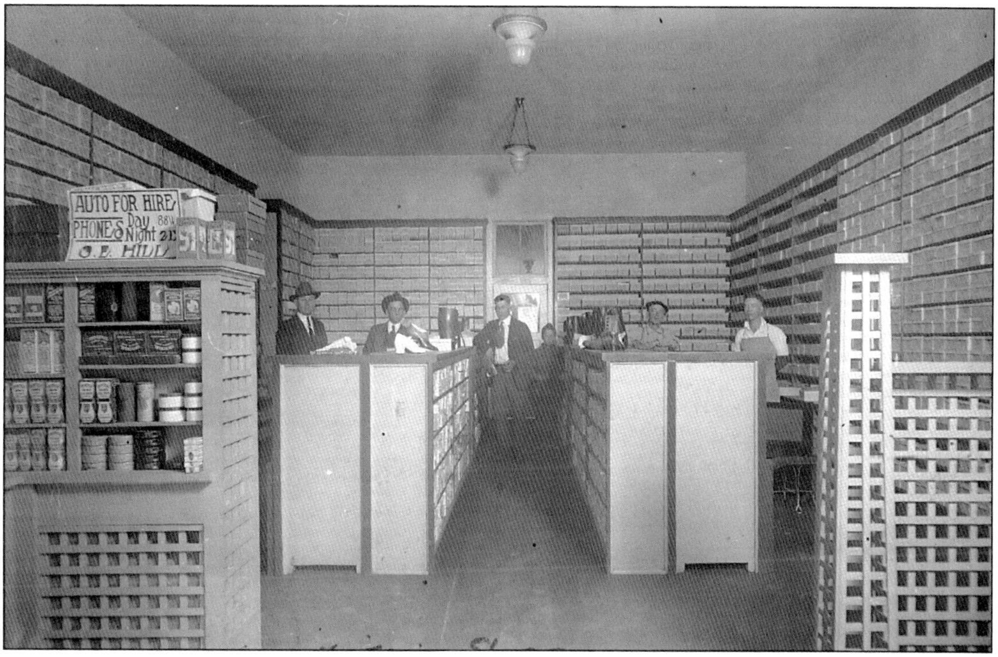

John Mehl came to Orland in August 1882, started the town's first cobbling shop, and later was the proprietor of his own shoe store. Prior to retiring on January 5, 1920, Mehl sold his shoe business to James M. Hinton and his younger brother H. P. Hinton of San Francisco. The interior of the Hinton Brothers Shoe Shop was photographed around 1920.

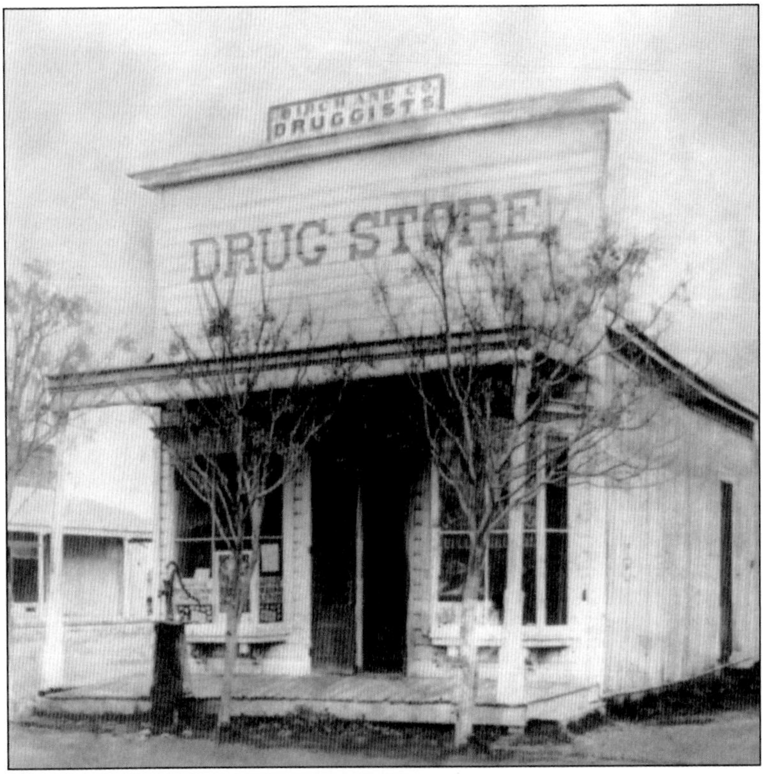

The Birch Drug Store was located at the southeast corner of Fourth and Walker Streets. Both John Wesley Birch and his wife, May (Cushman) Birch, were licensed druggists. John Birch opened his first drugstore about 1891, where he also tested eyes and prescribed glasses. The building was later moved (around 1913) to the rear of the lot and faced Walker Street as a cycle shop and auto body paint shop. (Courtesy Tom Birch.)

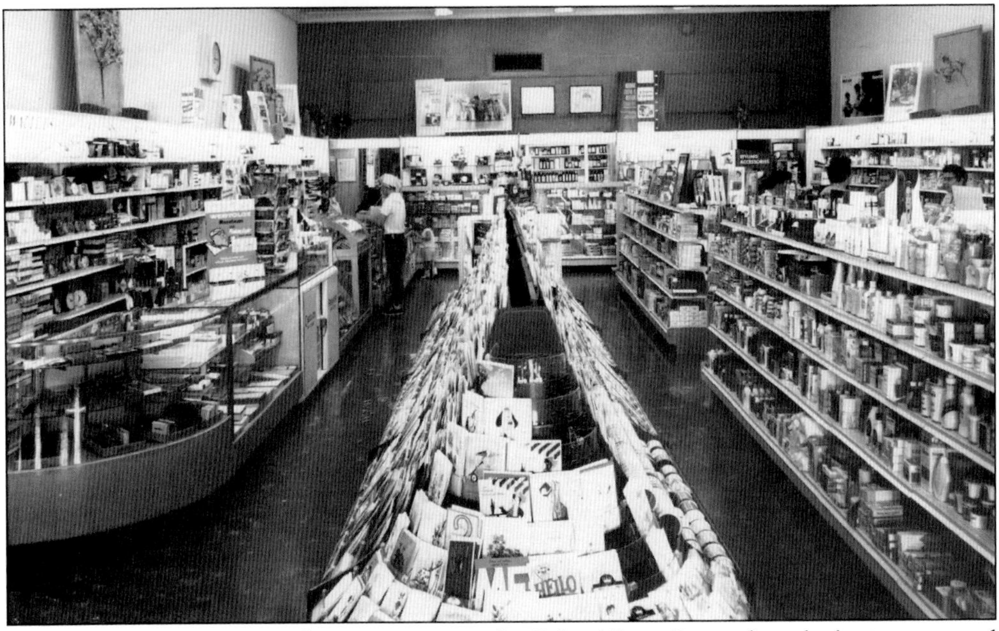

Harrington's Pharmacy was the name given to the Orland Drug Store when the business moved from the Barceloux-Iglick Building to 740 Fourth Street. Around 1918, Michael Harrington moved the business a third and final time one space north. The elder Harrington took in his son Frank as a partner in January 1928. The photograph was taken around 1961 when the Harrington family marked their 50th anniversary of business in Orland.

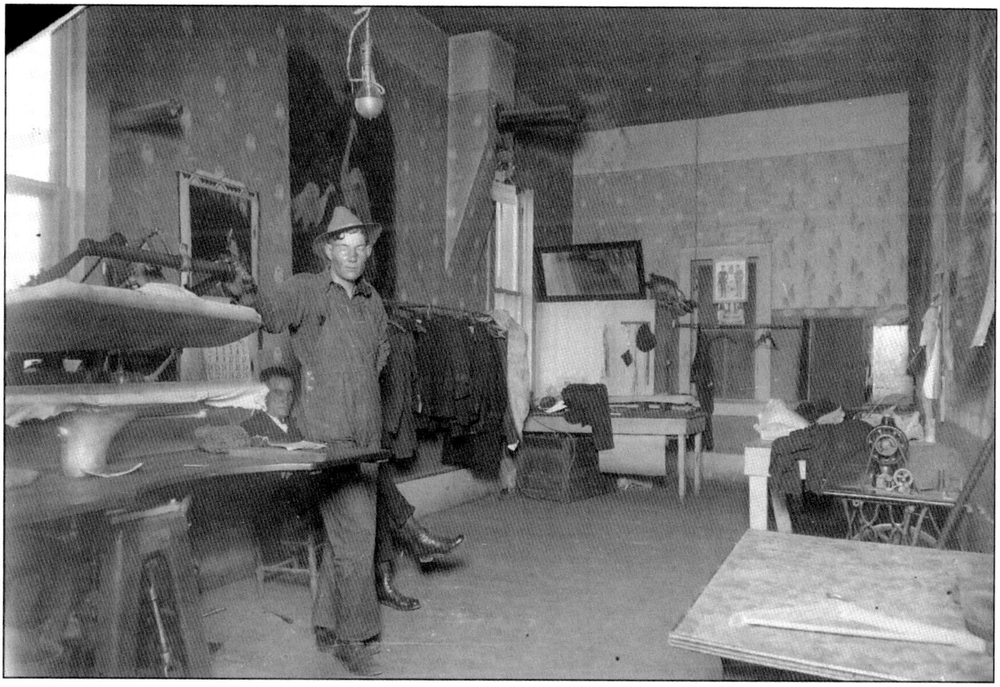

C. E. Carlson, the "Master Tailor," had his business in the Hotel Orland building before moving to the building just west of the Hotel Royal. Making clothing to order was Carlson's specialty, but he also did cleaning and pressing. The photograph was believed to have been taken in the early 1920s.

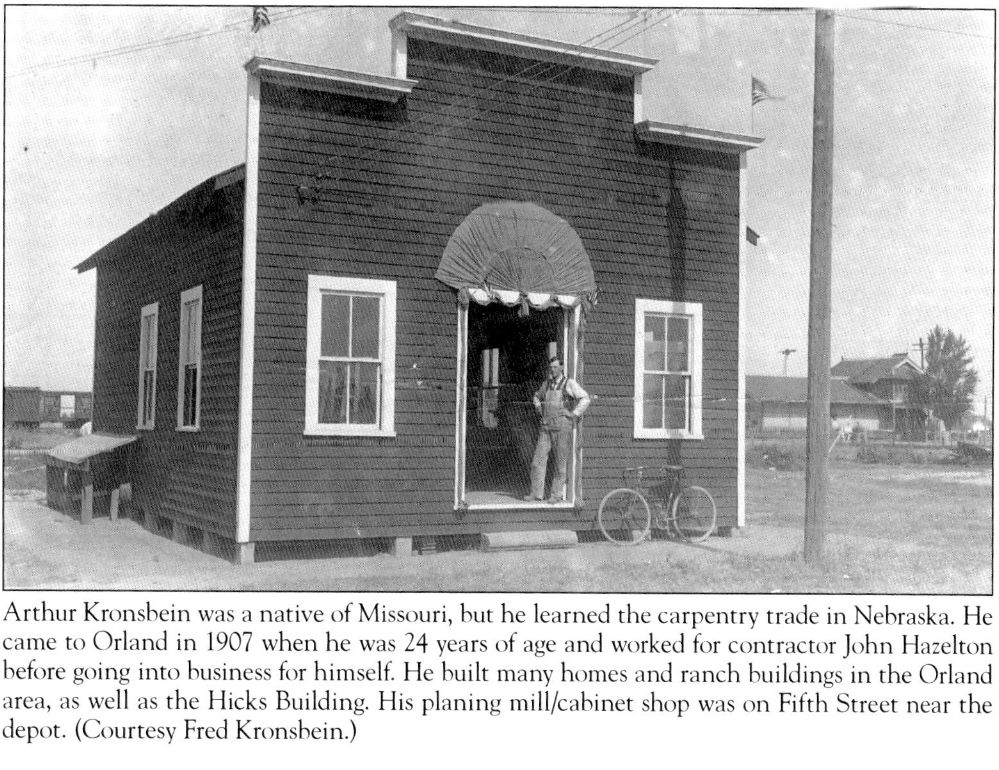

Arthur Kronsbein was a native of Missouri, but he learned the carpentry trade in Nebraska. He came to Orland in 1907 when he was 24 years of age and worked for contractor John Hazelton before going into business for himself. He built many homes and ranch buildings in the Orland area, as well as the Hicks Building. His planing mill/cabinet shop was on Fifth Street near the depot. (Courtesy Fred Kronsbein.)

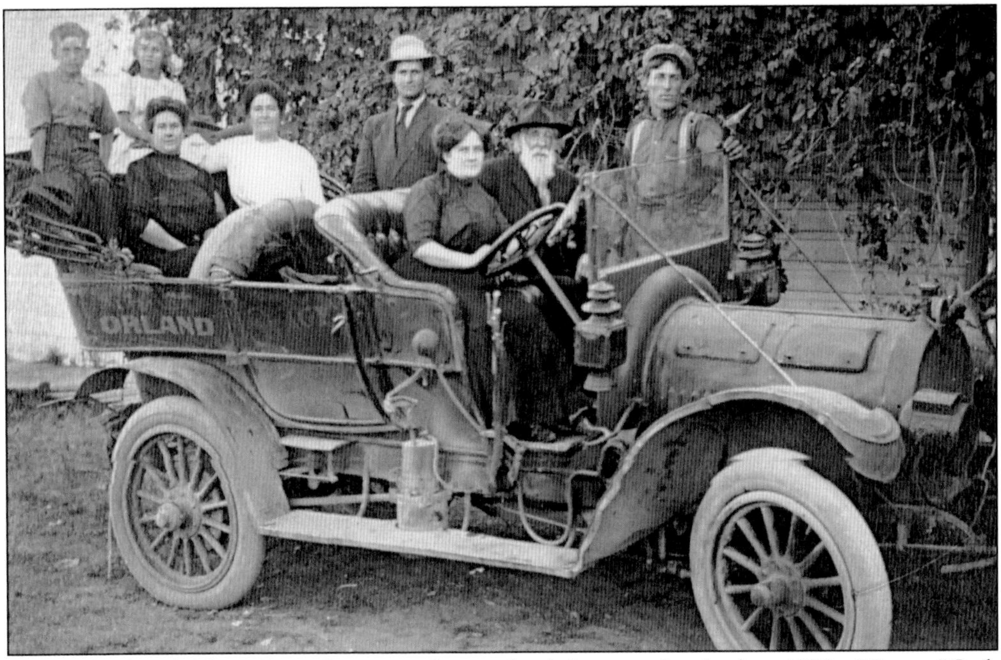

The Orland and Chico Stage Line was doing a brisk business by the late 1880s. "Cactus" Jack Houk expanded his successful Chico-to-Oroville and Chico–to–Hamilton City operation to include Orland and Willows. Pictured is Houk's Chico-Orland Stage about 1912. (Courtesy John Nopel.)

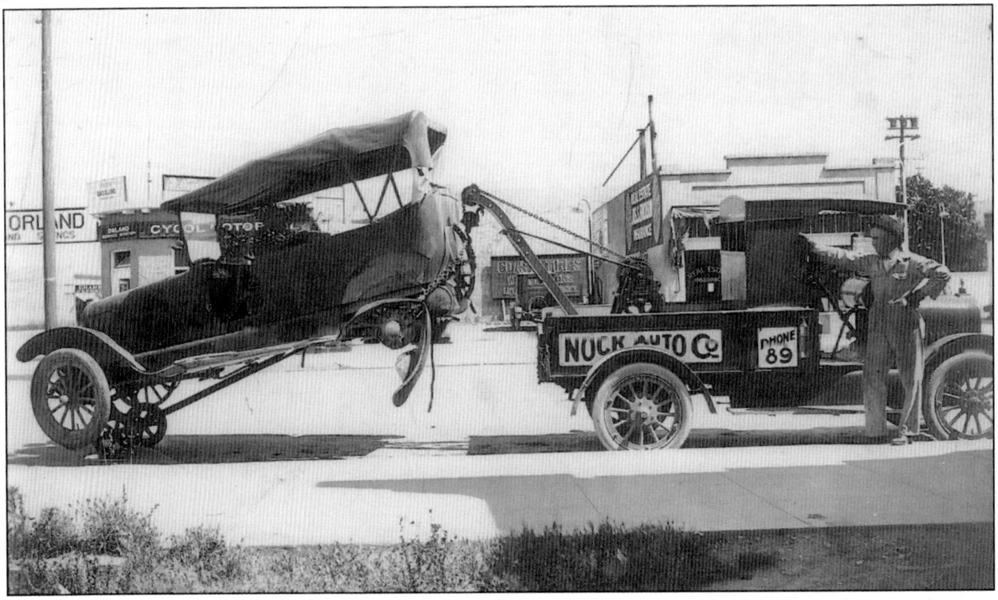

Helen Brantley and her young daughter Ruth escaped death on May 15, 1923. Brantley was driving to town and failed to see the approaching train before the car and occupants were thrown into the ditch by the roadside. Helen Brantley suffered a broken bone in her foot and was seriously bruised while Ruth escaped injury. Nock Auto Company sold tires and was the Hudson and Essex Motor Car dealer. The picture was taken near the eastern corner of Colusa and Fifth Streets. (Courtesy Ruth Falkner.)

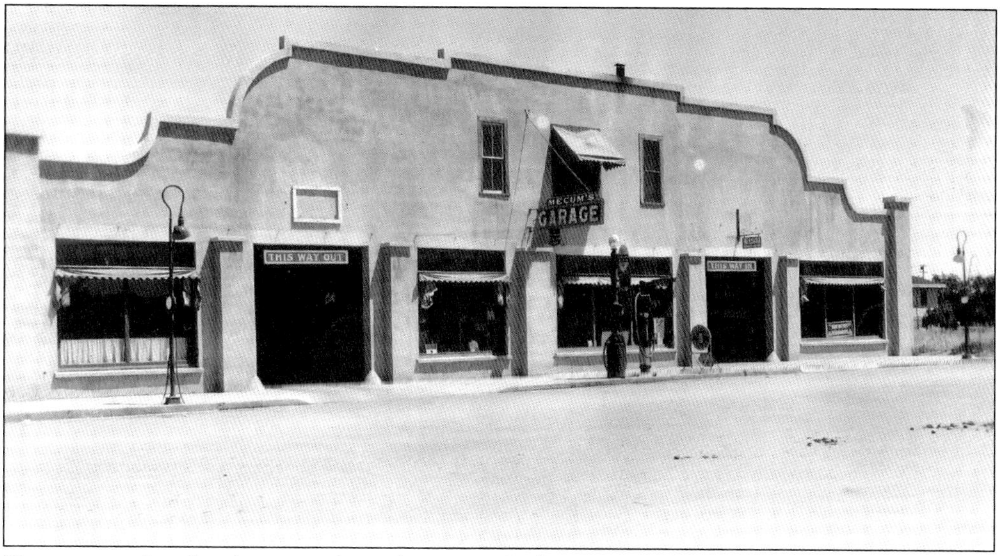

Outgrowing their local store and warehouse on Walker Street, the Poultry Producers of Central California moved into the north half of the spacious Mecum Garage on Fourth Street on July 31, 1933. The Poultry Producers would eventually use the entire building to house their inventory of feed, eggs, and chickens. The building was destroyed by fire in 1959. (Courtesy Bruce Gilmore.)

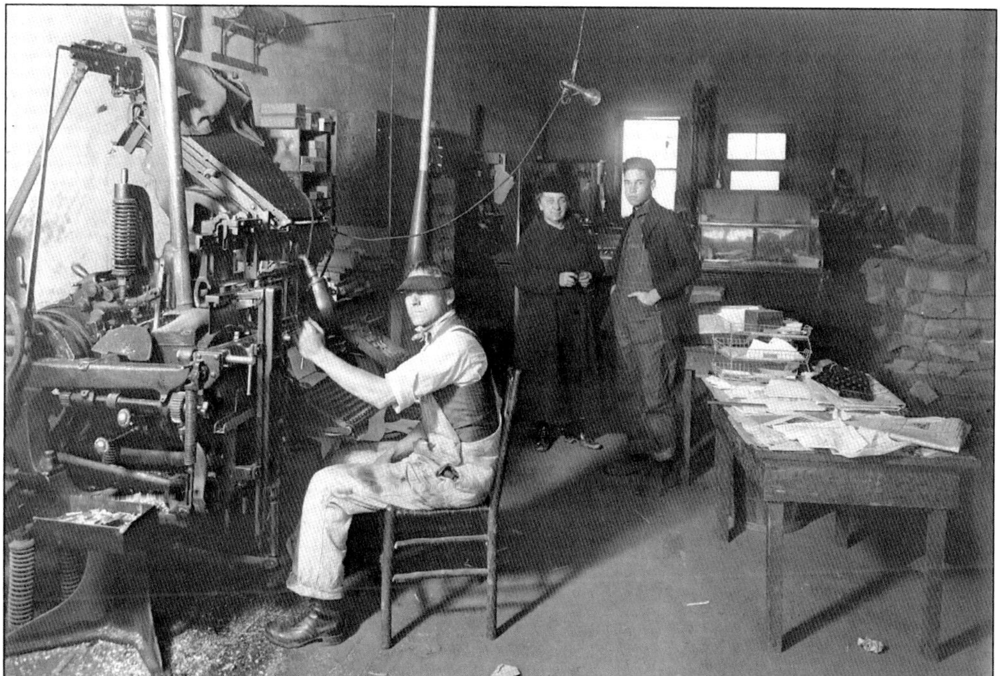

Printers had been setting type by hand for 400 years before Ottmar Mergenthaler developed his Linotype machine in the 1880s. These ingenious machines were used by the weekly Orland newspapers in the early 1910s. Pictured on the right is Donald Keene.

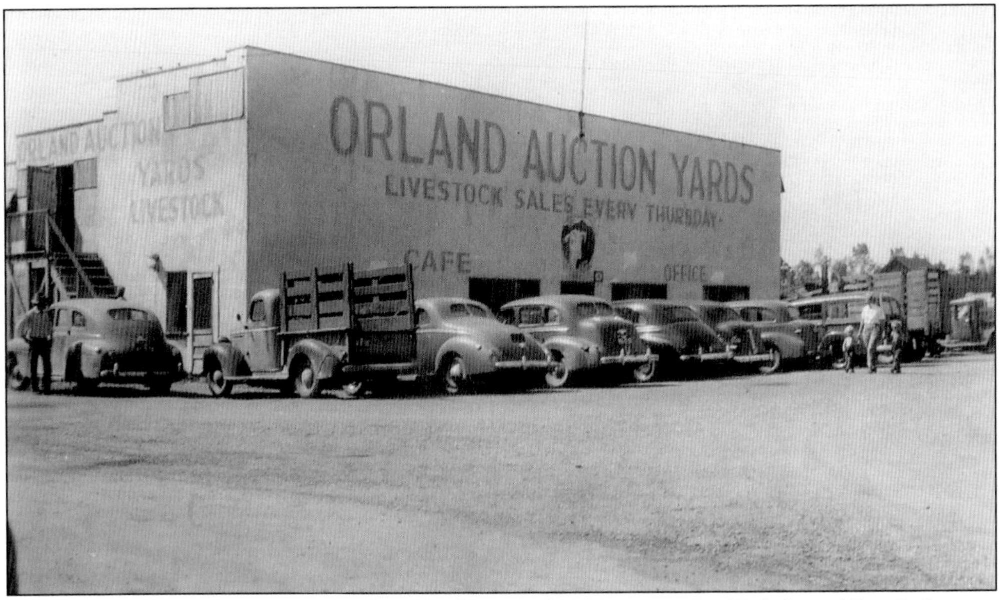

The Orland Livestock Auction Yard was built around 1939. Located at Eighth and South Streets, the yard sold beef cattle, feeder cattle, sheep, and hogs. Approximately 500 buyers and sellers would attend the Wednesday and Thursday sales. The yard employed 24 people and had a tremendous impact on the Orland economy. Owners included Charles Berry Sr., Harry Kubister, Ivan Stockton, Aaron Stockton, Bob Howard, and Scott Gleason. The yard, sold to Ed Lacque in 1977, burned down in 1979. (Courtesy George and Lana Trovao.)

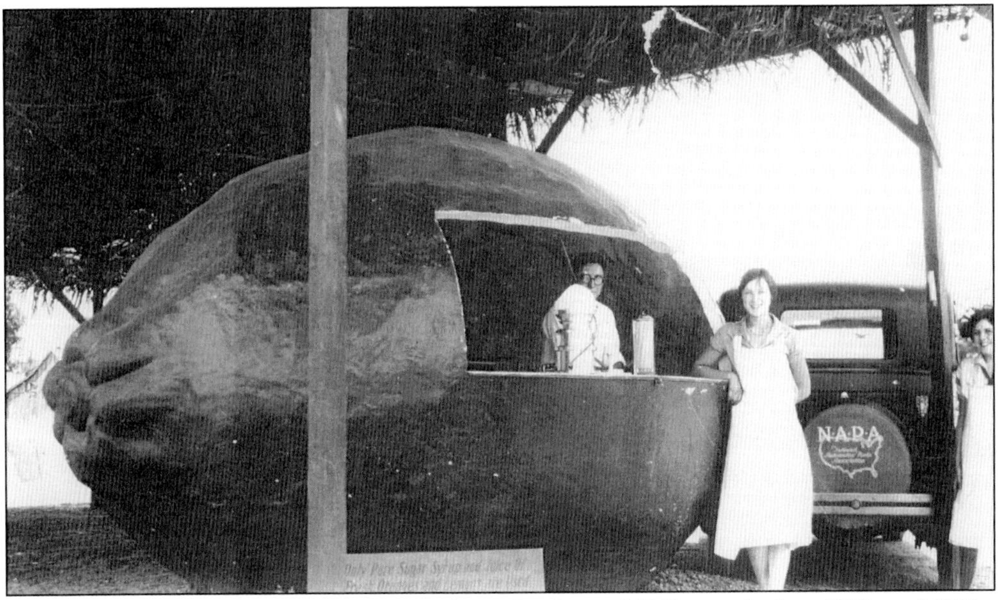

Jumbo lemonade stands were a common sight in the Central Valley in the late 1920s and 1930s. James Mills II used the stands to sell second-grade, cull, and surplus fruit from his vast lemon grove west of Maxwell. John Leonard was 20 years old when he bought his first stand. Orland's Jumbo Lemon stopped operation during World War II when it was difficult to purchase sugar. Pictured about 1928, from left to right, are John Leonard, Florence Leonard, and Gwen Thomason. (Courtesy Carol Baugher.)

Five

City and Community

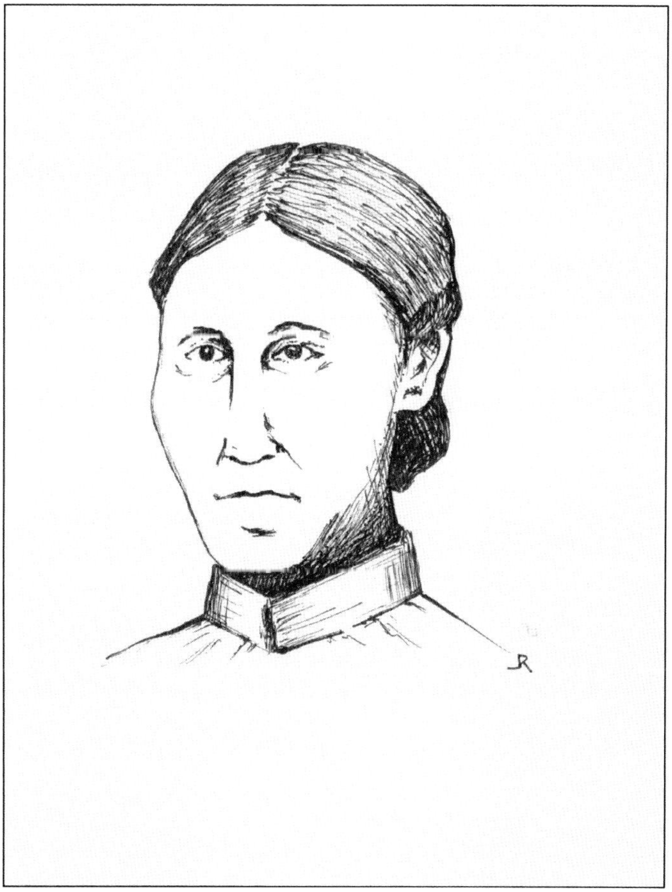

Anna Almira Springston was the wife of Emanuel Kesselring, a pioneer rancher of St. John and the Orland area. Emanuel was one of the first to plant wheat on the treeless valley floor of northern Colusa County, then known as the Colusa Plains. Moving to Orland in 1893, the Kesselrings entered into the hotel business and the public life of the community. Anna recognized the need for Orland's women to take a role in civic improvement and became a leading force in the organization of the Orland Women's Improvement Club. She was unanimously elected its first president on March 10, 1909. Anna passed away on September 4, 1927.

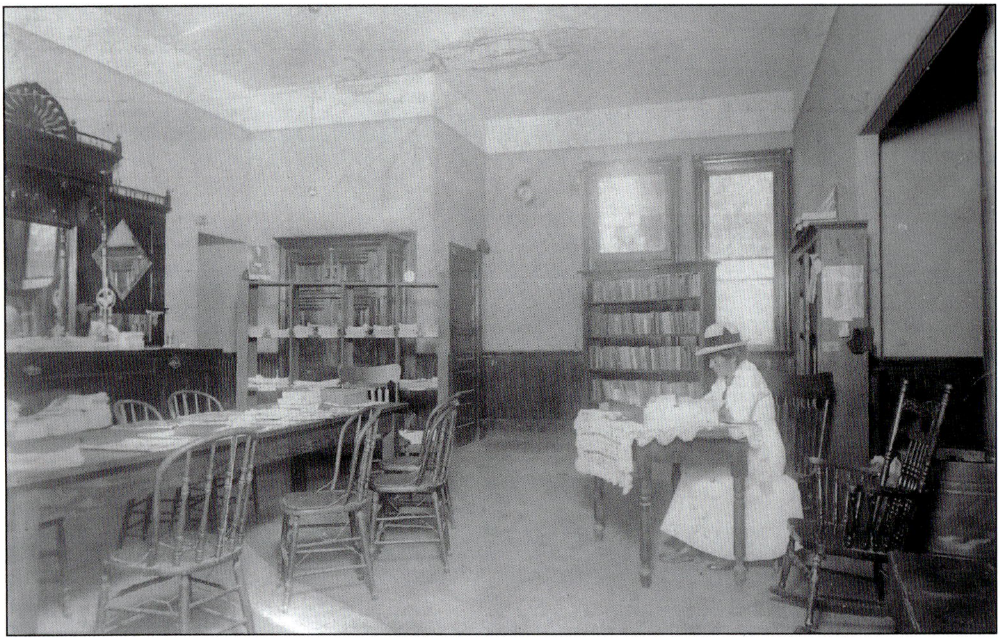

The Orland's Women's Improvement Club named a ways and means committee on November 9, 1910, to establish a reading room. Shared with a photographer, this room was opened in January 1911 with a "book shower and tea." A year later, the room moved to the old Hotel Royal, and Valerie Magnenat let out books each Saturday morning. This room had been the hotel bar, which can be seen at the left.

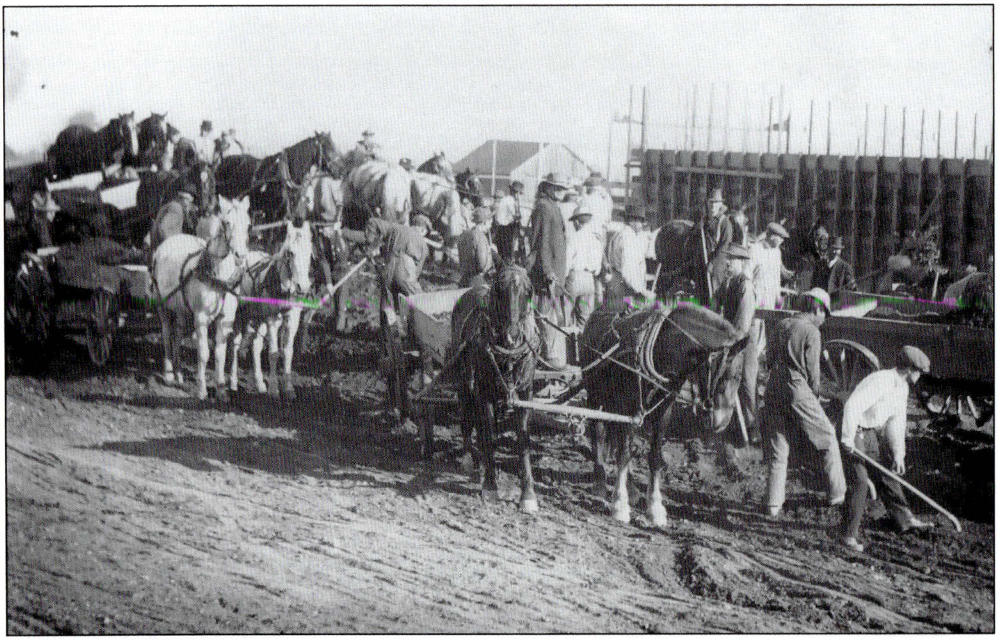

Orland's first community Work Day was held on December 3, 1916, to prepare the block where the Carnegie Library would be built. To fill the swale that ran through the property, soil was brought in by wagon from Stony Creek and from the mounds of excavated dirt beside the Orland High School gymnasium then under construction (pictured in the right background).

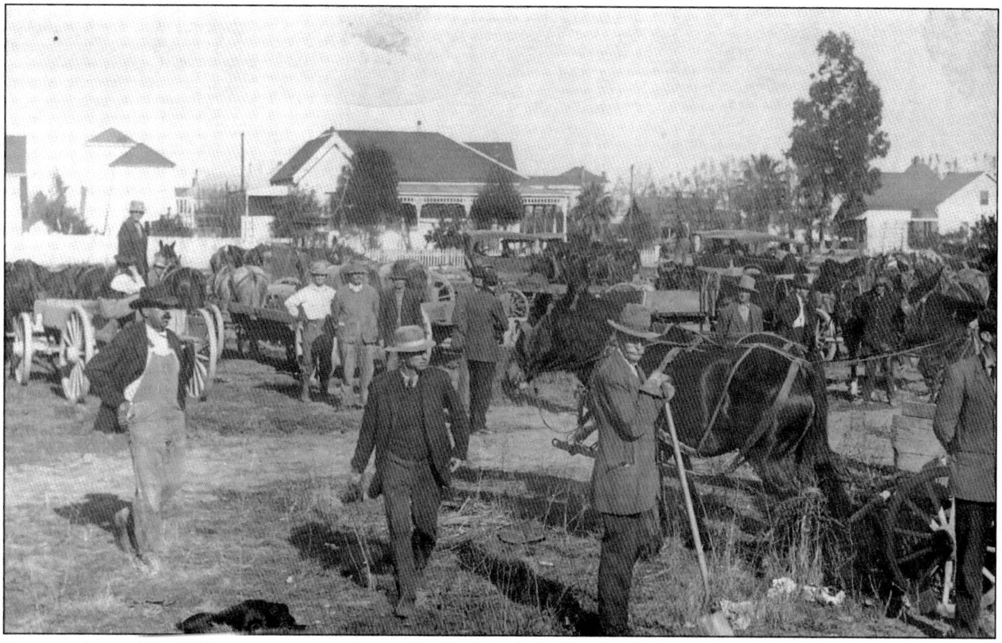

Pictured are Work Day crews ready to receive and dump the wagonloads of dirt. Pictured in the foreground from left to right are Ed Hale, owner of the Orland Creamery; Willard Clark, rancher and civic leader; and F. W. Sidener, county supervisor. The Orland Women's Improvement Club served dinner to the workers, who leveled the block in one day (December 3, 1916).

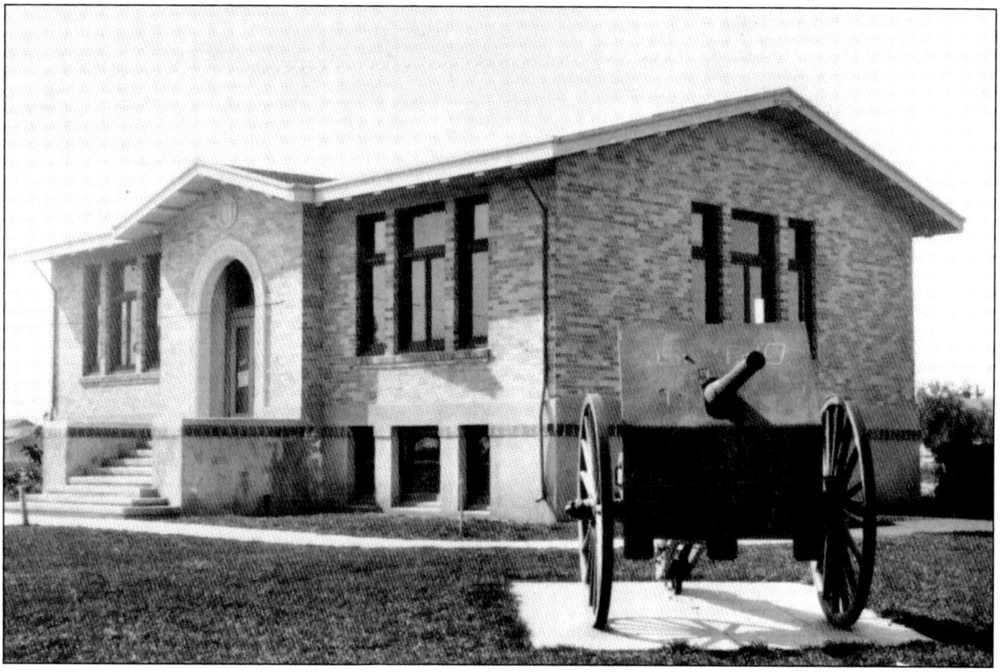

The city library was built in 1919–1920 with a Carnegie Foundation grant of $8,000 on lots bought and paid for by the Orland Women's Improvement Club before the city bonded itself for the remainder of the block for a city park. Construction had been delayed in an effort to obtain a larger grant but to no avail. The cannon was a World War I souvenir.

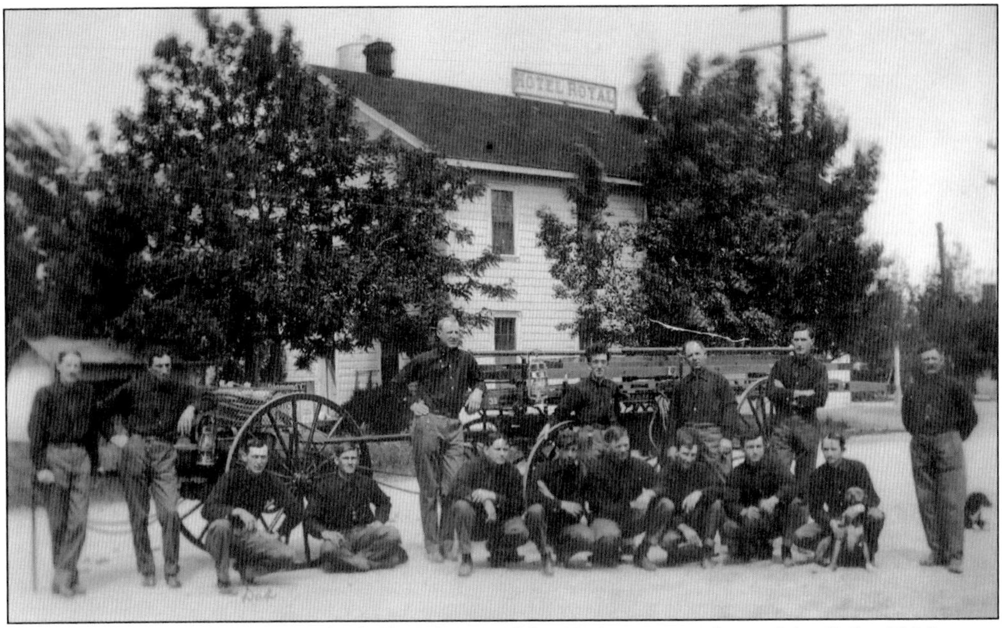

Chief Phil Noerager (fifth from the left) and most of the 22 charter members of the Orland Volunteer Fire Department are pictured in front of their first hook-and-ladder wagon. The department was formed after a devastating fire on June 19, 1911, nearly destroyed all of the business buildings adjacent to the Hotel Orland on Fourth Street. Noerager was the local manager of Northern California Power Company.

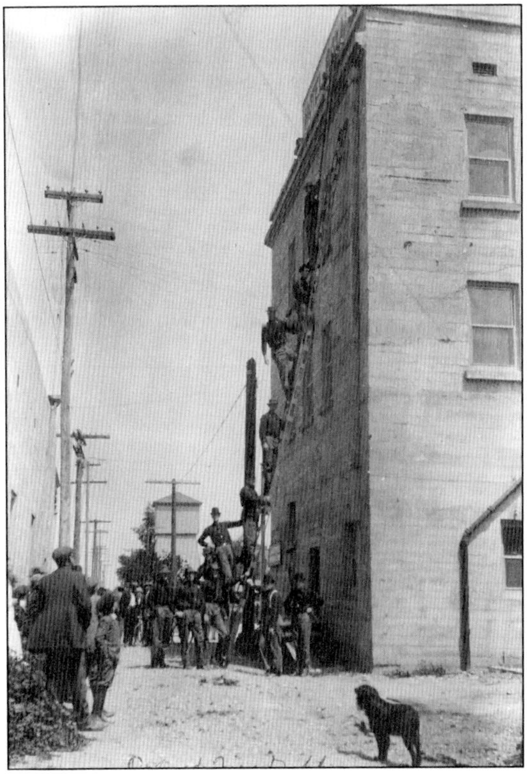

Early Orland firemen practice on one of their ladders in the alley at the east end of the Hotel Royal. Equipment on the new American LaFrance hook-and-ladder truck included one 35-foot rapid hoist ladder, one 20-foot wall ladder, one 16-foot wall ladder, one 14-foot roof ladder, 26 canvas and leather buckets, pike poles, tin roof cutter, fire axes, rope, crowbars, and fire lanterns. The truck was stored in Proctor Knott Hicks's building, which also doubled as the meeting place for the town council.

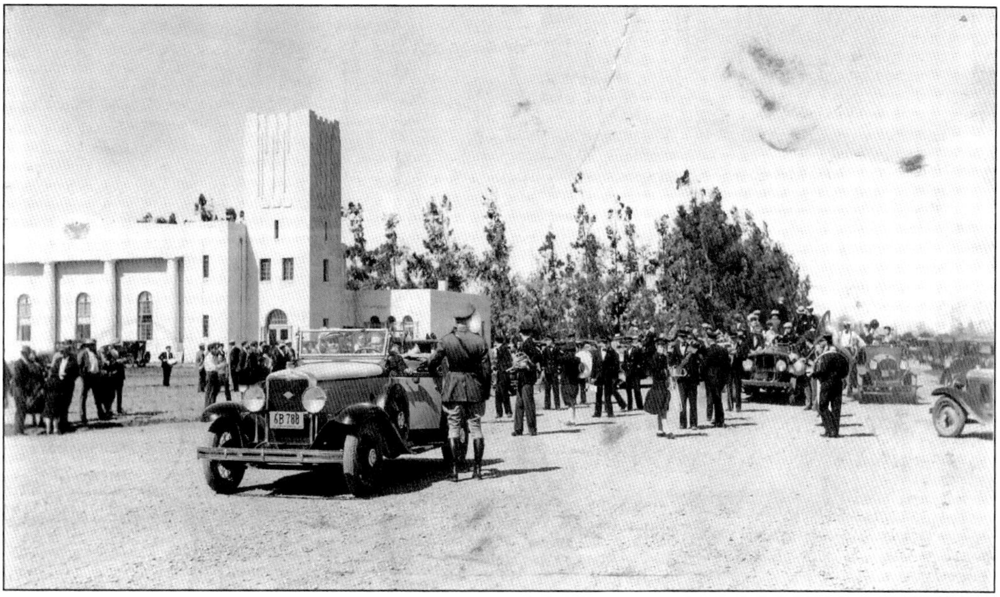

The 1939 Northern California Fireman's Association convention was held at the Orland Memorial Hall. Participants are shown at the start of a parade through downtown. Orland fire chief Harry Strawn is visible in the passenger seat of the 1932 Chevrolet in the left foreground. Behind the town band and to the right is Orland's first motor-driven fire truck. It was a 1.5-ton REO acquired in 1921.

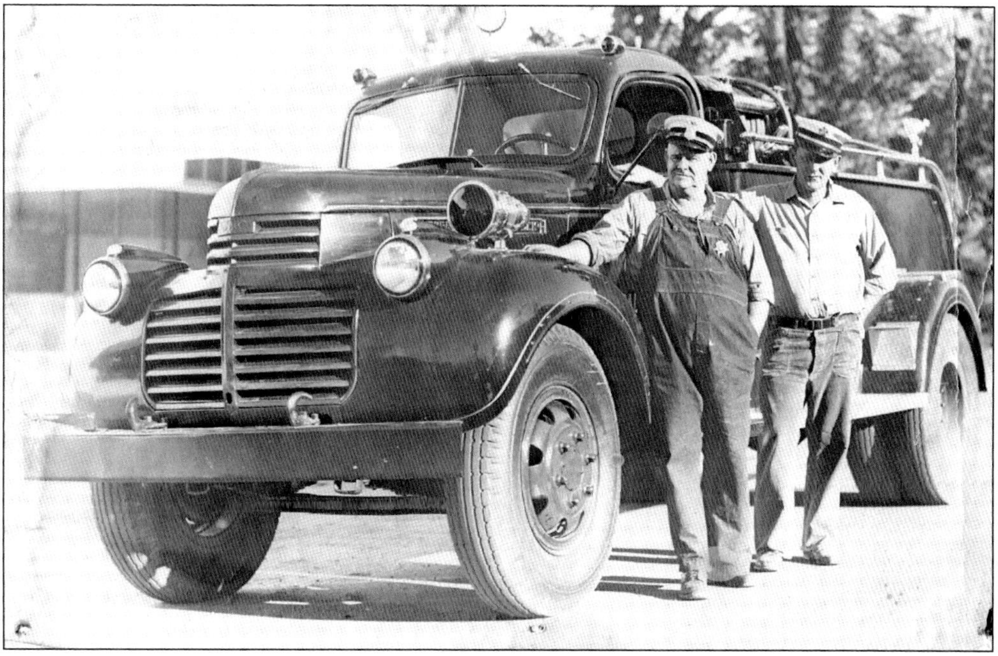

The formation of the Orland Rural Fire District took place in June 1935 to offer fire protection for the entire land of Orland. Pictured is a new GMC fire truck purchased by the rural district board in 1946 to replace an older Ford tank truck. Standing next to the truck are Harry Strawn (left) and Everett "Sharky" Schmidt. Strawn was chief from 1927 to 1936 and from 1937 to 1939, and Schmidt was chief from 1943 to 1949.

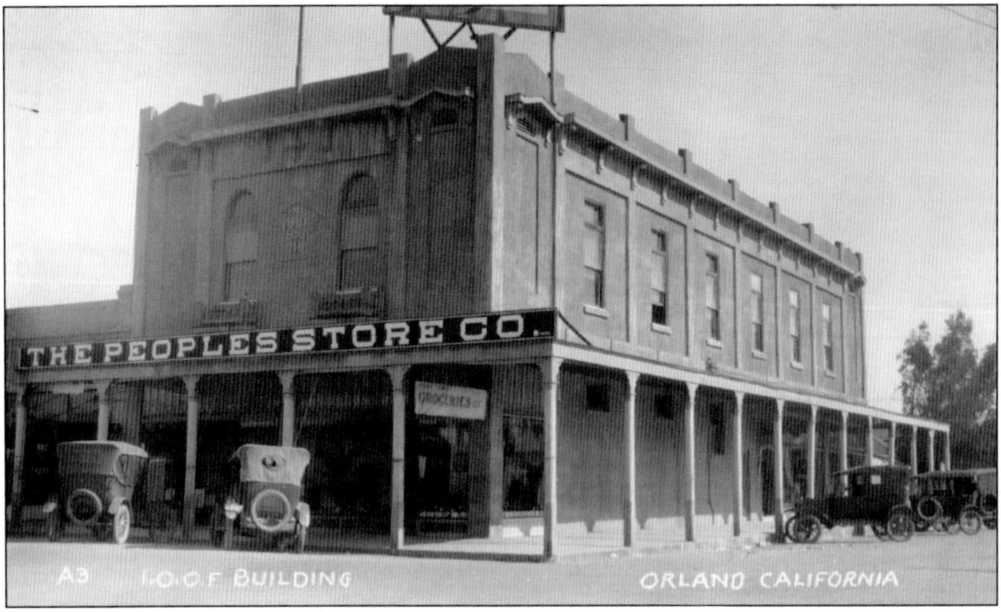

The dedication of the Odd Fellows Building at Fourth and Colusa Streets was held on November 11, 1910, and was one of the biggest and most successful lodge events ever held in Orland. The ceremonies began at 3:00 p.m. with A. J. Zumwalt of Willows presiding. At 7:30 p.m., there was a three-act comedy drama in the Orland Opera House followed by a grand ball and a supper in the banquet room of the new hall.

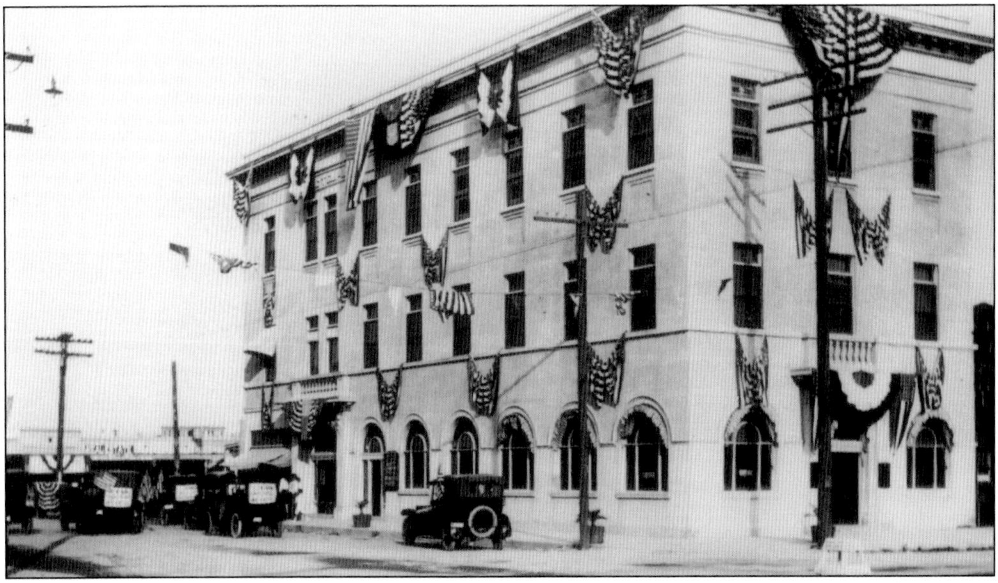

Optimism was high in February 1909 when Orland Lodge No. 265, Free and Accepted Masons, with 59 members and no money in the bank, decided to build a new hall. Through trades and real estate deals, the desired lot at Fourth and Colusa Streets was secured. The three-story building was designed by T. L. Stiles of San Francisco and was built for $21,500 in 1913. The photograph dates from late September 1917 when the automobiles carried large signs announcing a change in the Glenn County Fair dates. (Courtesy California History Room, California State Library, Sacramento, California.)

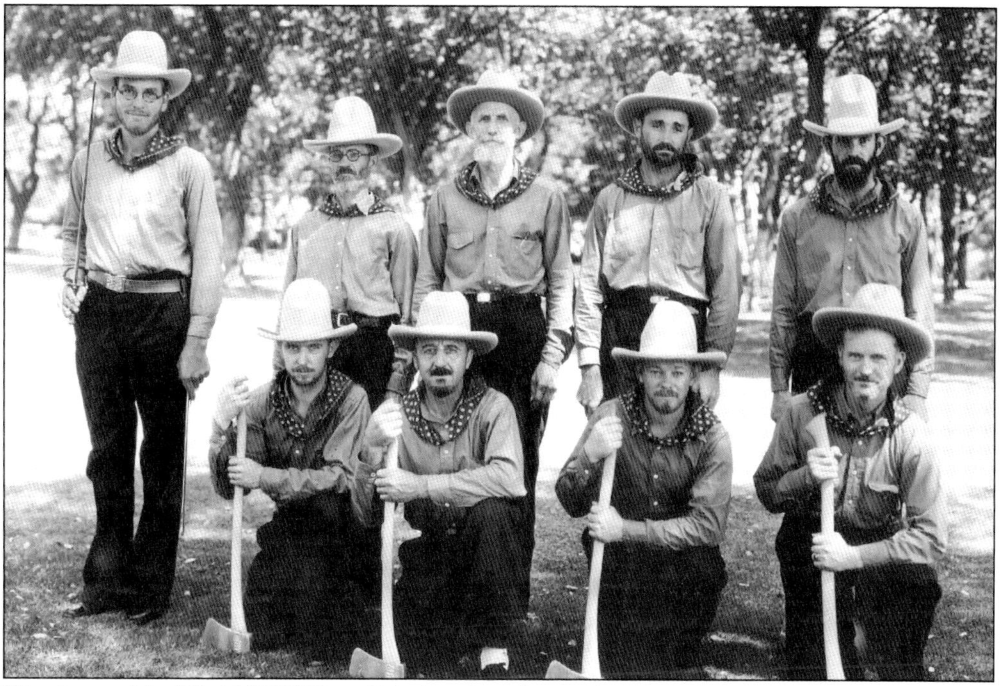

Woodmen of the World (WOW) and Modern Woodmen of America (MWA) were fraternal benefit insurance societies that had local camps in Orland and surrounding communities. Pictured is the Orland MWA's Whiskerino Drill Team at the 1931 state fair. The members are, from left to right, (first row) Ray Harrison, Ray Nighbert, Burdette Johnson, and Art Edwards; (second row) Bill Fellerson, H. L. Lundeen, Dr. C. C. Bihler, Russell Porter, and Jack Weber.

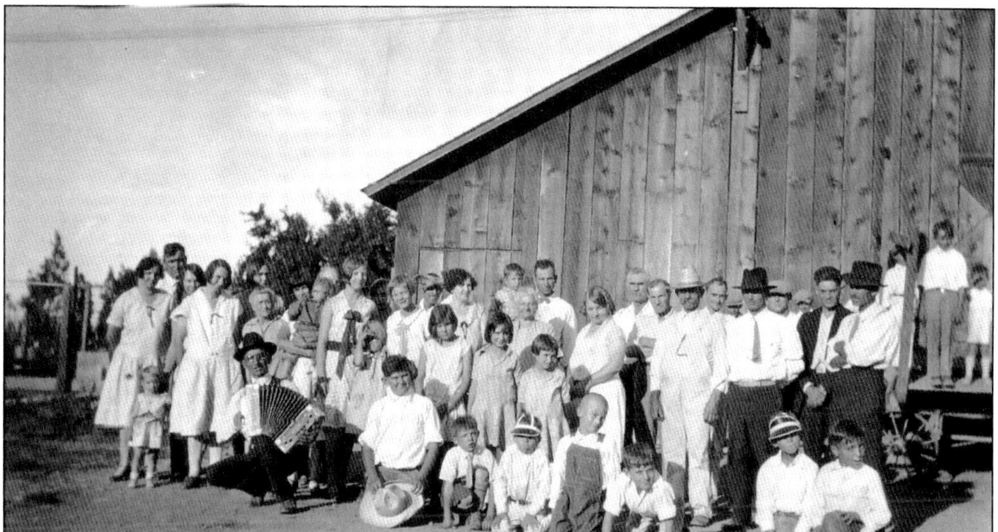

Reunions, picnics, and fraternal gatherings were important events for new immigrants to stay connected with family and those from their area of origin. Pictured is a gathering of Bohemian families and settlers in the Orland area at the Benda ranch north of Lake School in the early 1930s. The men were members of the ZCBJ, short for Zapadni Cesko Bratrska Jednota, a fraternal organization that provided ethnic solidarity for Czech immigrants. (Courtesy of Jim Slyh.)

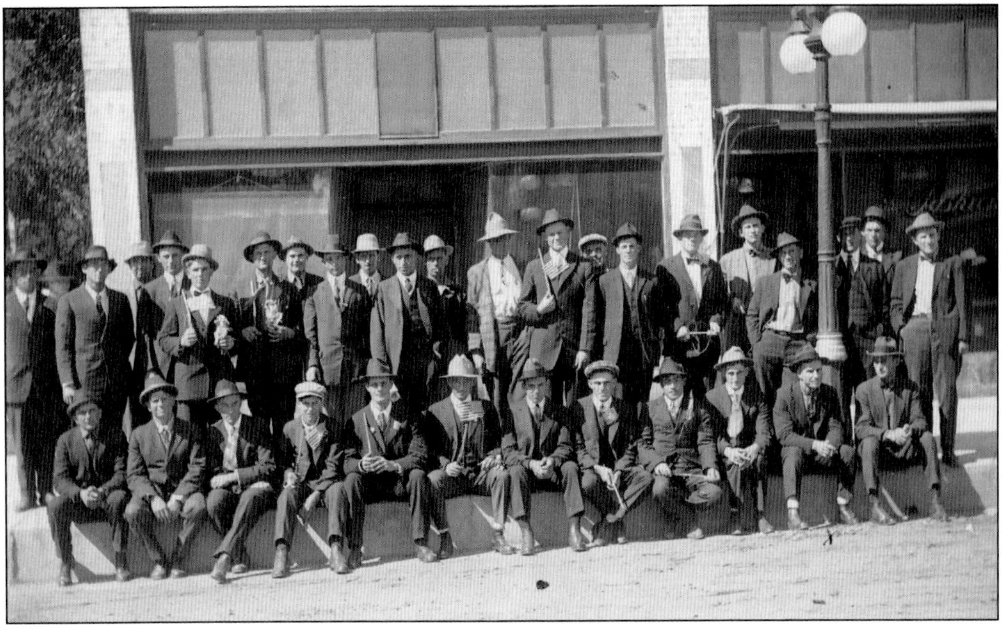

Patriotism ran high during 1917–1918 as a large number of Glenn County men enlisted or were called to active military service in World War I. On September 24, 1917, six hundred people turned out to bid the Orland men farewell. The upper grammar school students marched to the depot and gave the men several rousing cheers. Pictured are part of the 37 men from Orland and Glenn County ready to leave Willows for training camp. (Courtesy Geraldine Reager.)

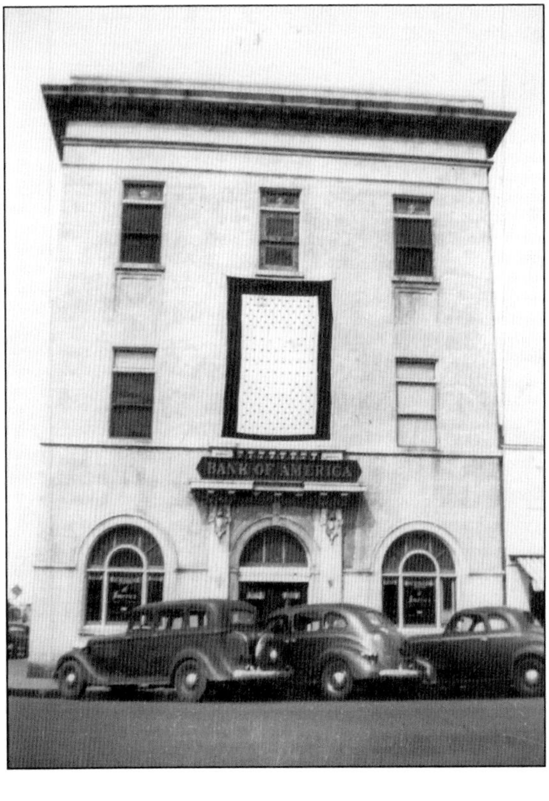

During World War II, a large "Son In Service" or "Service Star" flag was hung on the Masonic Temple to denote Orland's direct participation in the war effort. Each star represented a man or woman from the area in active military service. When the death of a serviceman occurred, a gold star was placed on the flag. The photograph was taken September 1942. A strong wind later destroyed this flag.

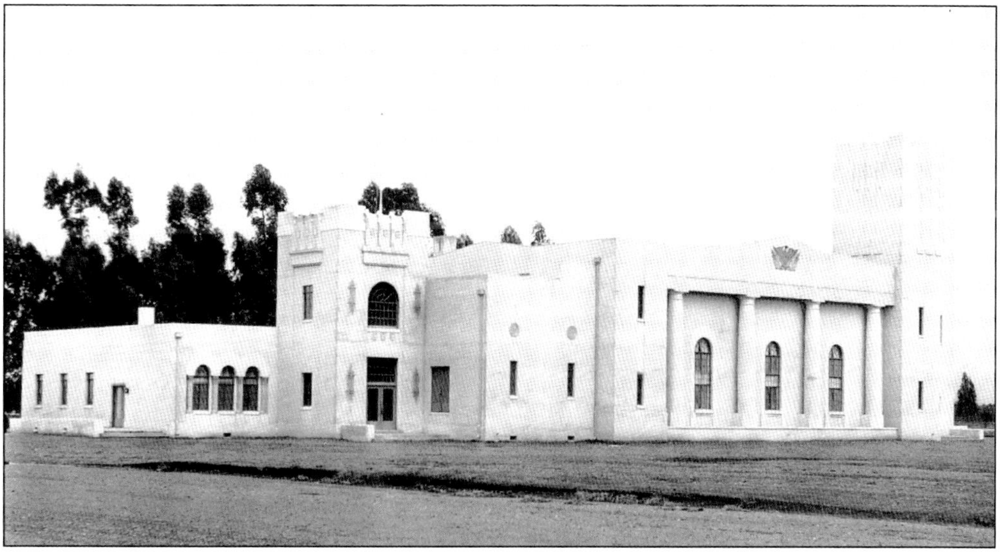

Representatives from the American Legion Posts of Orland and Willows met with county supervisors in 1922 and 1925 to request funds to erect Legion buildings in each town. The ground-breaking ceremony was held on April 17, 1930. The building was ready for occupancy the following March and dedicated on May 2, 1931. The walks, curbs, and gutters were added in 1935.

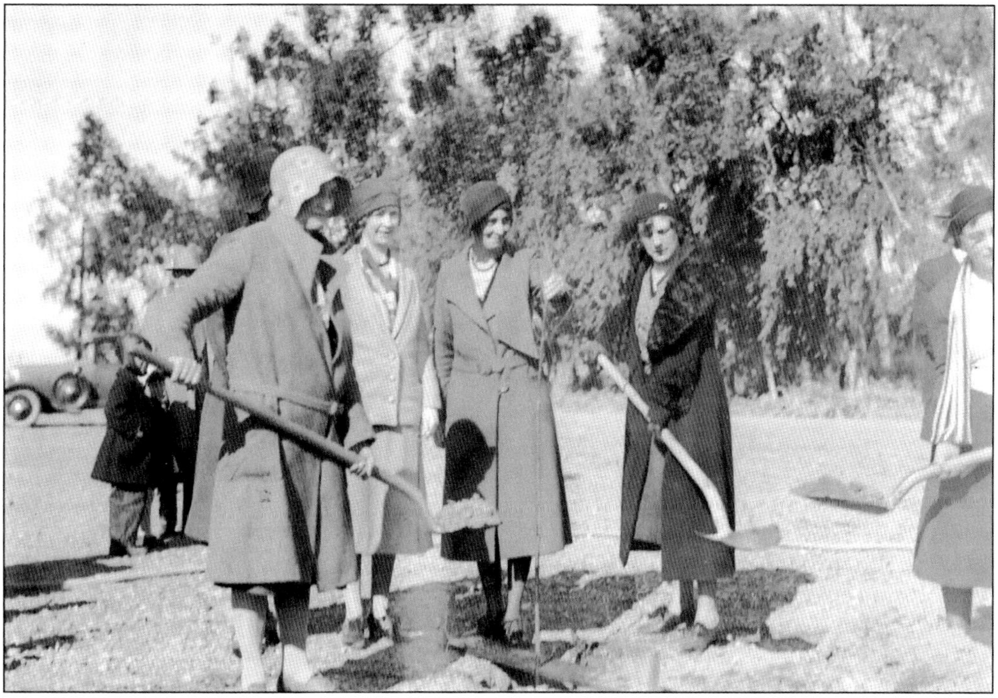

The landscaping of the new Memorial Hall began on February 22, 1932 (the 200th anniversary of George Washington's birth). Twenty-four local organizations joined in planting trees that formed a continuous line around three sides of the grounds. In March 1935, the project continued with the planting of 264 shrubs.

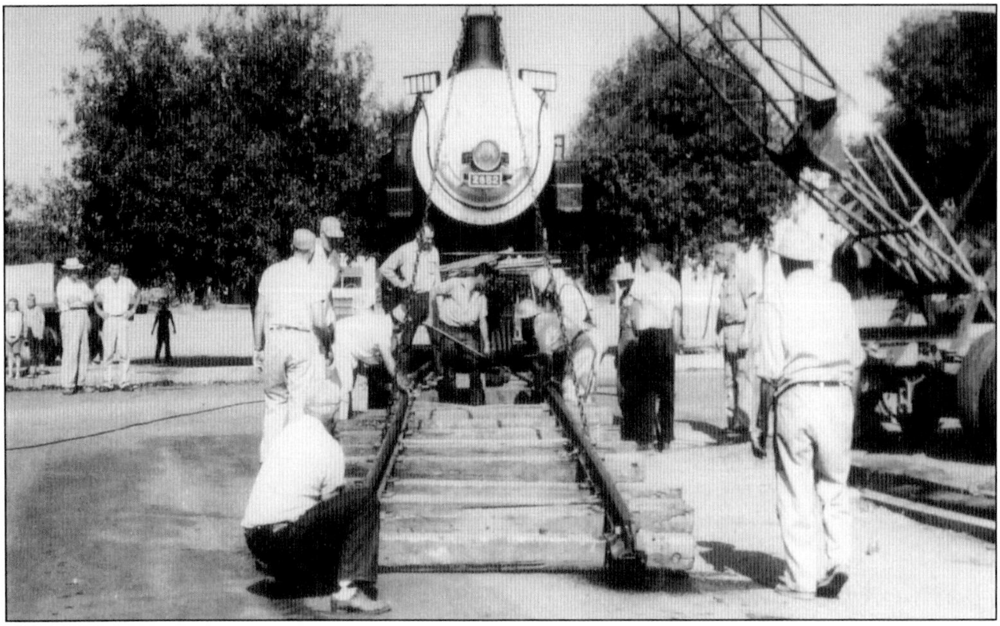

Southern Pacific steam locomotive No. 2582 was a donation to the people of Glenn County to mark the passing of the steam age. The 271,000-pound engine was moved from a siding by the depot to the Glenn County Fairgrounds on July 19–21, 1958. Volunteers and railroad employees used a winch truck, cable, and four sections of 35-foot rail to pull the engine and tender forward on its last run of 13 blocks. Engine No. 2582 is shown moving east through the Mill Street School yard.

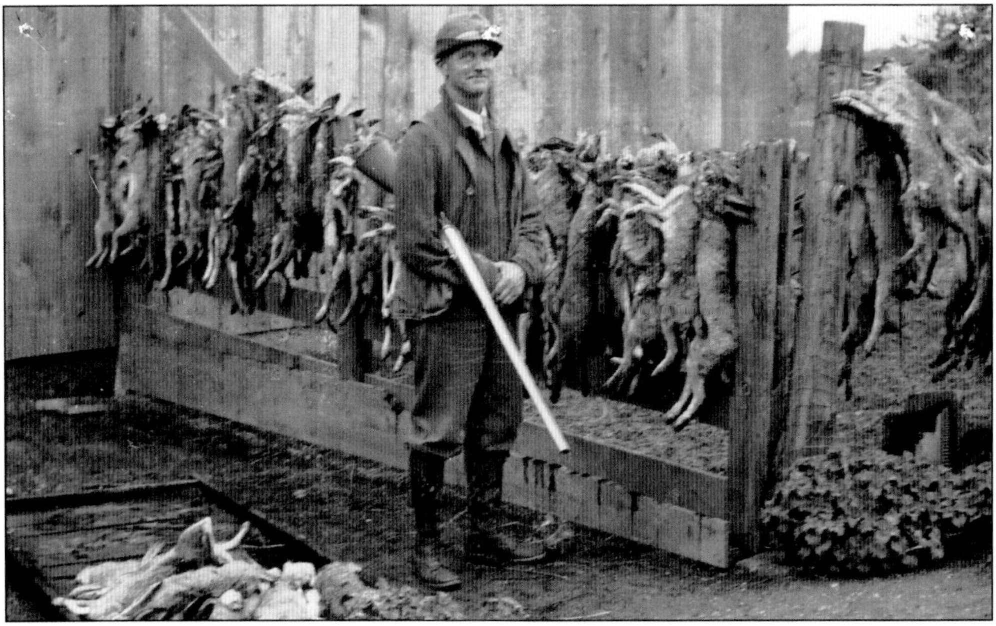

Black-tailed jackrabbits were a serious pest to agricultural crops at the beginning of the 20th century. "Rabbit Drives" were held during the 1920s and early 1930s to reduce the jackrabbit population. Pictured is Art Edwards at the Lemon Home School north of Orland after the February 18, 1934, rabbit drive.

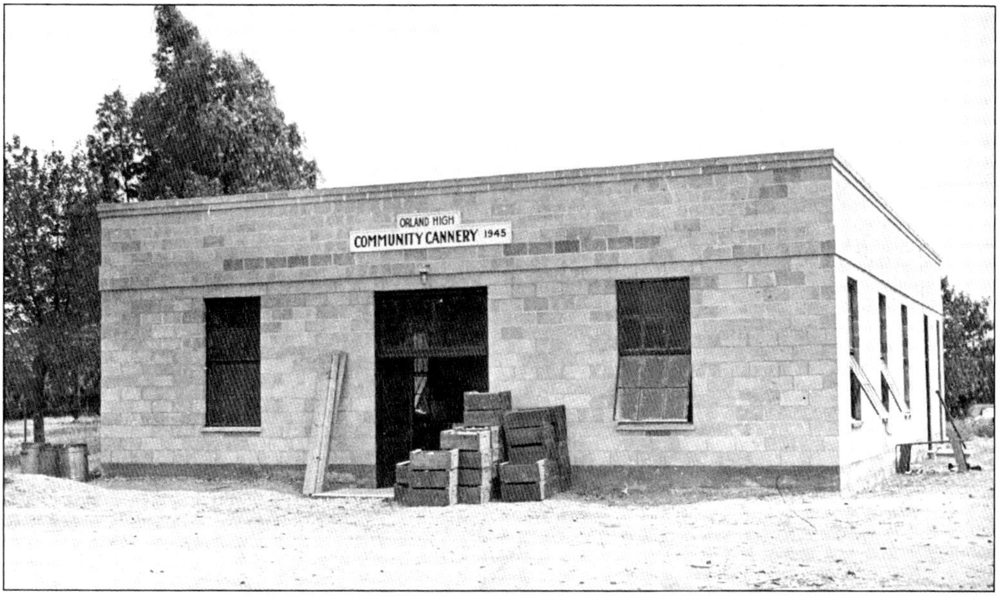

The Community Cannery was a 40-by-60-foot concrete-block building on the high school campus outside the southeast corner of the football stadium. Canning started on June 19, 1945, using equipment on loan from the Federal Food Conservation Program. During the next 18 years, foods canned included corn, peas, beets, apricots, peaches, pears, fig jam, beef, turkey, venison, salmon, and tuna. Members of the community made appointments through the high school office and had to bring their own pans, utensils, and sugar. During the peak years in the 1950s, the cannery operated two shifts and once topped 130,000 cans in a season. Art Alberico was in charge of the cannery. Pictured below are cannery employees Avanella Holt (left) and Emma Brun adding water to cans filled with fruit before sending them through the exhaust box. (Courtesy Orland Alumni Association.)

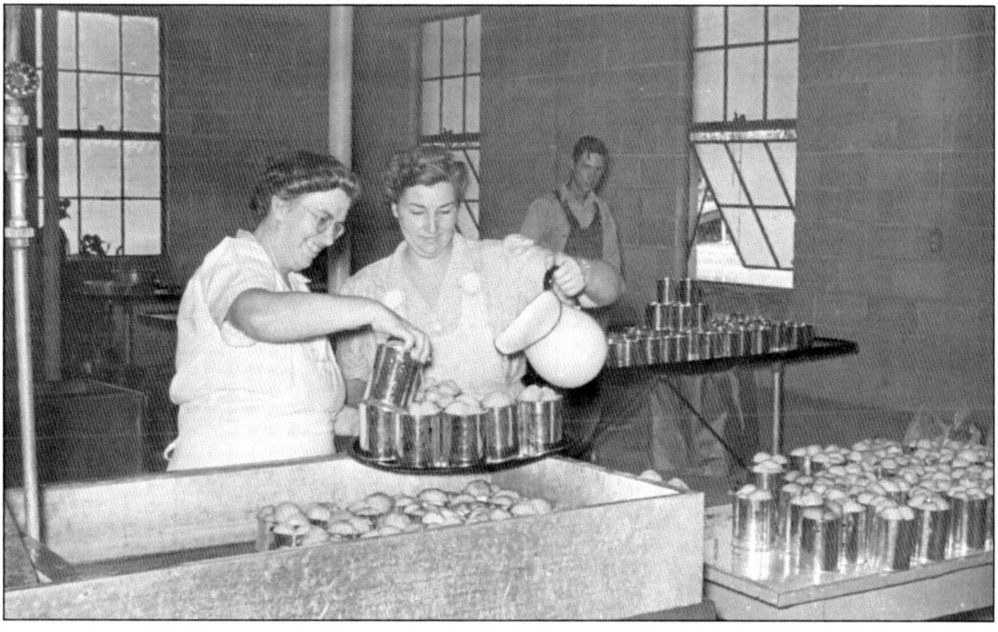

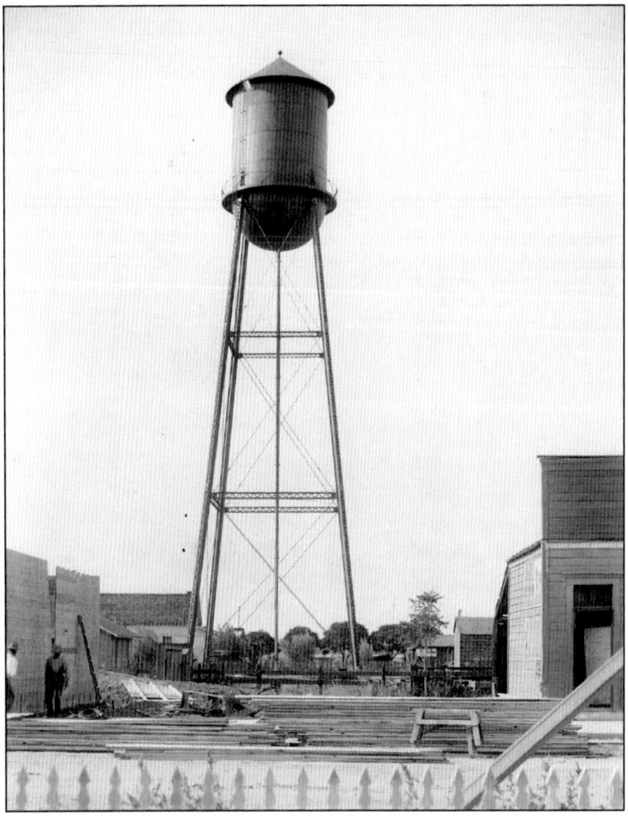

The municipal water system dates from 1912. The steel water tower was manufactured by the Des Moines Bridge and Iron Company of Des Moines, Iowa. The tank is 21 feet in diameter, 24 feet tall, and will hold 80,000 gallons of water. The workmen at left are putting up forms for Ed Hale's new creamery building.

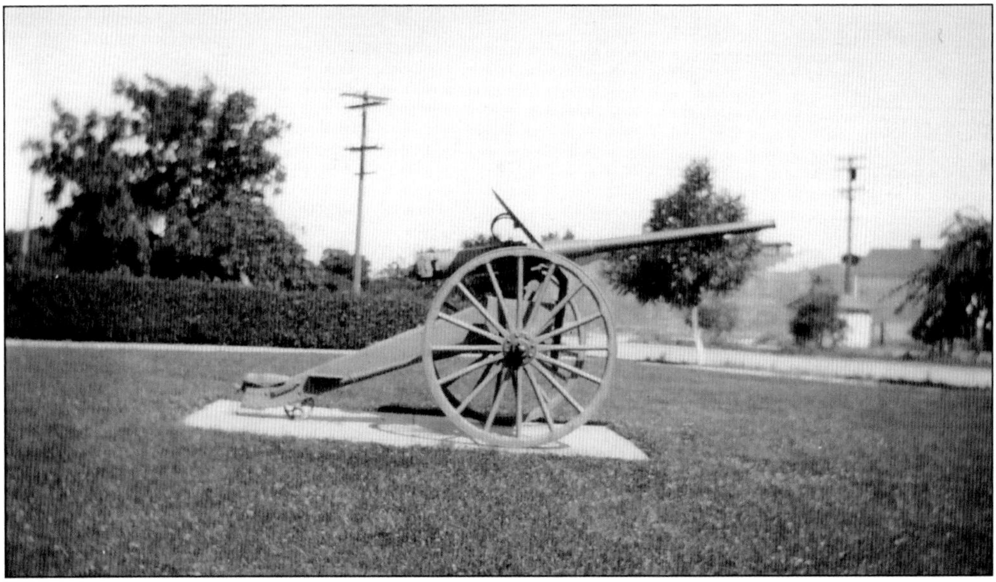

Orland's first artillery piece was a 24-inch cannon that saw action in France during World War I. The gun was secured through the effort of Sec. Edward A. Kirk of the chamber of commerce from the Benicia, California, arsenal. It was placed on display in Library Park during the summer of 1921 as a reminder of the heroism that went into winning the war. The cannon was donated to a World War II American Legion scrap metal drive in September 1942.

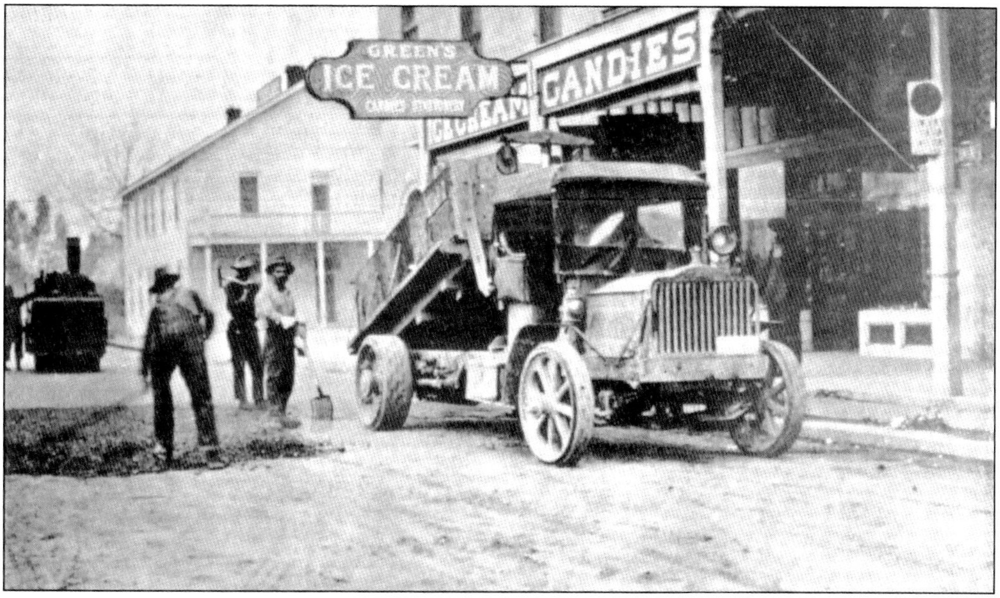

The paving of the business district streets in the early 1920s was met with bitter opposition because property owners were going to be assessed individually to pay for the paving in front of their property. Shown are the finest machines of those days spreading and rolling the blacktop, called "Warrenite," on Fourth Street near the Colusa Street corner. The community-wide "Paving Celebration" in May 1922 included a decorated automobile parade, a baseball game against Willows (the visitors won 13-7), a radio concert in Maple Hall (Masonic Temple), and a street dance with music provided by a 10-piece jazz band from Red Bluff. (Above courtesy *Orland Unit-Register.*)

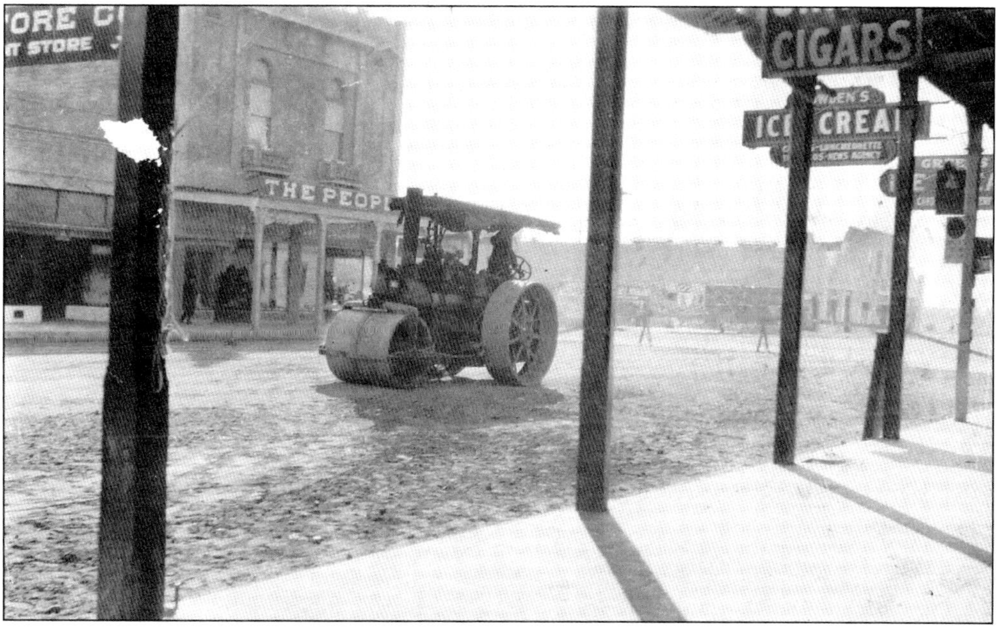

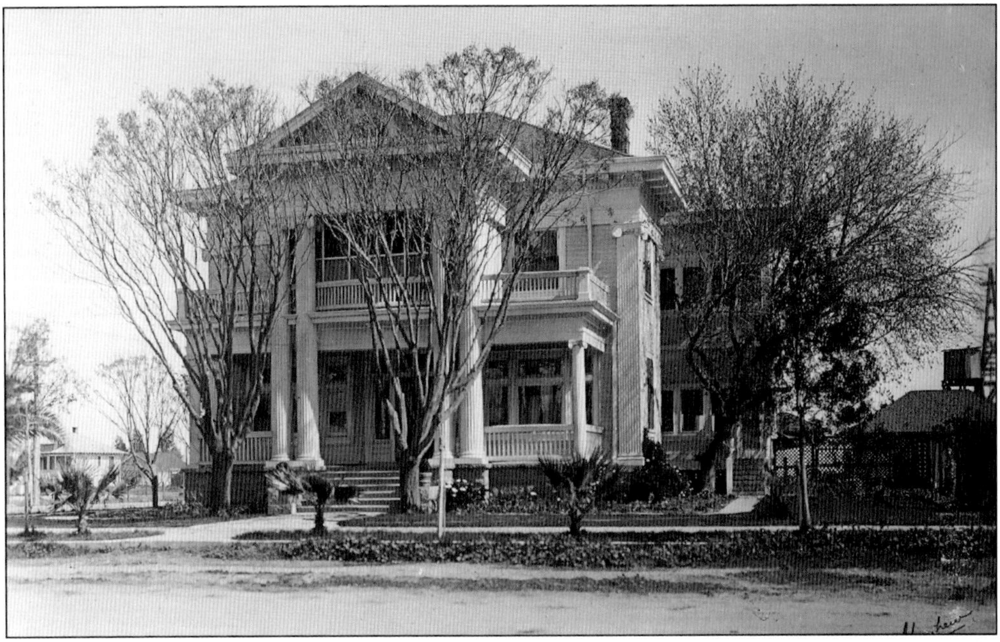

The Colonial house at the southeast corner of Third and Walker Streets was built in 1909 by Earl H. Mecum, a prominent Orland merchant. About 1917, the house was purchased by Allen T. Moore, whose family owned it until 1946. Moore was a sheep raiser and owner of the People's Store, a general store and grocery. After Moore's death, the house was sold and used as an apartment and restaurants. The landmark was dismantled in 1973.

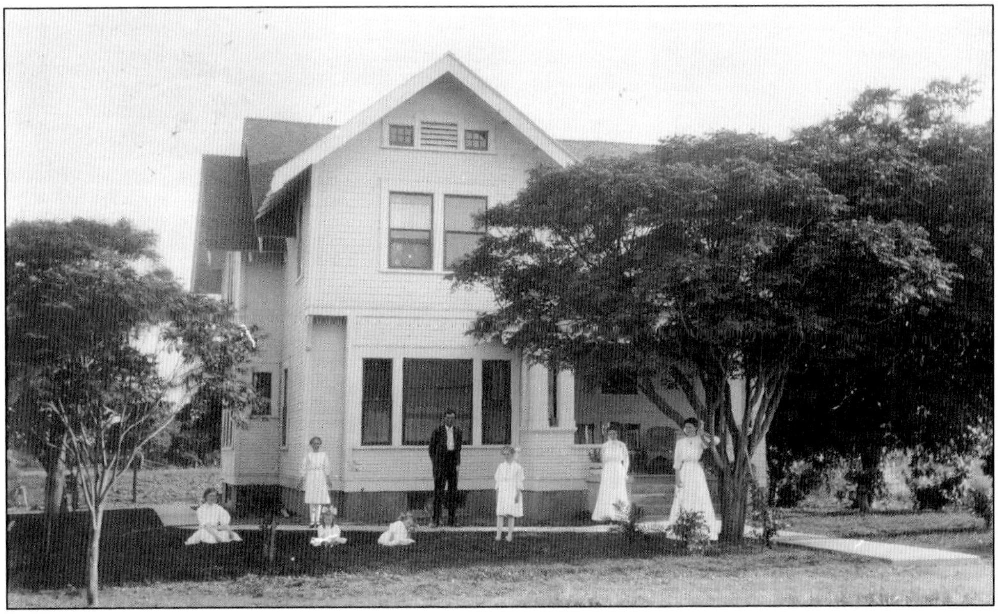

George Absalom Reager was a native and lifelong resident of the land of Orland. He was a farmer of wheat and barley, and a civic leader serving as one of Orland's early mayors. George and Evaline's East Walker Street home was completed in the spring of 1910 by Landis and Webster. Pictured from left to right are Ruth, Mary, Evalyn, Reba, George, Georgiana, Evaline, and Hazel. Fire destroyed the house on July 28, 1997. (Courtesy Arthalyn Kublick.)

Six

Schools and Education

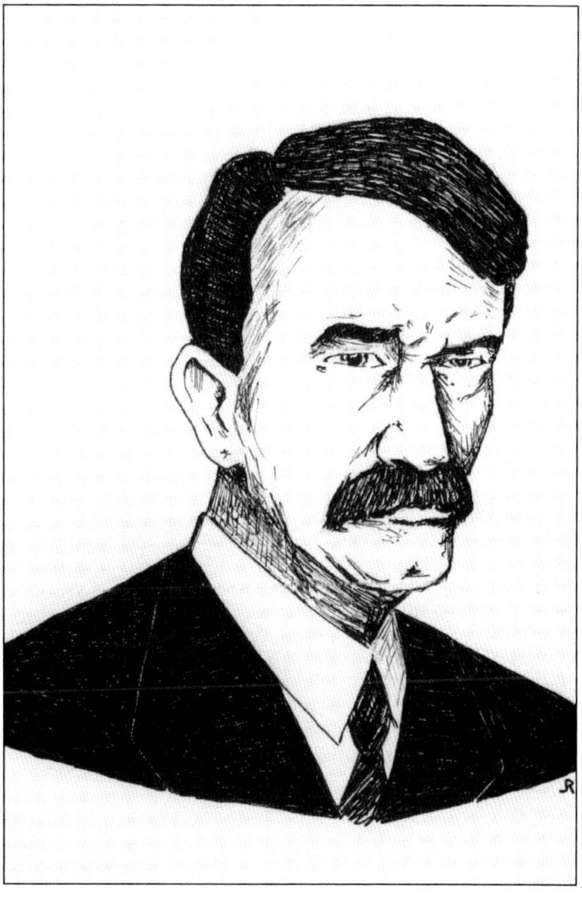

Prof. Jerome B. Patch was the founder and first president of Orland College (1882–1891). As a religious educator, he traveled about the West teaching, preaching, and establishing schools. He arrived in Orland about 1880 and arranged for a town meeting to discuss his proposed school. Receiving a favorable response, Patch then sold stock to local businessmen and area landowners to secure the necessary funds for constructing the brick building. The doors of Orland College opened for business in September 1882 with a student body of 26. Patch's famous standoff incident with Constable Gifford took place in the college in January 1884, and he was relieved of his teaching duties. When he died in March 1891, he was remembered for his unreasonable stubbornness and erratic, impulsive, and obstinate behavior. Others, however, recalled his organizing skills, perseverance, and energy for overcoming difficulties. Orland's most enigmatic character was undoubtedly Professor Patch.

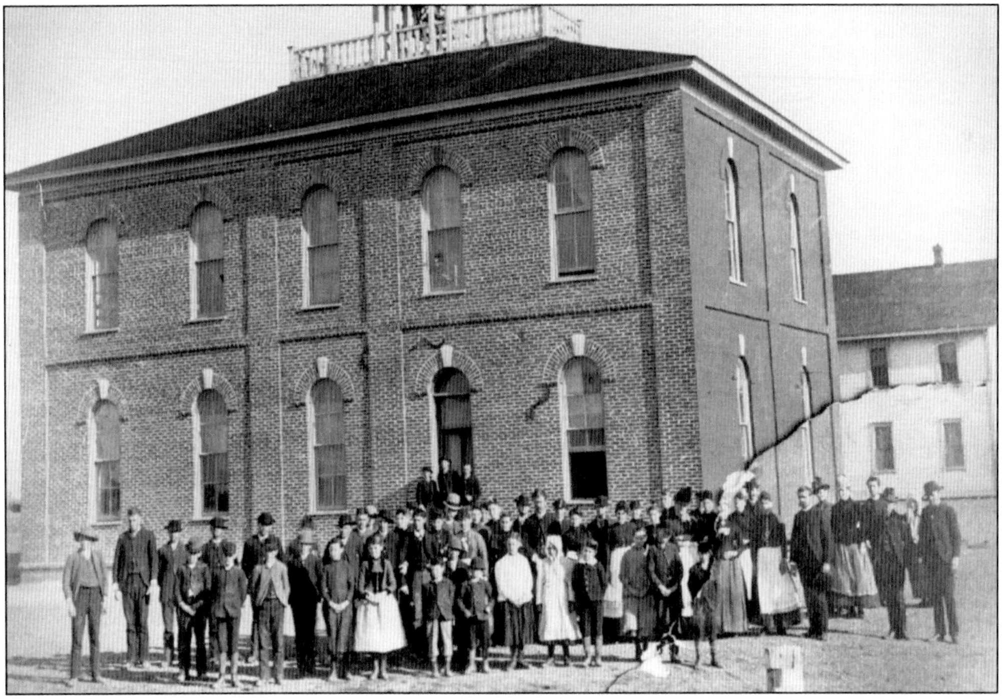

Orland College was located on 13 acres donated by Albert Papst across Walker Street just east of Woodward Avenue. Three bricklayers and Professor Patch, the founder of the college, constructed the two-story brick building for an estimated $10,000. The doors opened for students in September 1882. A two-story wooden dormitory was constructed directly behind the college and provided the needed housing for out-of-town students. (Courtesy Thelma White and Special Collections, Meriam Library, California State University, Chico.)

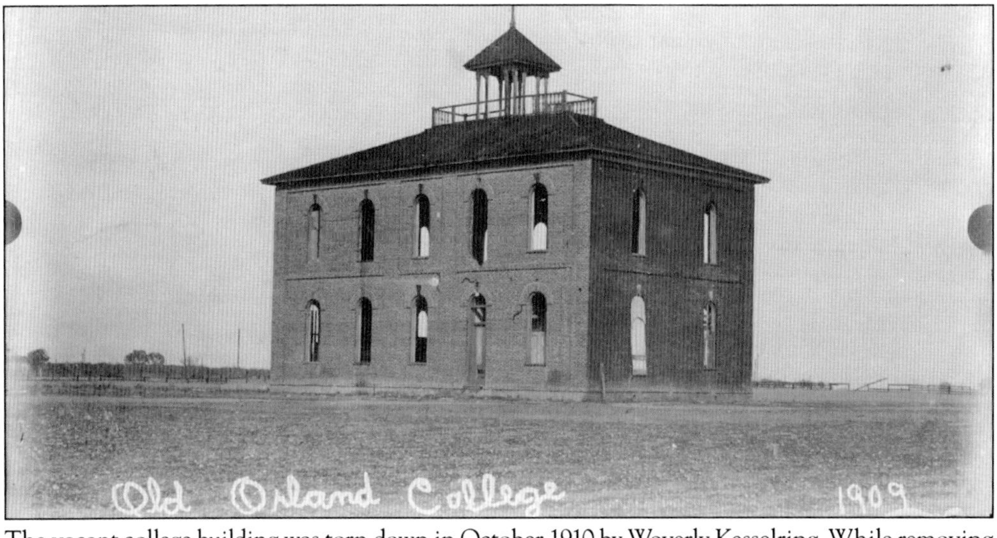

The vacant college building was torn down in October 1910 by Waverly Kesselring. While removing a brick wall, the cornerstone was discovered that had been placed there 30 years previously by Professor Patch. A small Bible that had belonged to Annie Patch, the deceased wife of the founder and first principal of the college, was found to be well preserved. The bricks were used to build two houses in the 400 block on Fourth Street.

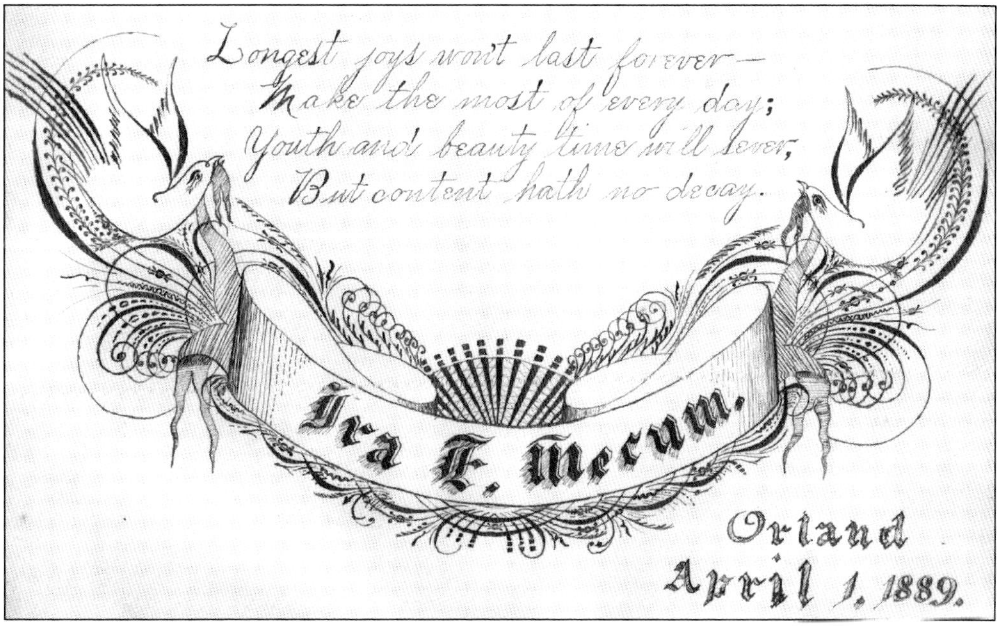

Small, hardbound, autograph books were popular in the latter half of the 19th century. Friends, schoolmates, and teachers were asked to sign their names, and most added a short poem or verse. "Josie" (believed to be Josephine Taylor) was a student at Orland Normal during the 1888–1889 academic year when she asked Ira Mecum to sign her book. He became a successful Orland merchant and early automobile dealer.

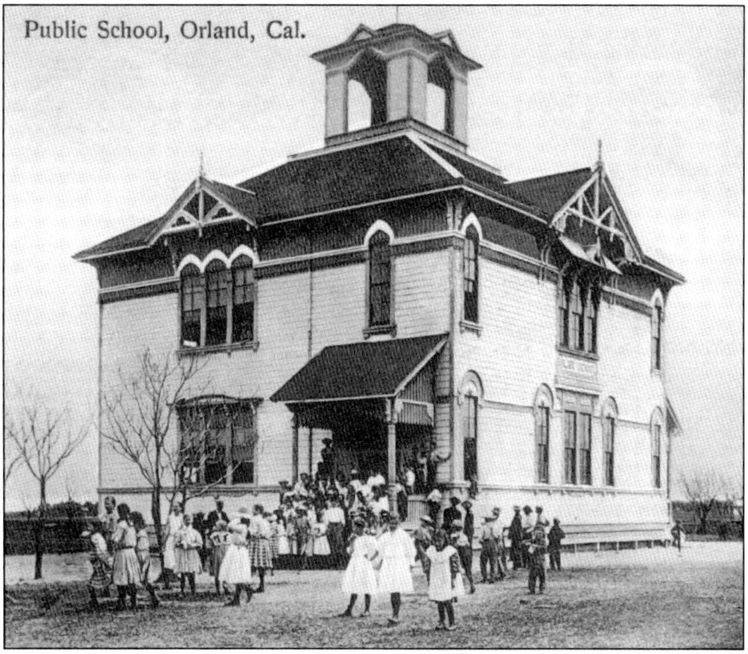

The second Orland Grammar School was built in 1884 following the approval of a $5,000 bond measure by area voters. Money ran out during the construction of the two-story wood-framed school, and the upstairs was not completed until 1895 when the second-story rooms became the first high school in Orland. "Old 1884" was vacated during the winter of 1910–1911 and torn down February 22–23, 1912.

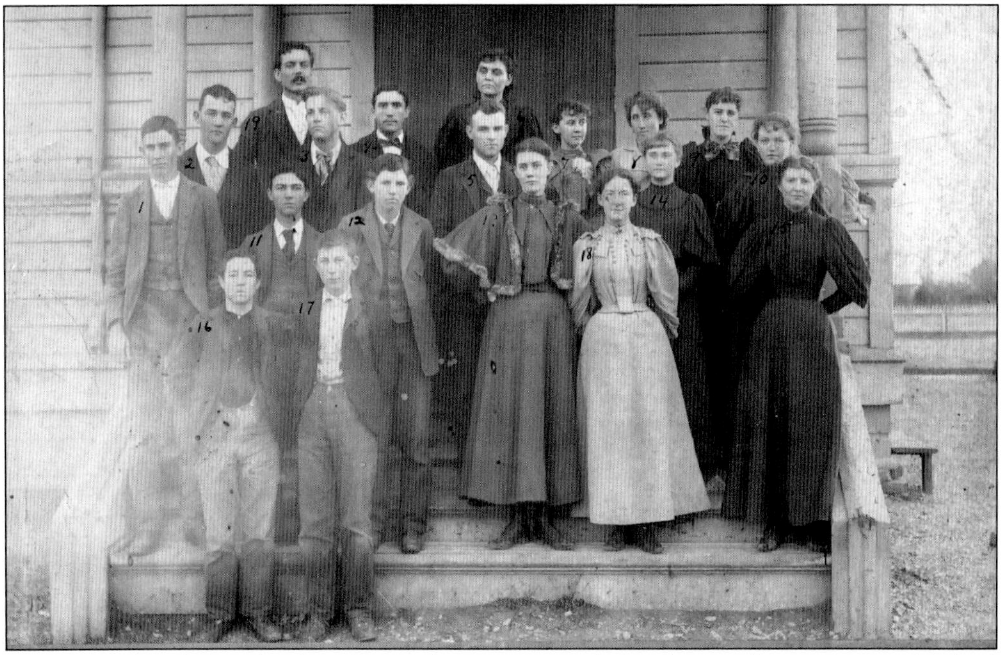

This posed shot, believed to have been taken in 1898, includes the very first graduates of Orland High School. It was taken on the steps of the Victorian school. As named on the back of the photograph are, from left to right, (first row) Edward Masterson and Hartwell Brown; (second row) John Birch, Willie Mattocks, Jesse Hamor, Laura M. Christian, Maude Hightower, and Helen Hamor; (third row) Bryron Hicks, George Mortenson, Otis Cobb, Richard Chilton, Hadassah Cleek, Maude O'Hair, and Myrtie Brown; (fourth row) principal-teacher Frank Reager, Delia Reager, Bertha Downen, and Netti Scribner.

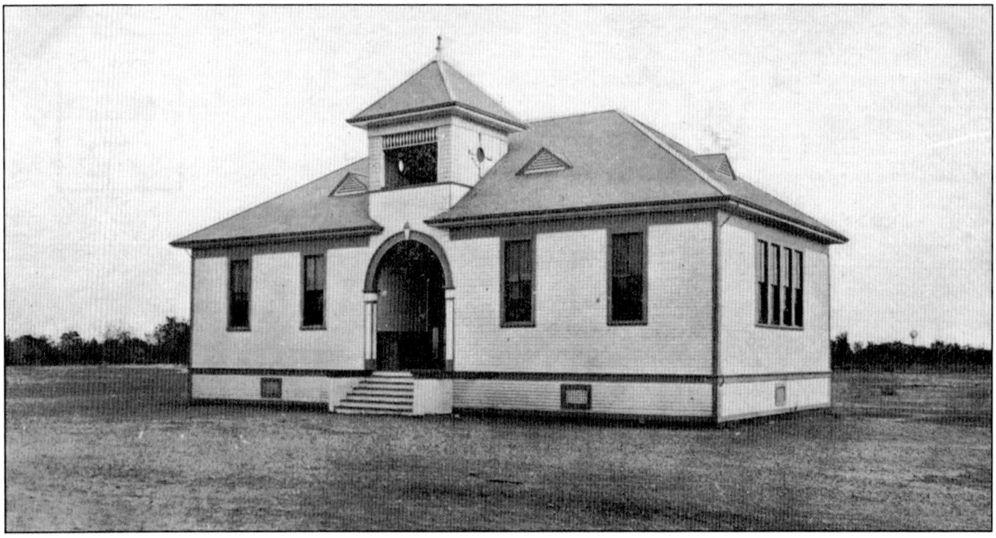

The first Orland High School building was located on the block immediately south of the grammar school. The one-story school was completed in 1903, but an increase in population resulted in overcrowded conditions after only 10 years of use. The last class to graduate from the old high school was the class of 1914—known as the "Big Six." The elementary school district used the building until 1929, when it was considered a fire hazard and torn down.

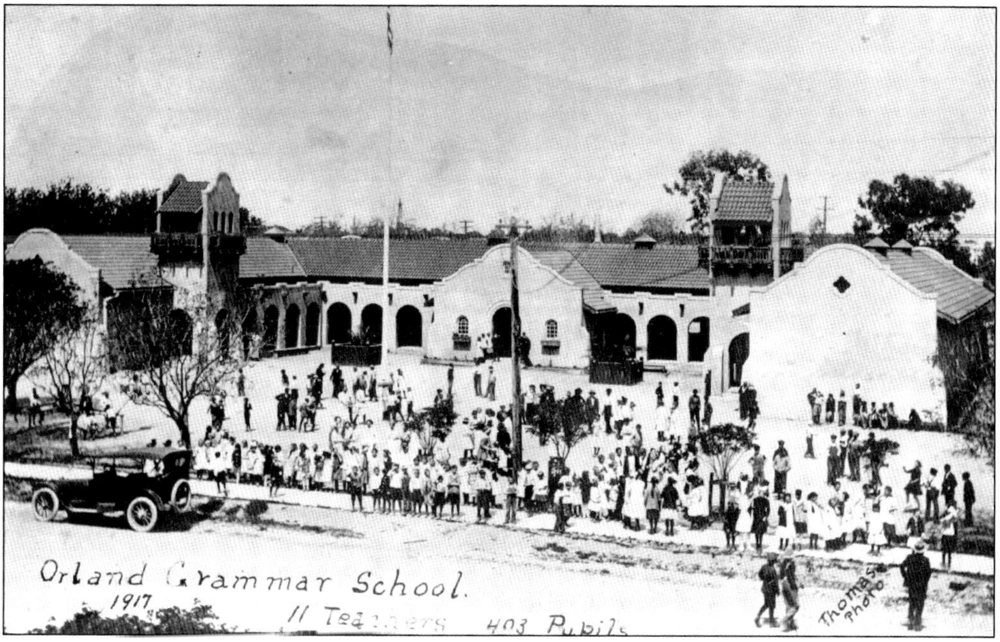

The mission-style grammar school was designed to look like an old mission church of Hispanic California. The Mission School Building, built to replace the two-story Victorian grammar school, was constructed in 1910 for $27,000 and over the objections of many taxpayers who complained it was a waste of money and would never be filled. In the bottom photograph, the Victorian school is seen on the right, as it was moved to the east side of the school block for construction of the Mission School Building. In 1939, the school name was changed to honor May V. Reager, Orland teacher for 27 years. The building was torn down in 1974 because it did not meet Field Act specifications. The school bell hung in the east red tile-roofed bell tower.

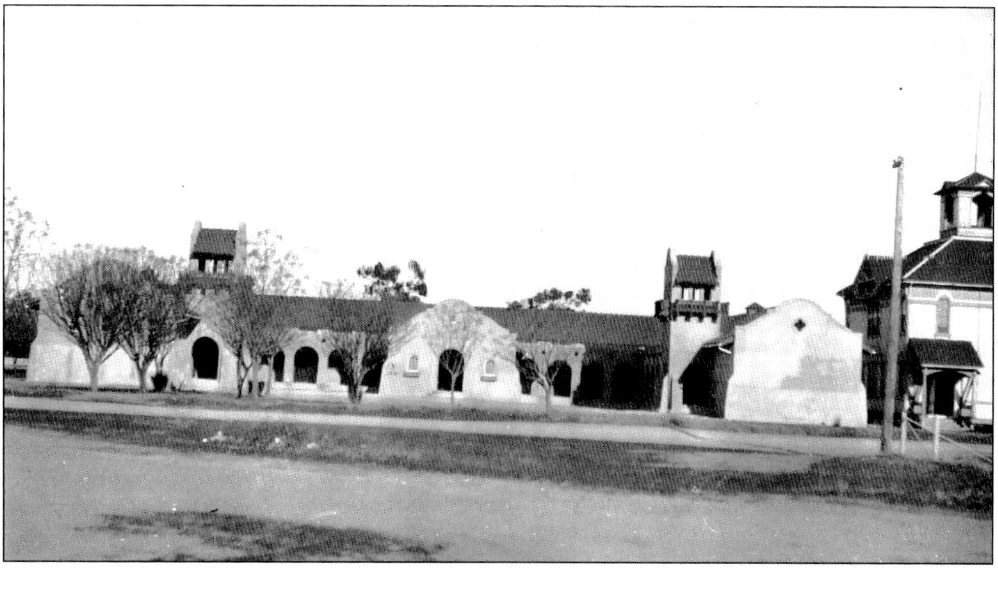

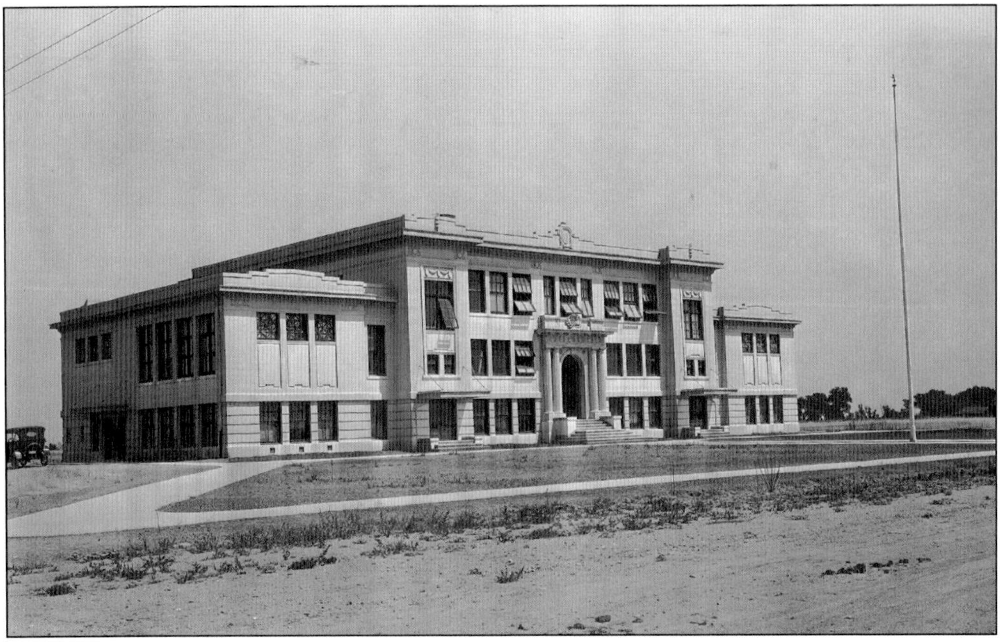

The Orland High School campus was brand new in 1915 and stood blocks north of the town. In fact, there had been quite a fight over putting it "way out in the country." The streets were gravel, the front lawn area was gravel, and the only nearby trees were those to the north along Hambright Creek. The building was torn down in 1974.

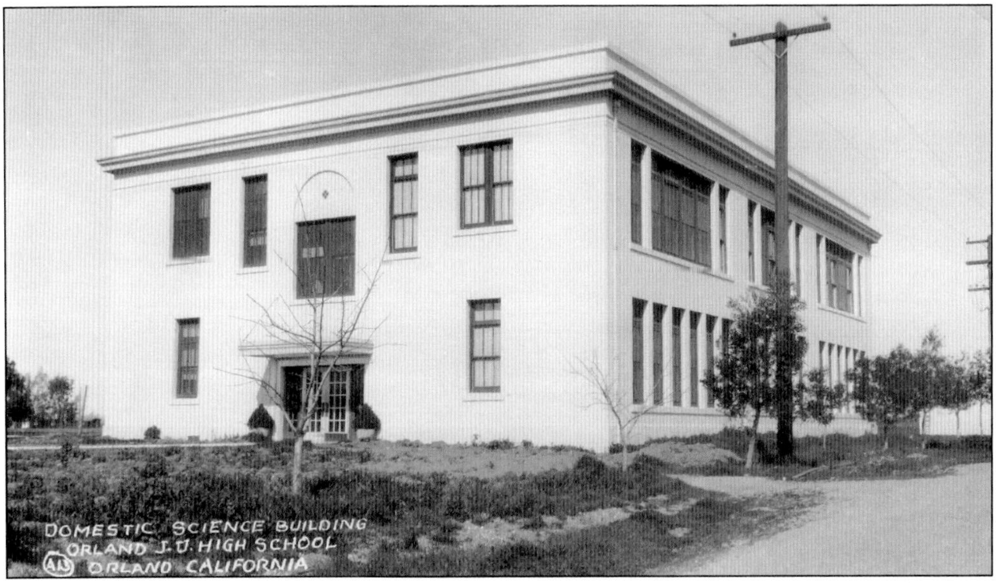

The Annex was a two-story classroom building located to the east of the old Orland High School main building. It was designed to house the domestic science and domestic art departments, several general use classrooms, and a teacher's room. The building was constructed in the early 1920s and was torn down in 1975. (Courtesy Orland Alumni Association.)

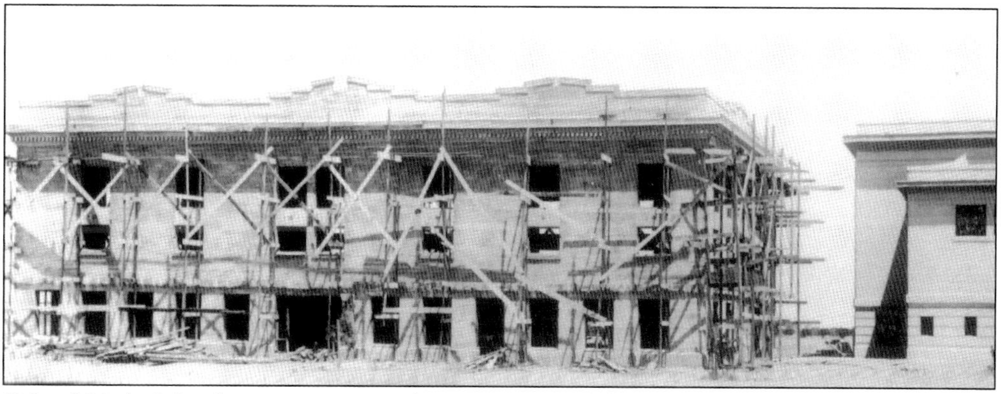

Orland High School trustees approved construction of the manual training and gymnasium building in August 1916. Instructor Herbert Busse drew the plans and then had his students involved in the construction of the reinforced concrete structure when they started school that fall. The photograph shows the building under construction on the high school campus in 1917. (Courtesy California History Room, California State Library, Sacramento, California.)

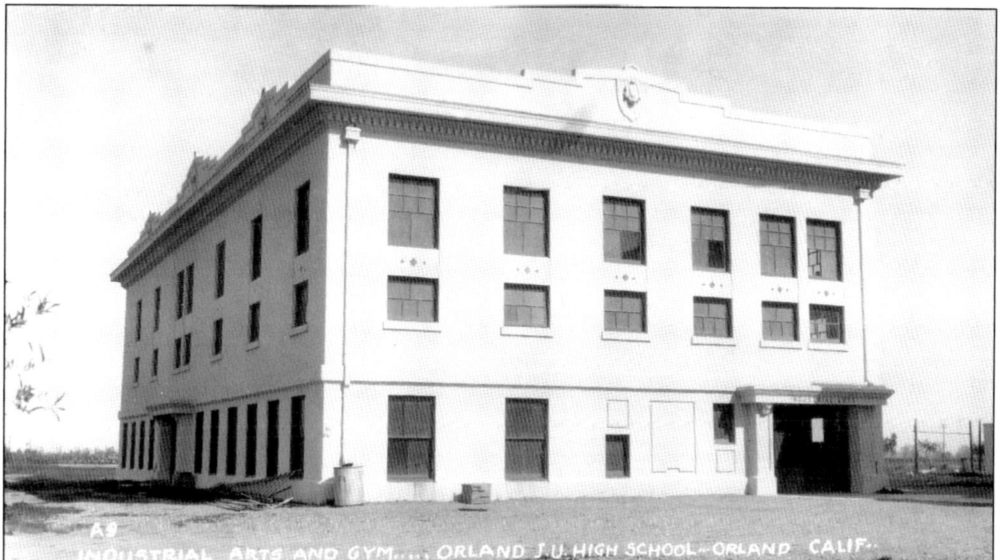

The completed manual training and gymnasium building was dedicated on February 9, 1918, with a doubleheader basketball game against Princeton. Orland won both games. The lower floor had a carpenter's shop, a sawing and planing room, a forge room, a kiln and fuming room, and a storage room. The upper floor was for physical culture and athletic work. (Courtesy Orland Alumni Association.)

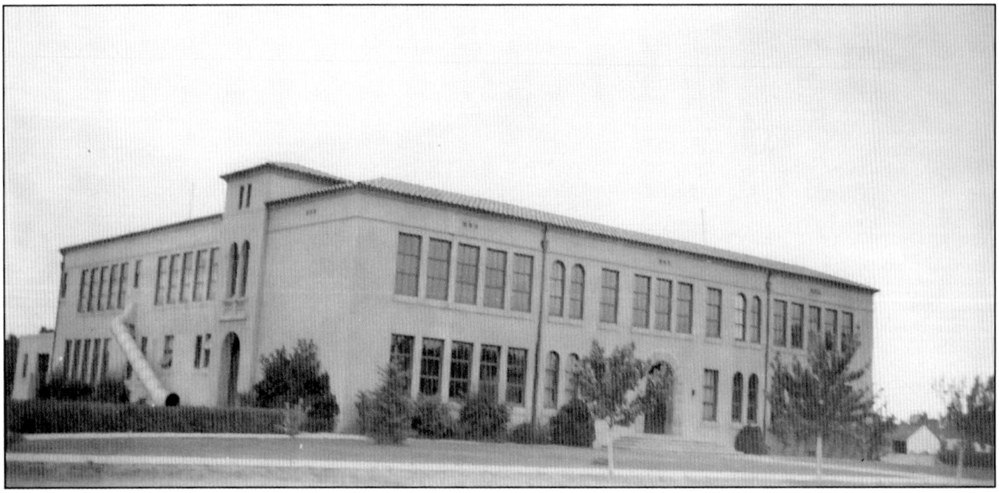

This two-story concrete grammar school building with a tile roof was constructed in 1920 just south of the Mission School Building. The new building contained a full stage and an auditorium with 1,200 seats. Note the exterior fire escape (large tube) on the east-facing side of the building.

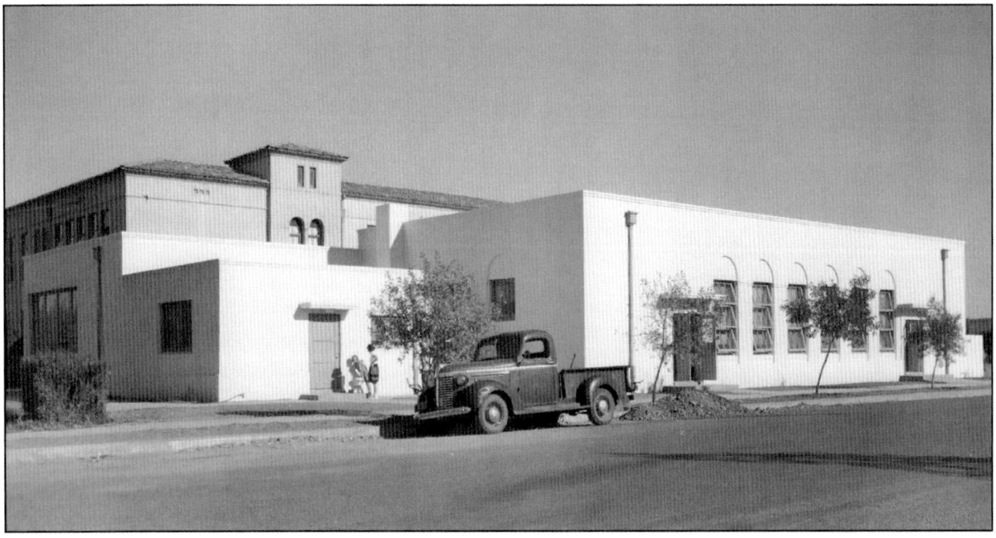

After months of negotiations between Orland First Baptist and school officials, the elementary school district was able to acquire the lot adjacent to the two-story grammar school on August 31, 1934. Removal of the church allowed for the construction in 1946 of a kindergarten classroom, a cafeteria dining room and kitchen, and a heating plant. The contractor expected the project to cost $80,000. (Courtesy Orland Alumni Association.)

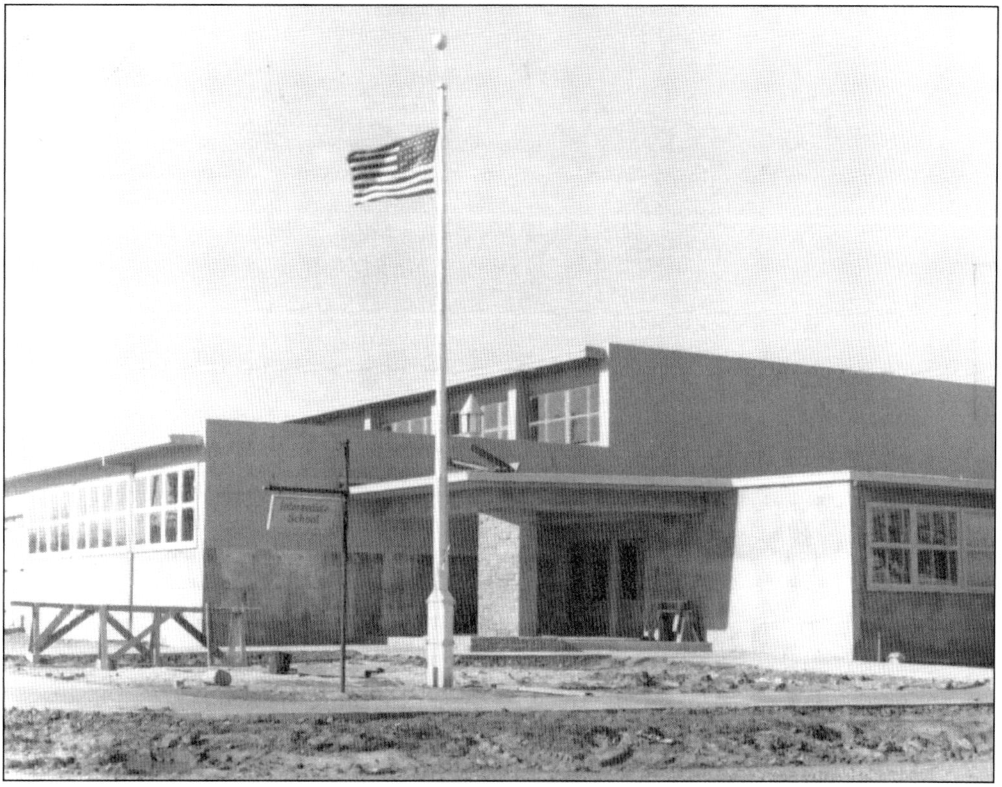

The Orland Intermediate School was built in 1949–1950 at the southwest corner of Marin and Chapman Streets. On March 14, 1950, the elementary school trustees named the new junior high school in honor of Charles Kirby "Chick" Price for his 37 years as superintendent of Orland Public Schools. (Courtesy Orland Alumni Association.)

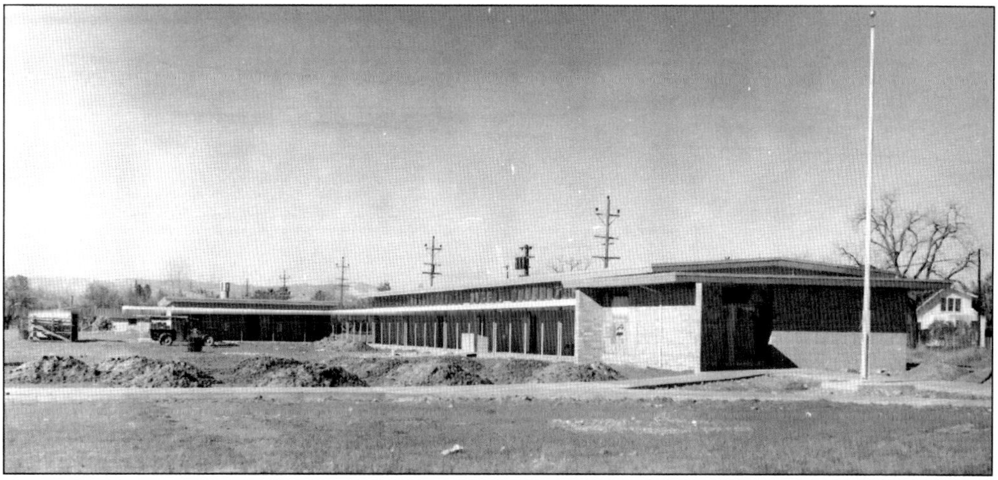

Ground was broken for a new Orland elementary school on June 11, 1951. Because the school site was across the street from the Glenn County Fairgrounds, the school board named the new school Fairview School. The new facility cost $129,091.42 and helped relieve crowded conditions within the lower grades of the Orland Elementary School District. (Courtesy Orland Alumni Association.)

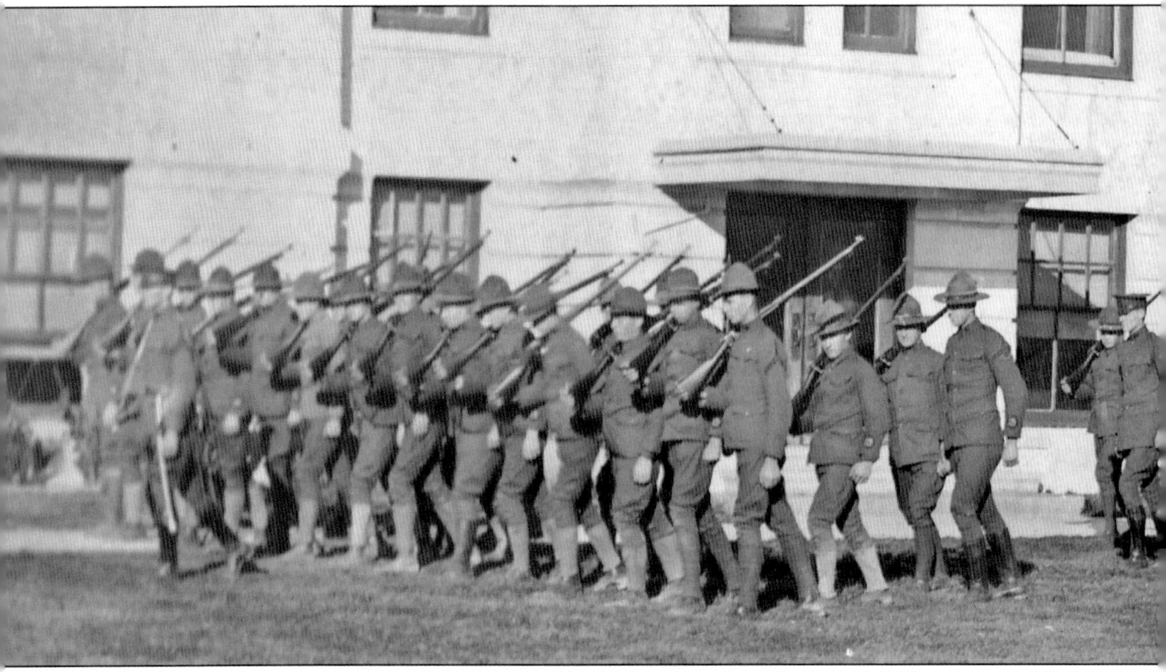

A cadet program was organized at Orland High School in the fall of 1919. When cotton khaki uniforms arrived, the boys wore them to school everyday. The rifles issued were Spanish-American War–vintage Kreg-Jorgensen .30-40 caliber, but very few were ever fired. The photograph shows

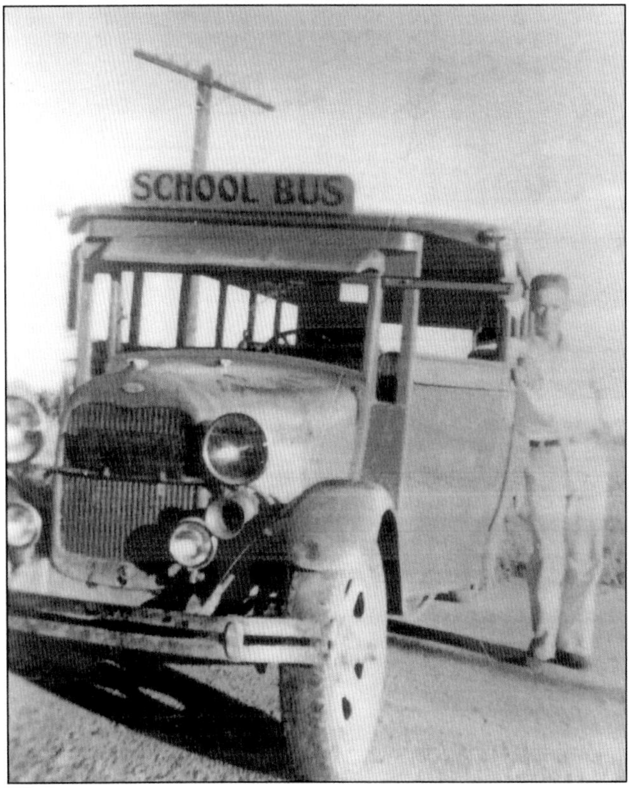

Orland's first school bus was the enterprise of Sam Boot, Orland High School class of 1929. He charged the student (or family) about 25¢ a week for riding in the 1929 Ford bus in 1935–1937. During the Depression, Boot accepted food, like chickens, in payment for the bus fare. When the school district purchased their first bus, Boot became the driver and maintained district buses until he retired in the late 1940s. (Courtesy Bill and Barbara Boot.)

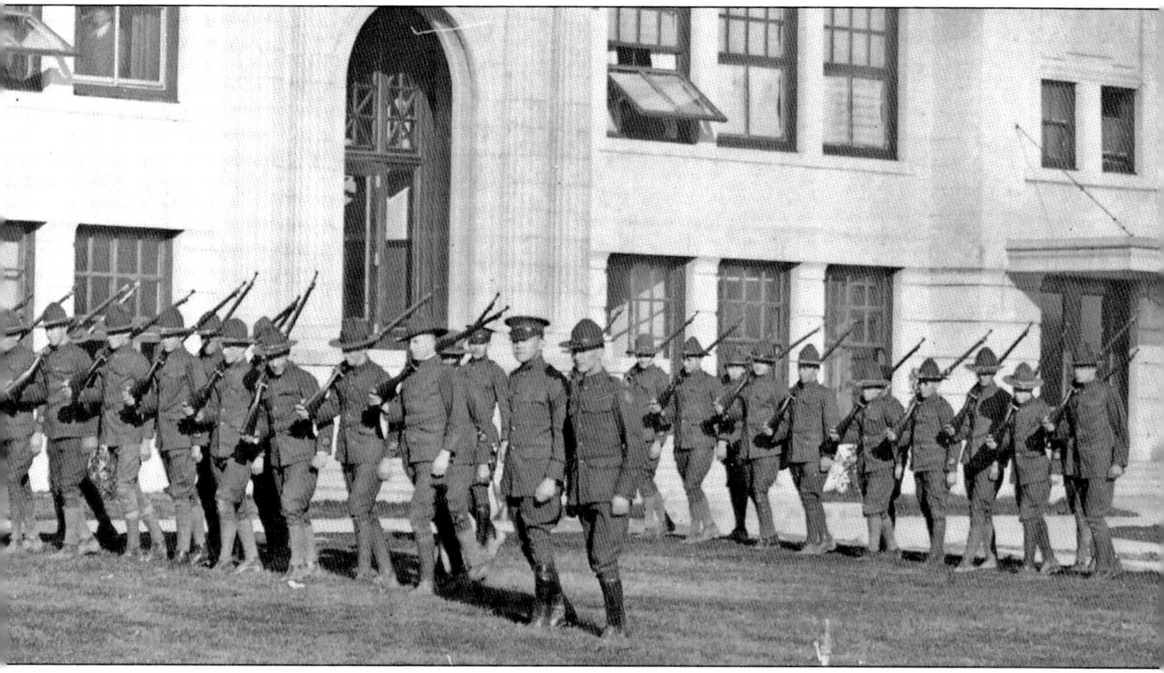

the cadets marching during the 1919–1920 school year in front of the school's main building. (Courtesy Orland Alumni Association.)

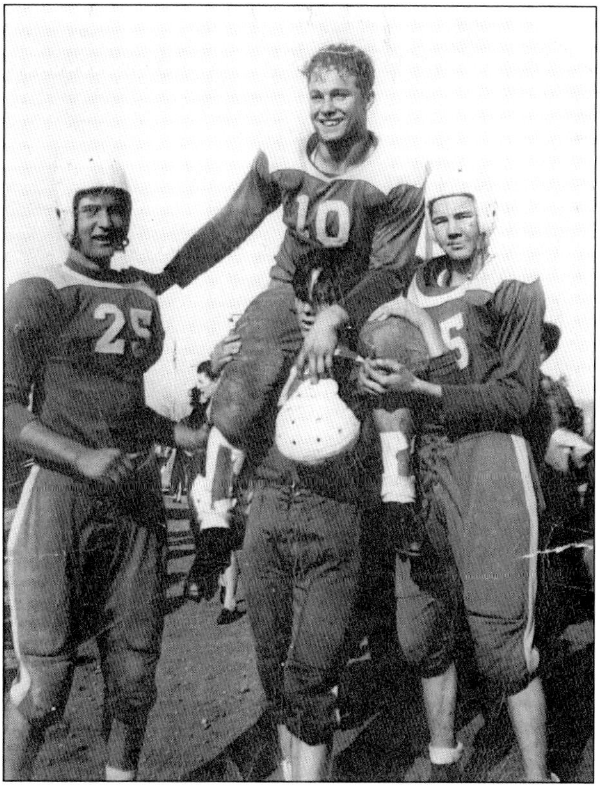

The first game of football ever played in Orland by the high school team was on October 22, 1921, at the old fairgrounds near Eighth and Sacramento Streets. On November 23, 1944, the Trojans beat Fort Bragg 13-0 to complete the school's first undefeated season. Darrel "Ole" Johnson is shown being carried off the field after the victory. Johnson's teammates are, from left to right, Bill Cook, Gene Cufaude, and Kenneth Whitsett. (Courtesy Reuben Barclay.)

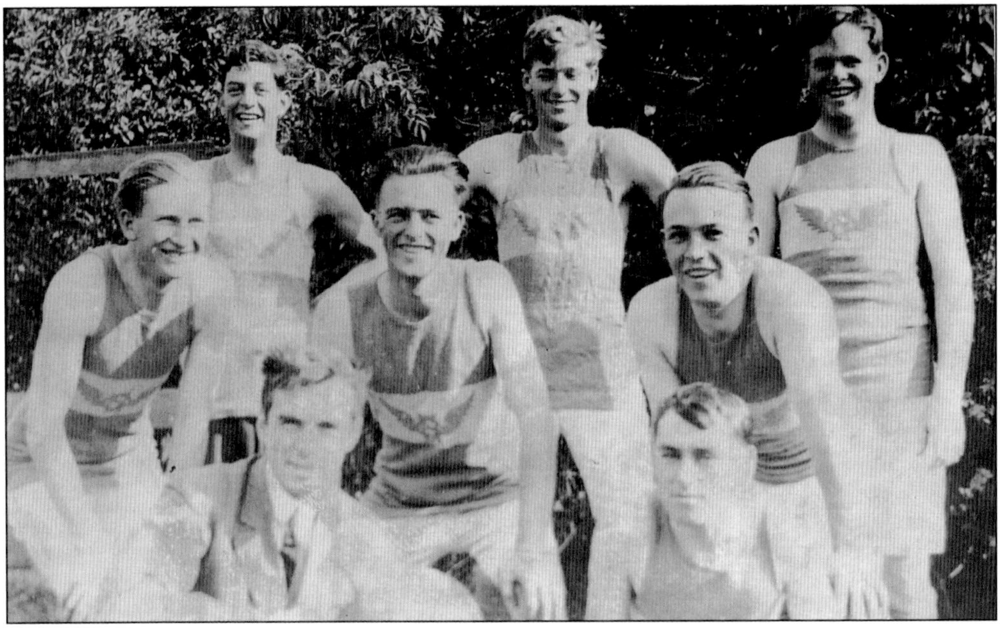

Orland High School's first championship pennant was earned by the boys' basketball team that won 11 of 15 games played between October 1913 and February 1914. The team members are, from left to right, (first row) Ralph McMasters (commercial teacher and coach) and Ralph Fotheringhame; (second row) Joe Erickson, Kenneth Morrissey, and Emerson Martin; (third row) Robert Aitken, Arnold Faltings, and Marc Morrissey.

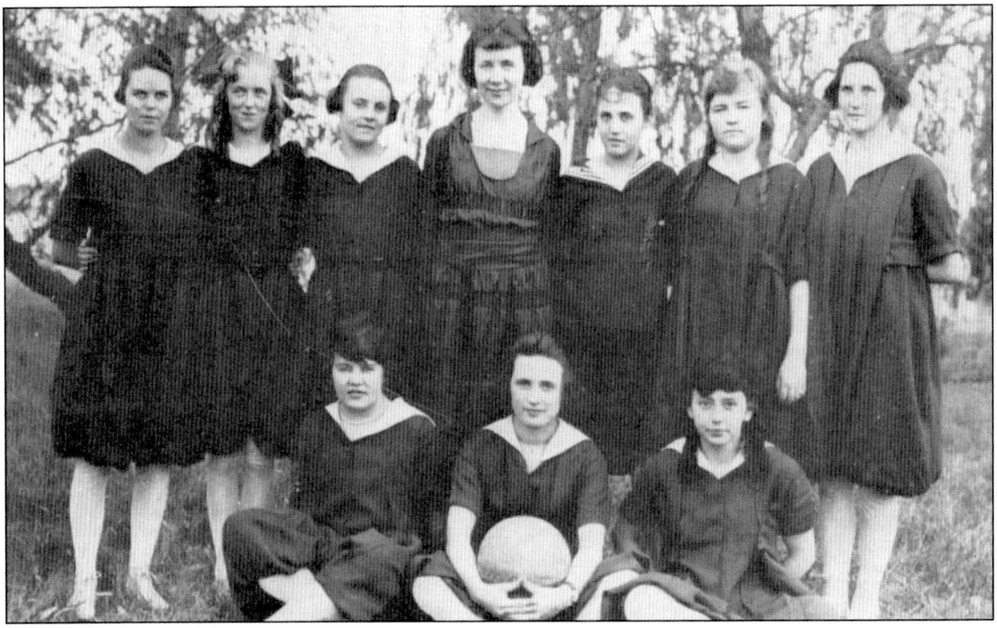

The 1919–1920 Orland High School girls' basketball team had a season record of 7 wins, 2 losses, and 1 tie. This record was good enough to claim the championship title of the Northern California High School Athletic League. Coached by Mabel Finch, team members were Charlotte King (captain), Madeline Wadsworth, Helen Reager, Helen Holt, Marion Long, Fairy Bentz, Mildred Chapman, Margaret Rankin, and Pauline Chapman.

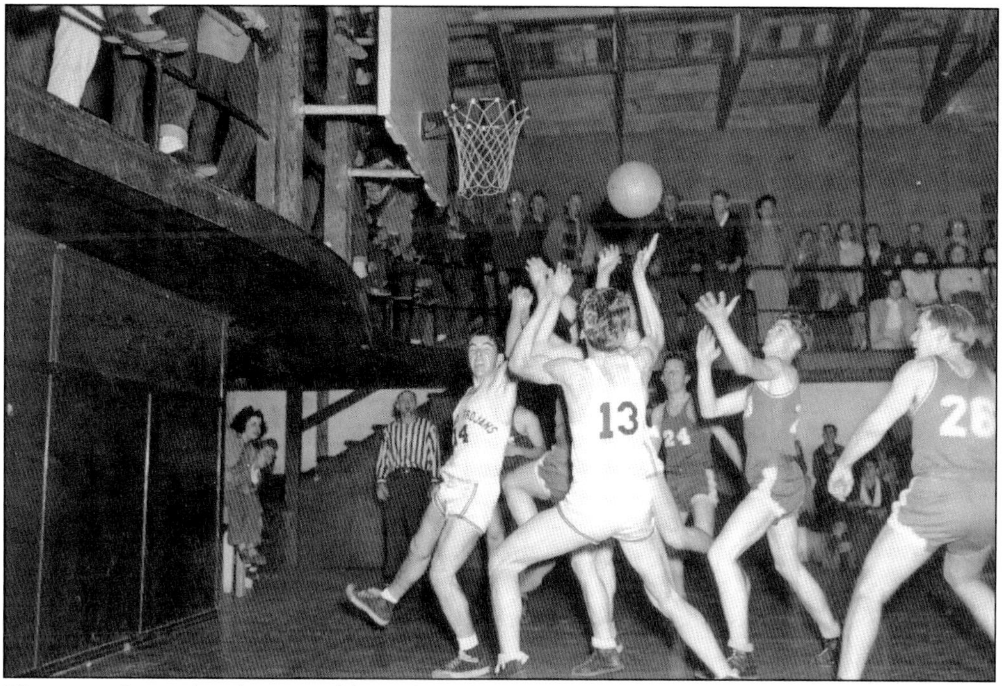

This view shows the players and how close the student body was to the action in the old high school gymnasium. Lawrence Aguiar (No. 14) and Otto Terkildsen (No. 13) were members of the 1946 Trojan varsity basketball team. (Courtesy Joe and Shirley Erickson.)

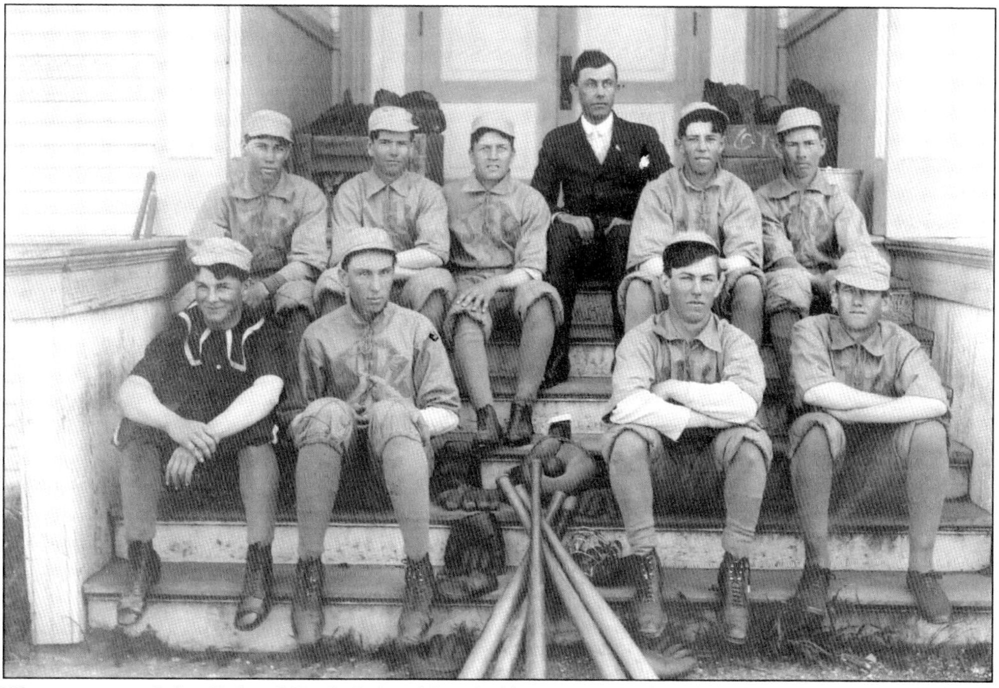

This picture of the Orland High School baseball team was taken in front of the school during the 1906–1907 season. It appears there was just enough equipment and players to field a team. (Courtesy Orland Alumni Association.)

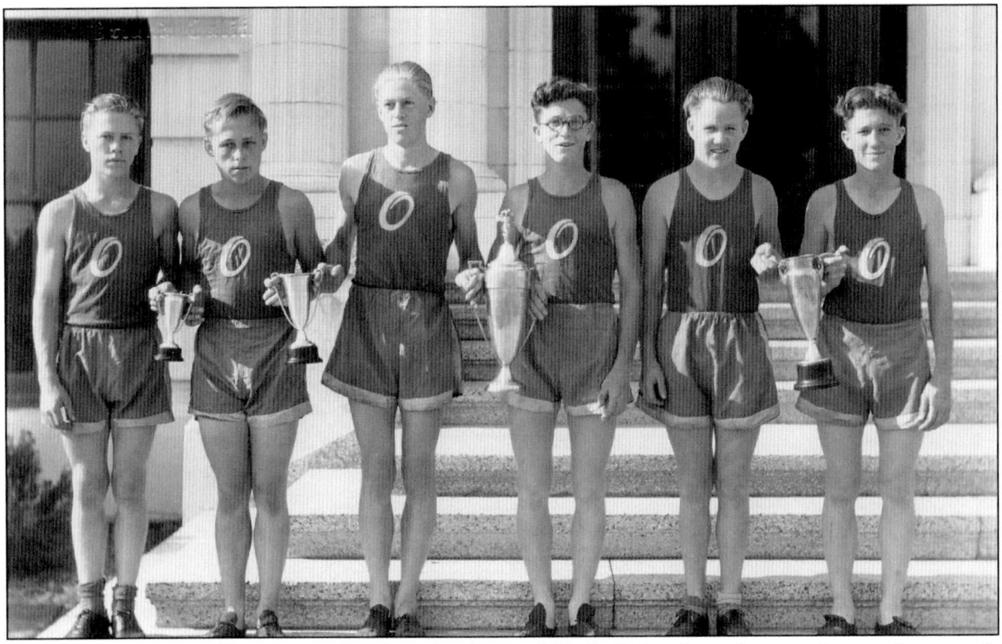

Coached by Granville "Granny" Siler, the Orland High School track team beat other north valley schools to claim the 1931 Northern California High School Athletic League Limited Championship and retain possession of the silver cup won the year before. Members of the team were Victor Howard (captain), Francis Cramer, Ancil Hall, Alva Whipple, Gordon Weidemier, Fred Reimann, Albert Kafer, and Marvin Seavers. (Courtesy Orland Alumni Association.)

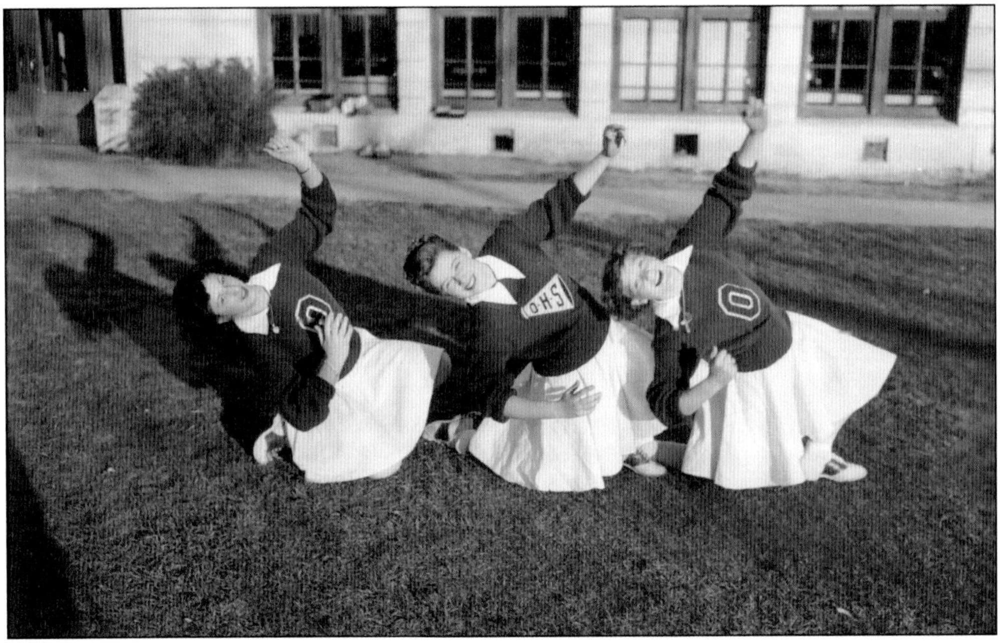

Orland High School has been fielding athletic teams since the early 1910s. In the fall of 1919, the "Yell Leader" was an elected official of the student body and could be held by either a boy or girl. Pictured from left to right, the 1947–1948 school cheerleaders are Garnett Royce, Ruby Medina, and Mildred Roman. (Courtesy Joe and Shirley Erickson.)

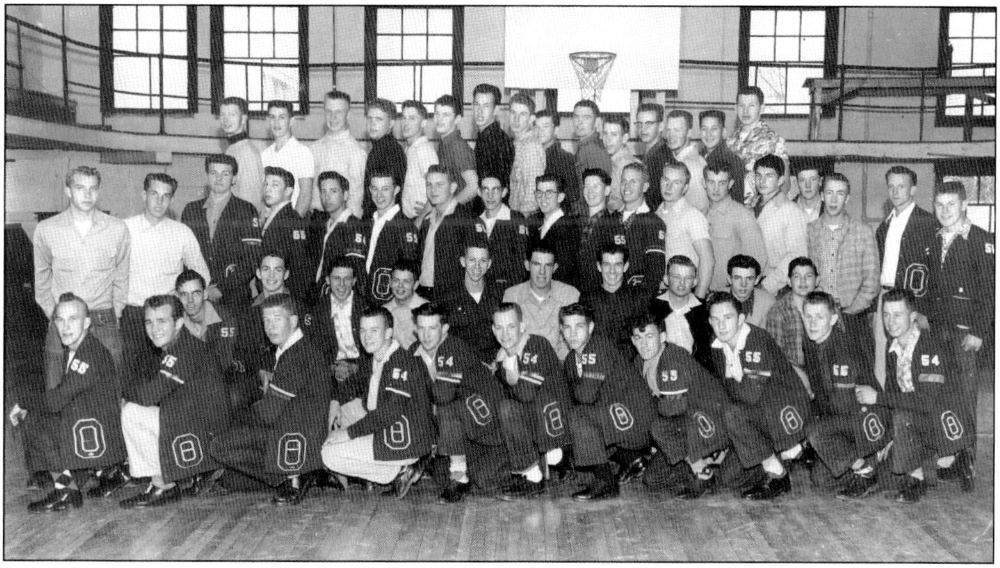

Block letters were awarded to boys and girls playing on the Orland High School teams starting in 1927. Several years later, references to "Block-O men" are found in the Orland newspapers. Pictured above is the Block O group photograph from 1954 under advisors and coaches Robert Russell and Clayton Wolfe. During the early 1950s, Block O sponsored the annual Boxing Show, Daisy May Day, and barn dance, and held fund-raisers to pay for the new football scoreboard. The Circle O group, pictured below, was changed to the GAA (Girls' Athletic Association) in 1950–1951. Girls received points for participation in team and individual sports in school tournaments. Pictured below are the 1954 GAA members with advisor Patricia Milton (second row, far left). The activities these members might have participated in were the annual faculty versus volleyball game, sock hop, Valentine's Day dance, school-color dance, aquacade, and annual dance revue. (Both courtesy Orland Alumni Association.)

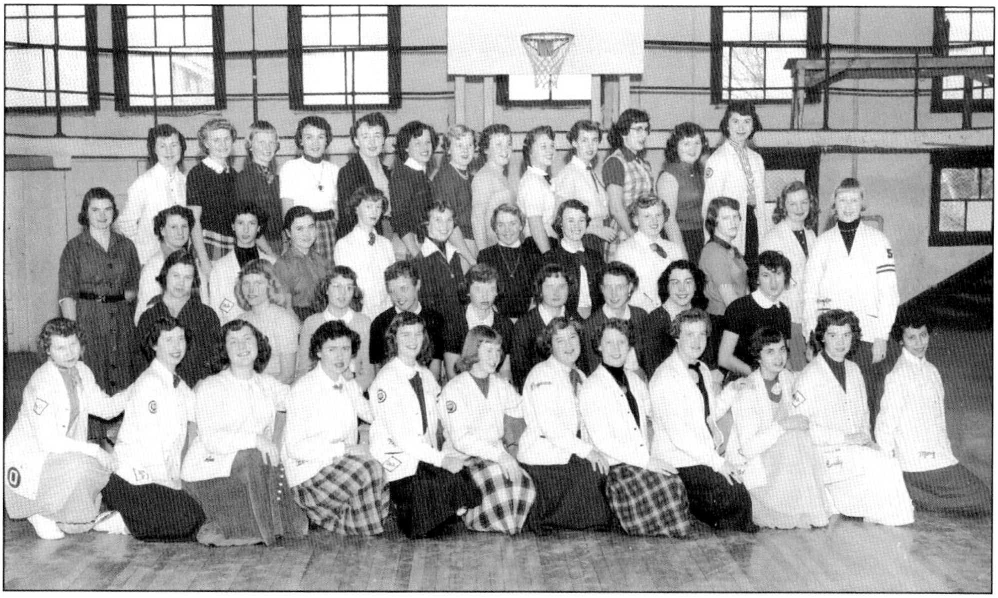

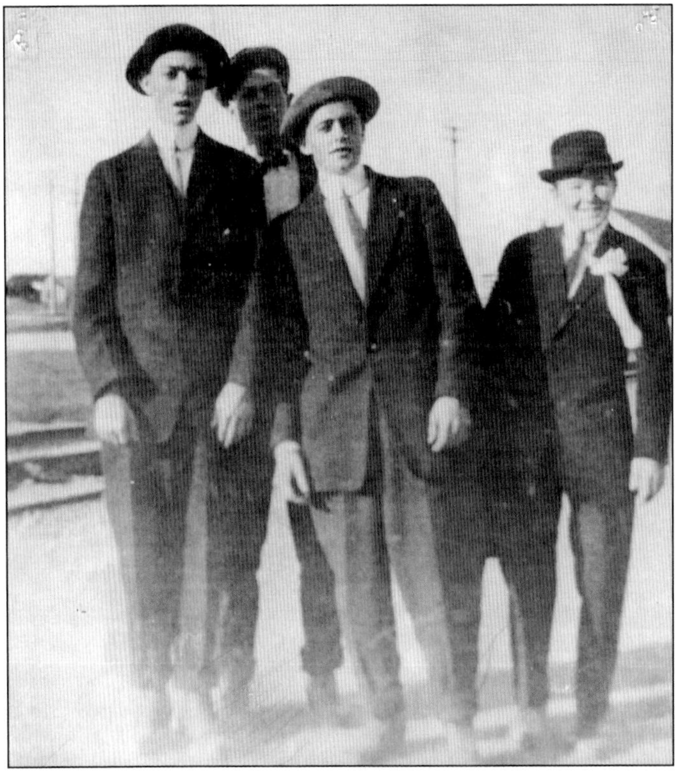

Prior to the chartering of the Future Farmers of America at Orland High School in 1929, there were agricultural clubs in 1915 and classes starting in 1917. In this photograph, several of the first members from these agricultural clubs are at the depot ready to leave for a meeting in Berkeley, California. The members are, from left to right, (first row) Paul Ehorn, Kenneth Morrissey, and Elwood Baugh; (second row) unidentified.

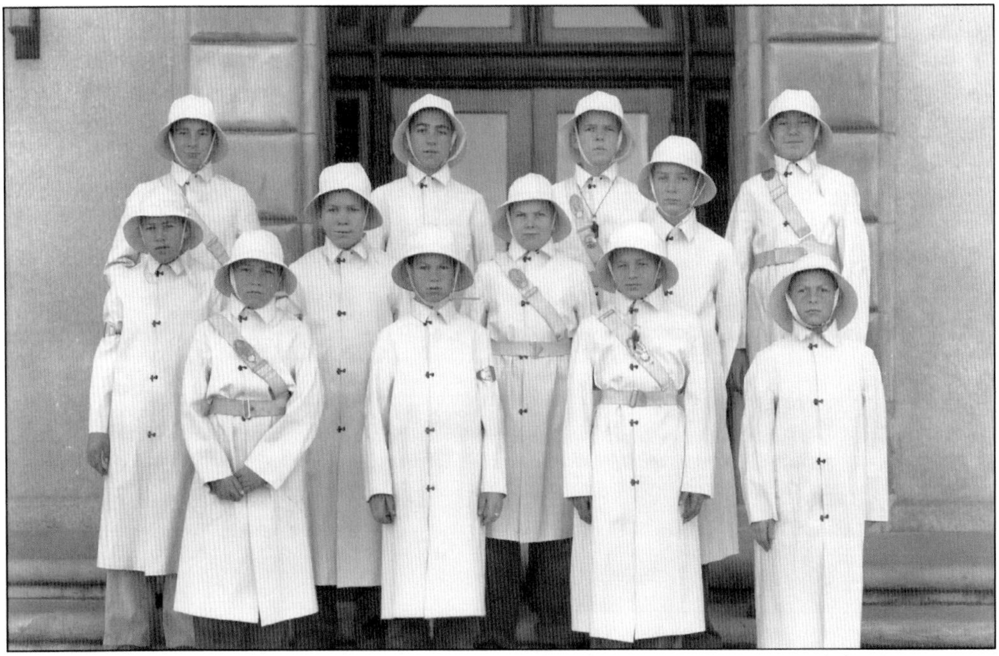

The Safety Patrol was a national program started by the American Automobile Association (AAA) in 1920. The program's purpose was to help schoolmates at hazardous crossings near schools. Patrol members did not stop traffic but waited for safe gaps in traffic to let schoolmates cross streets. This Orland group of Safety Patrol members was photographed in 1939.

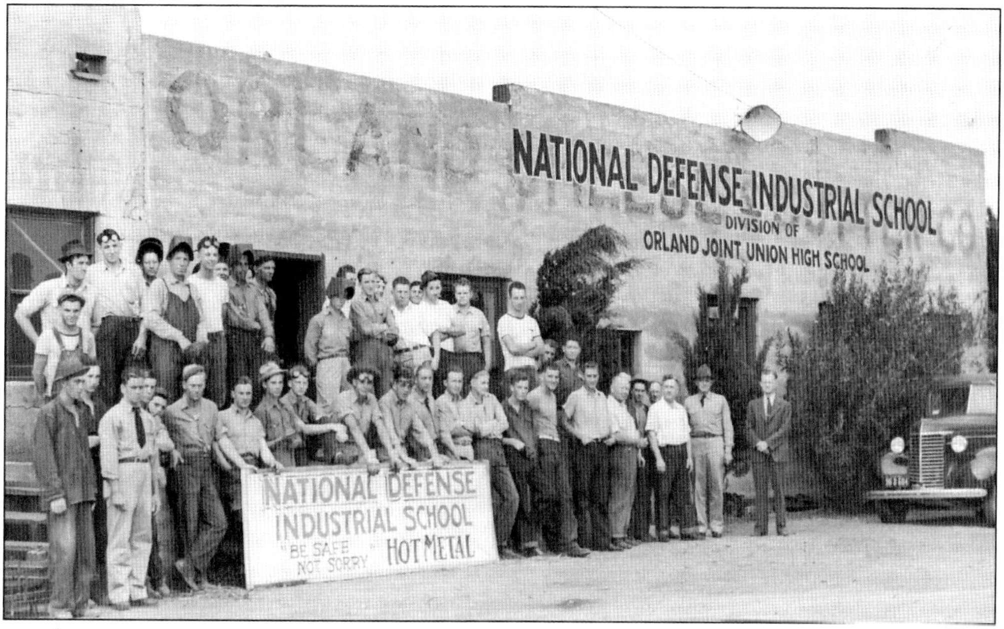

Word was received in January 1941 that Orland had been approved for a federal trade school to be built on the high school campus. Plans were hurriedly completed and ground broken February 3, 1941, for the 13,500-square-foot building adjacent to the existing shop building. While construction was underway, vocational classes were held in the former Orland Cheese and Butter building at Fifth and Colusa Streets. (Courtesy Orland Alumni Association.)

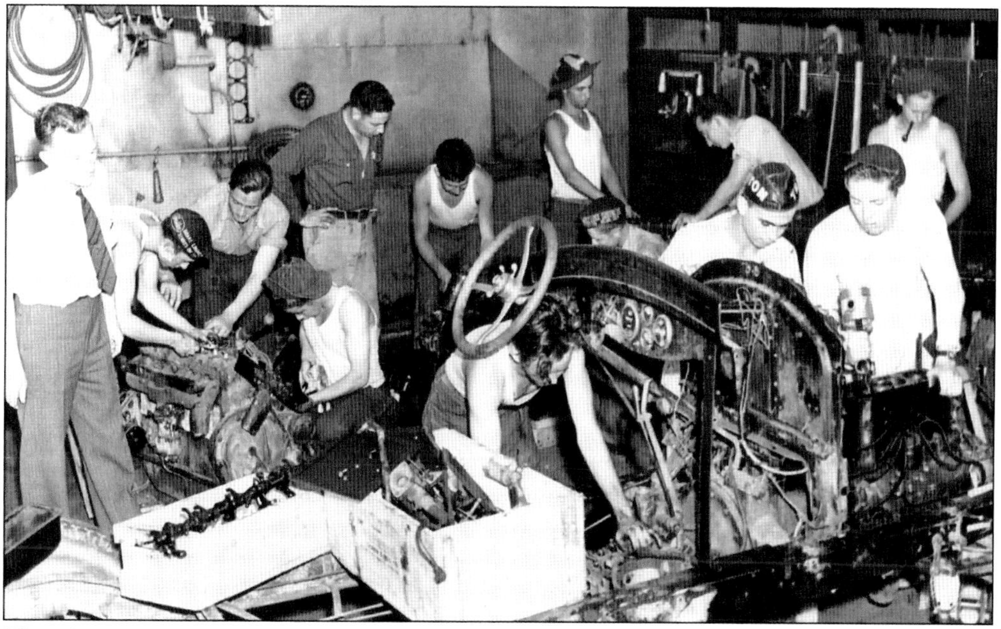

The 1941 spring semester for Orland's night school got underway on February 3. A new course among the 25 offered was auto mechanics for Civilian Conservation Corps (CCC) boys as part of the national defense program. Machine shop was also taught as a national defense course. On the extreme left is H. O. Williams, Orland High School principal. Three of the young men are wearing the floppy blue-denim CCC hats. (Courtesy Orland Alumni Association.)

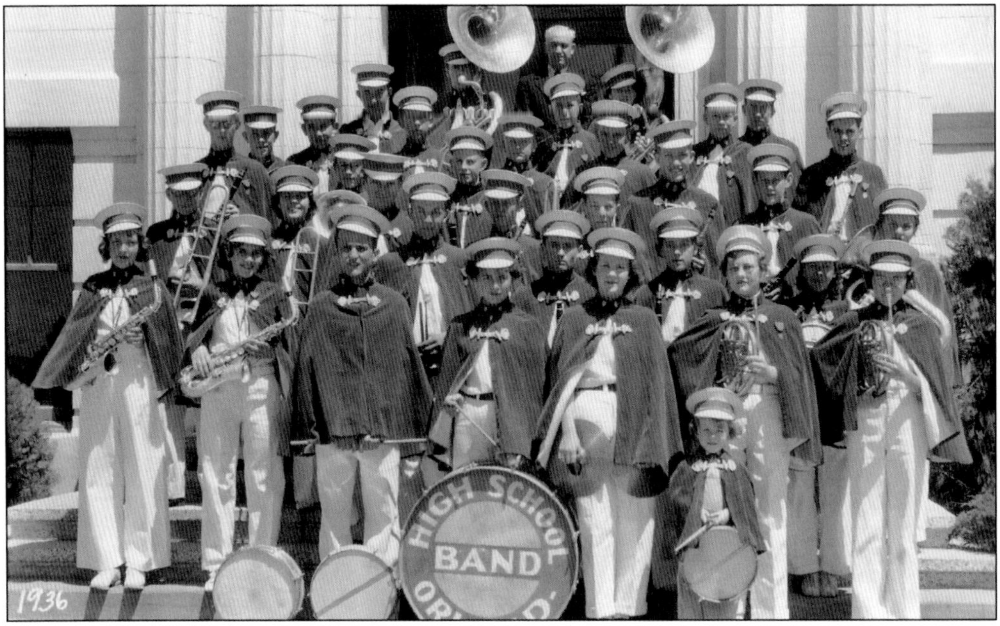

Dick Terrell was the popular music teacher in the Orland schools during the 1930s and 1940s. Students enjoyed his classes and found him to be "lots of fun." In the late 1930s, the band made too much noise in its third-floor room and was relocated to the basement of the Memorial Hall for classes. Terrell is pictured in the seventh row, center in this 1936 photograph. (Courtesy Orland Alumni Association.)

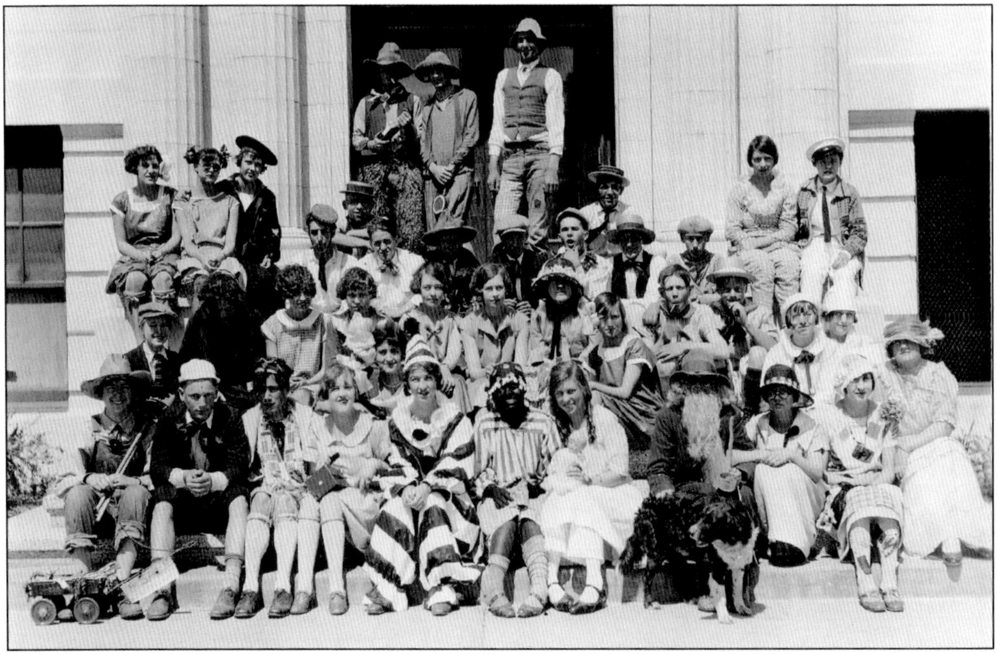

Jinx Day was observed in the 1920s and 1930s as a day for members of the senior class to dress up in odd attire. After a morning of classes, the seniors would take the afternoon off and motor to One Mile Dam in Bidwell Park, Chico, for an afternoon of swimming. Pictured are members of the class of 1923 in their costumes. (Courtesy Orland Alumni Association.)

Seven

CHURCHES

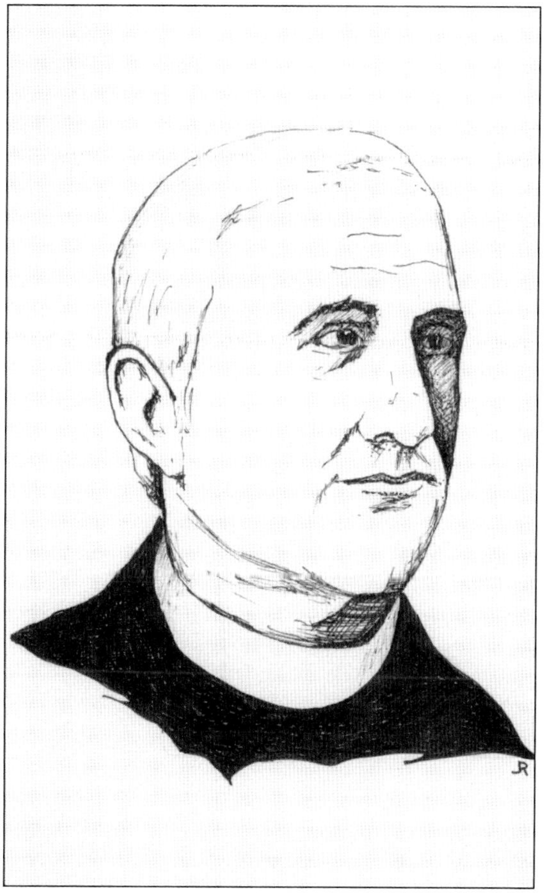

The Reverend Fr. Michael Walrath came to Colusa County in 1877 and was a tireless apostle in the performance of his duty for the next 35 years. After the construction of a new Colusa Catholic Church, creation of the Colusa Catholic Cemetery, enlargement of the pastor's residence, and building of a stable for his horse-and-buggy, Father Walrath turned his attention to the new railroad towns being established on the west side of the valley. For example, Father Walrath said Mass in the new Willows church on March 1, 1879, and the new Maxwell house of worship in 1881. In 1884, he continued his building program and helped construct St. Dominic's Church in Orland at the corner of A and Colusa Streets. The church was dedicated on May 3, 1885, by Bishop Patrick Manogue of Sacramento. Father Walrath was transferred to Woodland, Yolo County, in 1912 but was remembered for using a hand-car to travel on the railroad tracks between valley towns. This mode of travel was discontinued when he interfered with the time schedule of the overland trains.

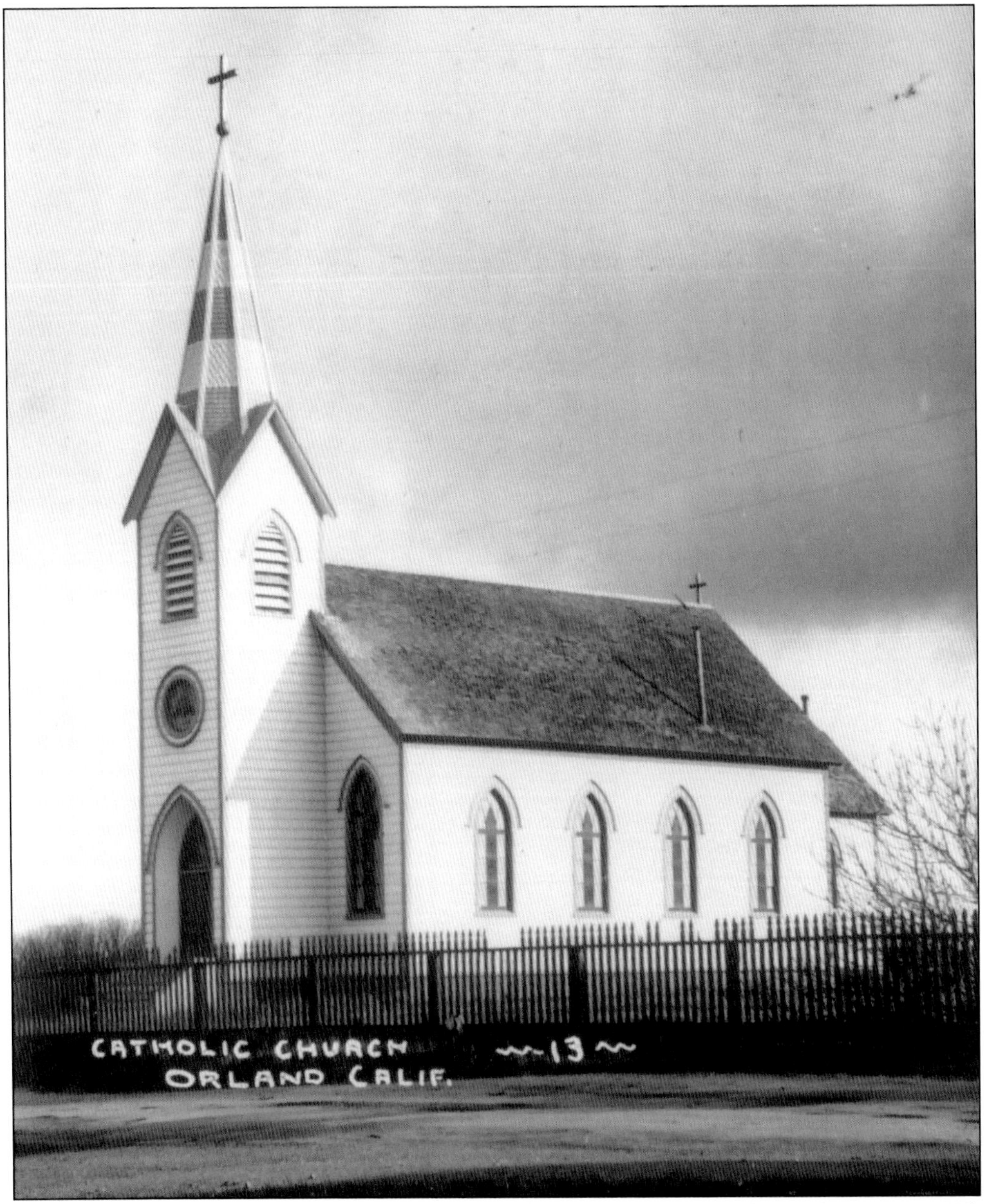

St. Dominic's Catholic Church was the oldest public building in Orland, dating from 1884–1885. The first Mass was said in the nearly completed church on December 23, 1884. The church was built under the direction of Fr. Michael Walrath and was a mission church of Willows until Fr. William Coen became the first resident priest. Rev. Fr. Cornelius C. McGrath of Willows, who was a carpenter before entering the priesthood, built the altar that was part of the church for 64 years. During the 1947 fire of the church building, Orland volunteer firemen were able to remove the altar and sanctuary fixtures through the rear entrance. Heat from the fire scorched the varnish on the pews, and they suffered water damage from the water poured on the blaze. The congregation had been considering building a new Catholic church as the original edifice had proven too small. The plan had included using the old wooden building as a parish hall. (Courtesy California History Room, California State Library, Sacramento, California.)

Fire destroyed the old St. Dominic's Church on March 13, 1947. Construction of the new church began on December 17, 1948. The California mission–style building was designed by architect Harry Devine of Sacramento and was built by contractor Gordon Weems of Willows. The church was completed and blessed by Bishop Robert Armstrong on Sunday, September 25, 1949. In the Peter Richter photograph below are, from left to right, (adults in front) Bishop Robert Armstrong, Diocese of Sacramento; Fr. Patrick Donnelly; Fr. Anthony Dosch; Msgr. Thomas Kirby; Fr. Andrew Coffey; and Paul Lathrop; (altar boys in back) Nick Kraemer; Ben Kraemer; Frank Harrington Jr.; Dan Kraemer (holding cross); Robert Mudd; and Fred Perez. (Right courtesy Jack Bucke; below courtesy Joanne Overton.)

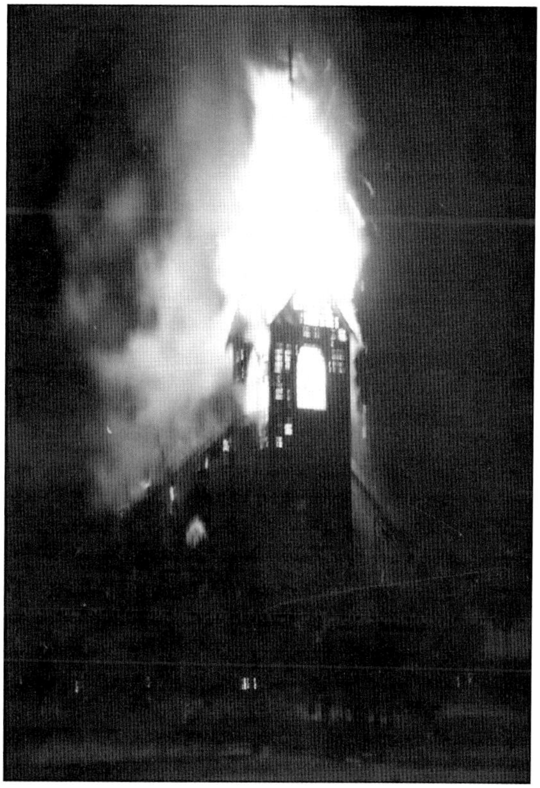

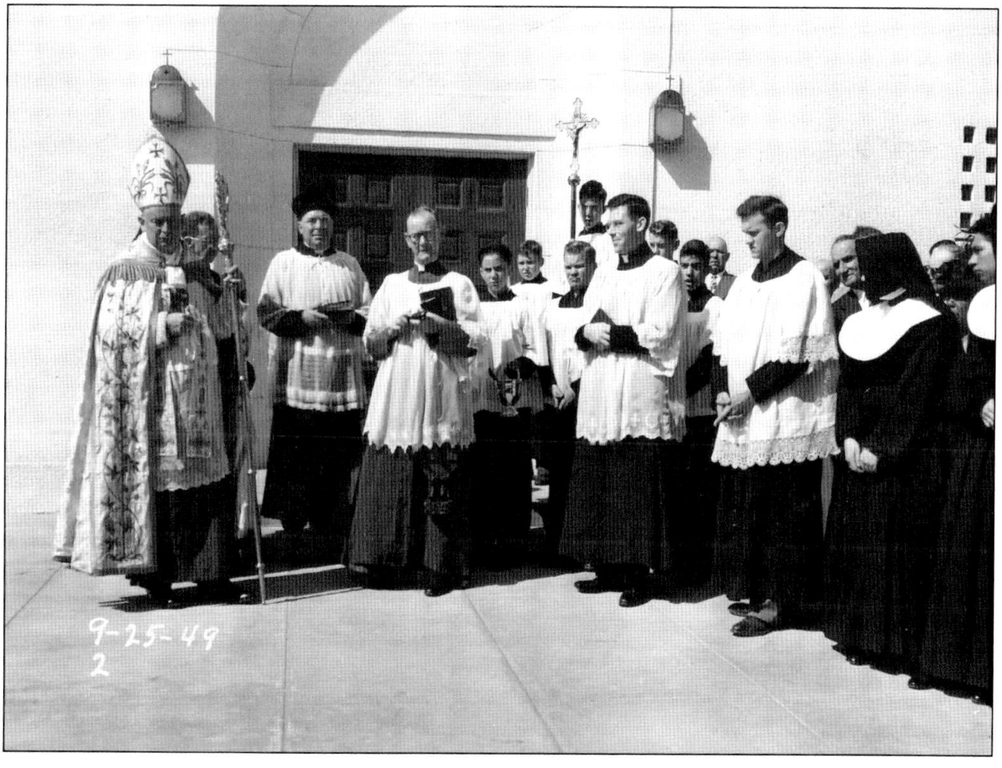

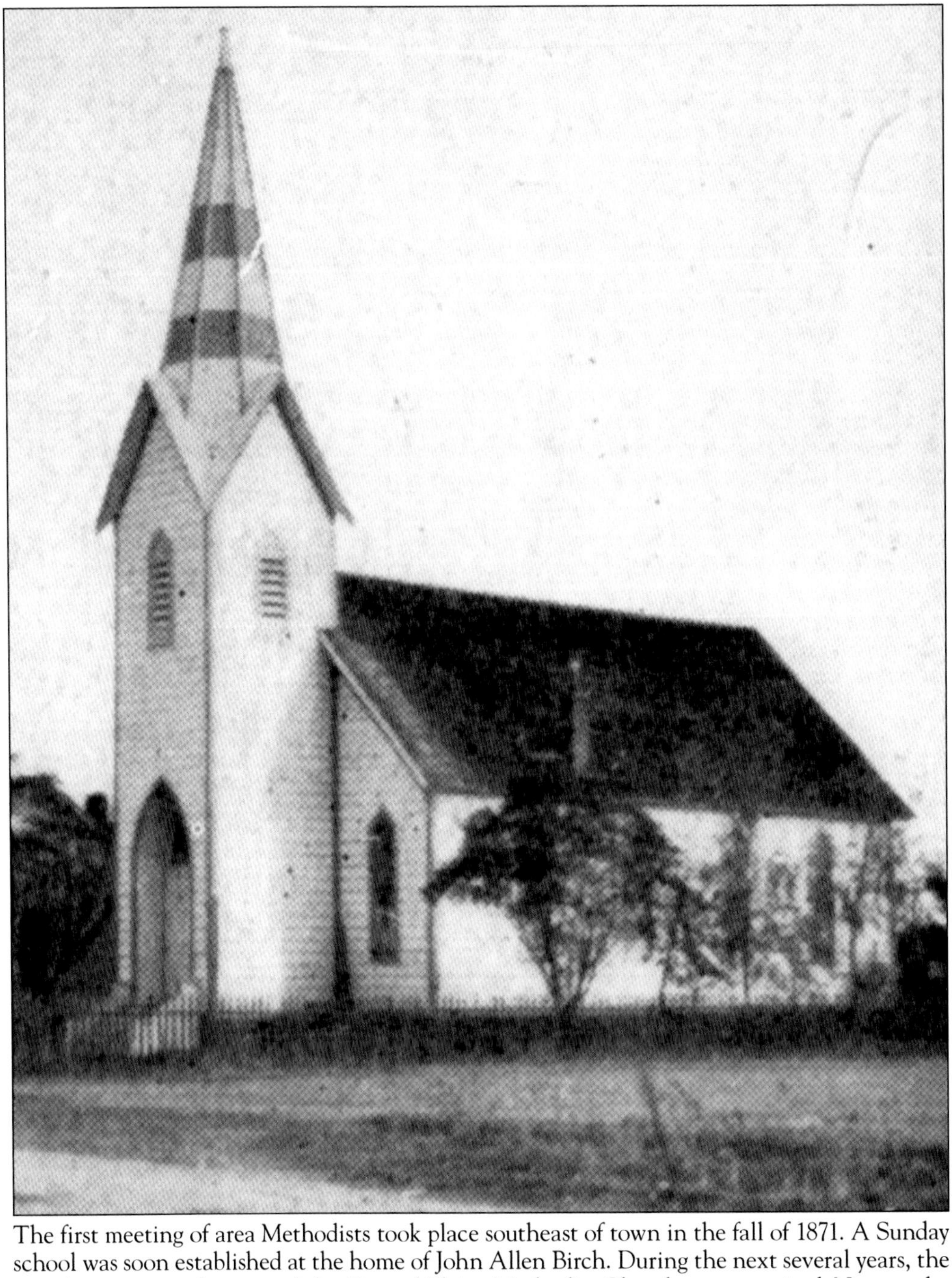

The first meeting of area Methodists took place southeast of town in the fall of 1871. A Sunday school was soon established at the home of John Allen Birch. During the next several years, the preaching services began and the Central Plains Methodist Church was organized. Next to the Birch ranch was property owned by Rev. John Rice. Here was built in 1874 a two-story church structure where the services and school work were on the upper story and the pastor's home was on the lower. With the coming of the railroad, many of the ranchers, like Birch, moved into the new town, and services were held in an old schoolhouse. The Southern Pacific Company donated a site at the southeast corner of First and Colusa Streets; a church costing $1,000 was erected in 1884.

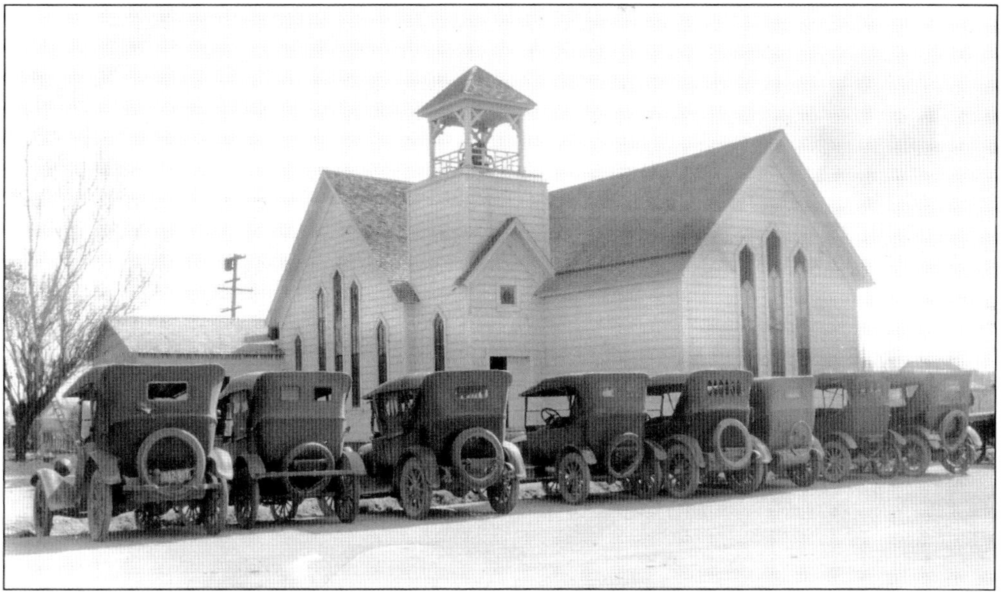

The Orland Methodist Church was the second church in Orland and was built parallel to St. Dominic's Catholic Church at the north end of the same block facing Colusa Street. The two churches were enough alike to be considered twins. In 1913, the Methodist church was rotated to face First Street, the sanctuary was enlarged with a balcony, and the steeple was removed. The building was used until February 1938, when it was sold to Henry Click for $150, torn down, and hauled away.

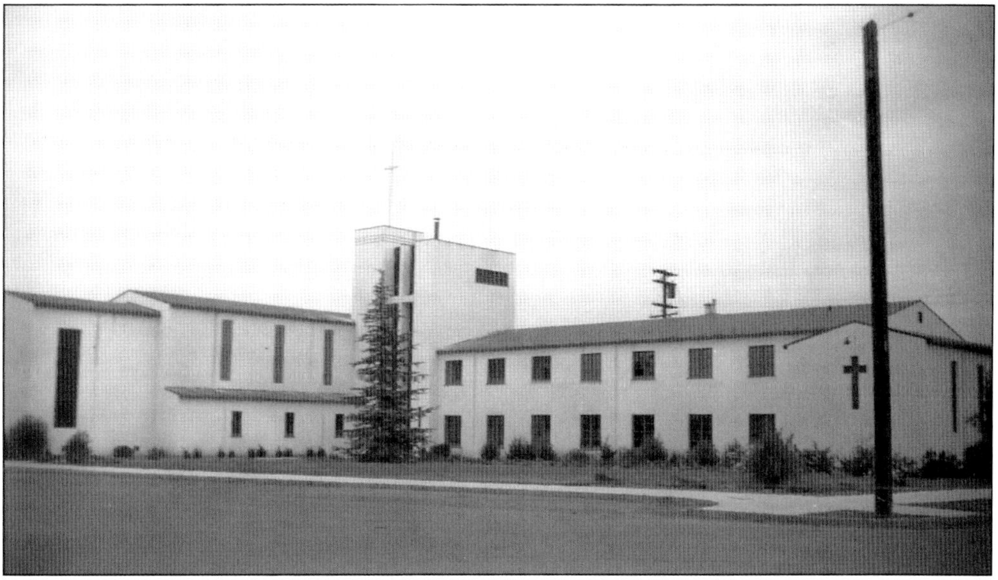

In the fall of 1928, a committee of Methodists and Presbyterians began a serious study of the possibility of a union. The proposition was voted upon favorably by both congregations the following March, and they first worshipped together as the Federated Church of Orland in May 1929. Their church building was constructed in 1937 and dedicated on February 20, 1938.

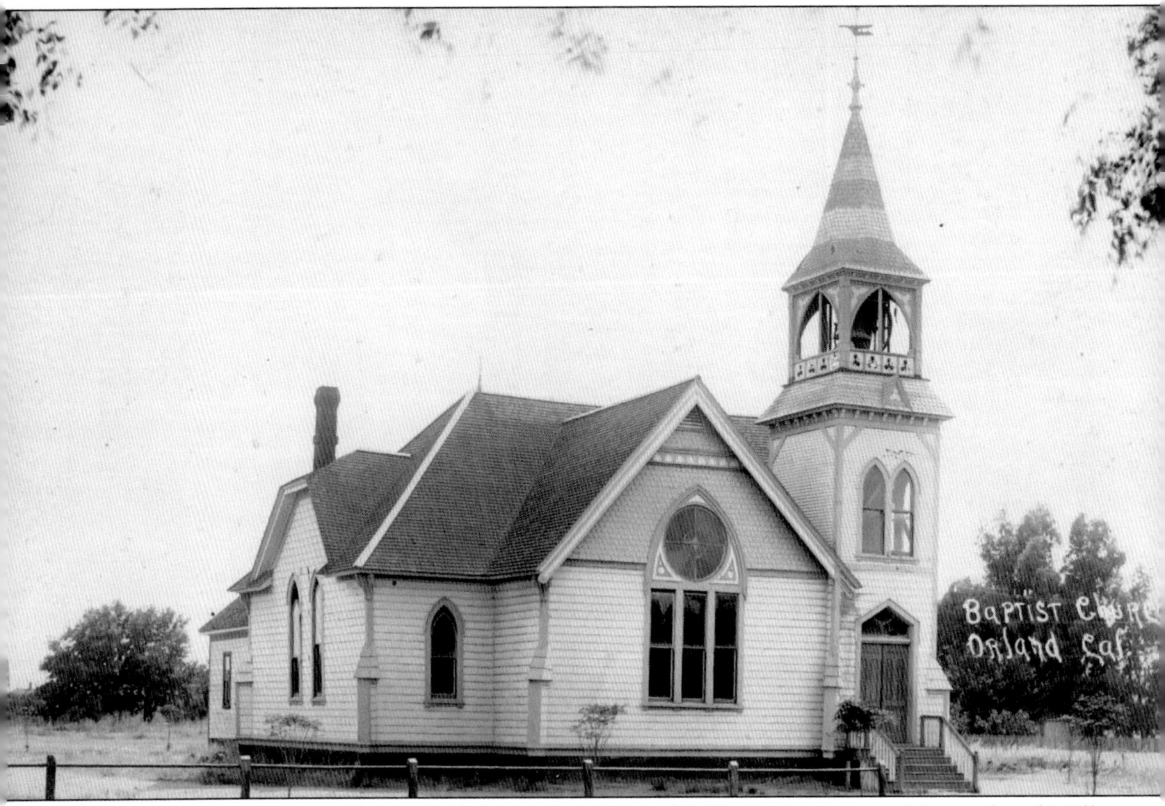

The First Baptist Church was built in 1888–1889 at the southeast corner of Second and Mill Streets at a cost of $3,160. The church had been organized in March 1873 as the Stony Creek Baptist Church by Rev. A. J. Cummings and Rev. J. M. Johnston. It was the first church in this part of the country, and the congregation met in the Plaza School. The following year, the church joined with the Stony Creek IOOF Lodge in a cooperative effort to build a two-story building on 16 acres of land acquired from H. W. Steuben. The IOOF Cemetery on County Road P marks the site of the partnership between Baptists and Odd Fellows. With the coming of the railroad and the expansion of the village, the Pacific Improvement Company donated land for the establishment of the town's third church—Orland First Baptist Church. In the early 1930s, when the elementary school district needed to expand, the Baptists purchased the vacant Trinity Presbyterian Church for $2,400. First services in their new church were on May 19, 1935. The church was dismantled between October and November 1934.

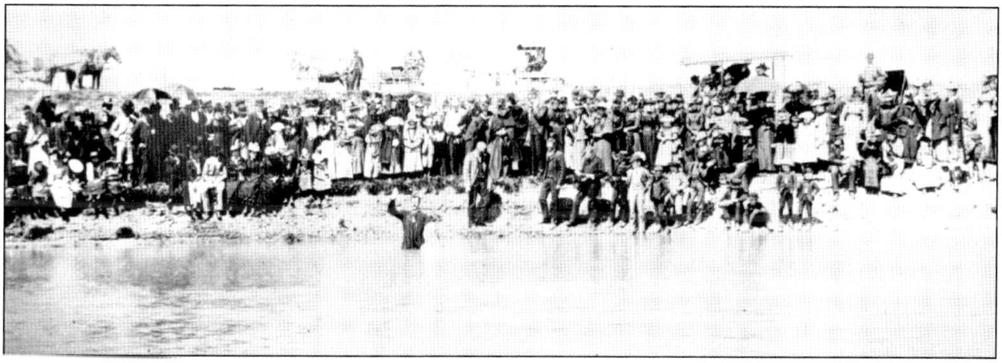

Pictured is a baptism on the north bank of Stony Creek in 1892. The Reverend Frank Baker, pastor of the Orland First Baptist Church from 1888 to 1904, is seen baptizing Janie Gafford. After church revivals, all those who made a confession of faith would meet near the Highway 99 West bridge to be baptized in the waters of Stony Creek. (Courtesy Special Collections, Meriam Library, California State University, Chico.)

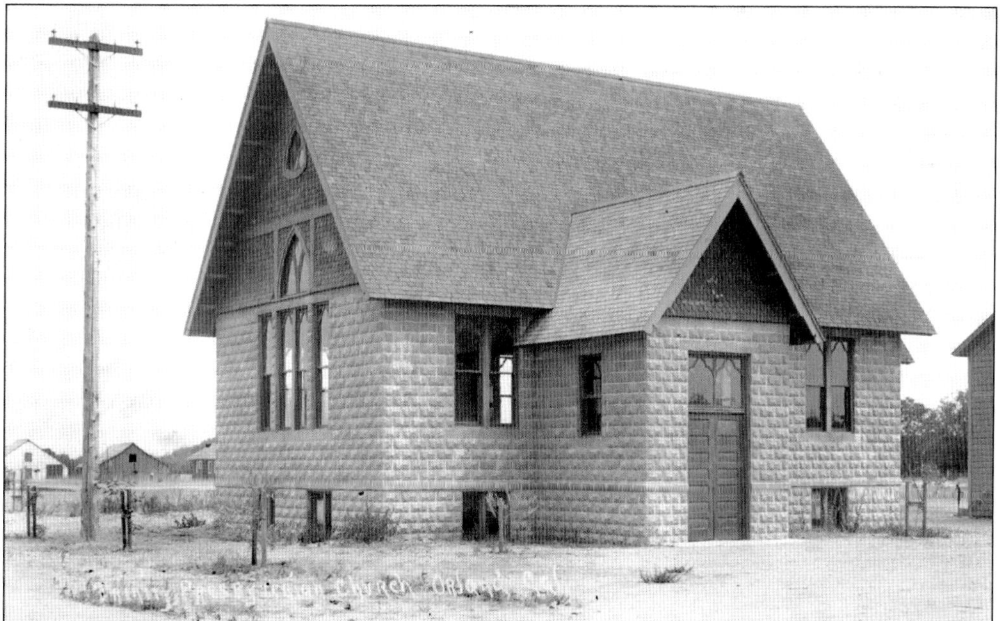

The cornerstone of the Trinity Presbyterian Church was laid on December 11, 1910, before a large gathering of spectators. The building committee invited Ella Tolley, vice president of the Ladies Guild, to officiate at the service. The congregation was then meeting in the Odd Fellows Hall and had hopes of dedicating the completed building by the following Easter. It would take several years before the early English–style church building would be completed.

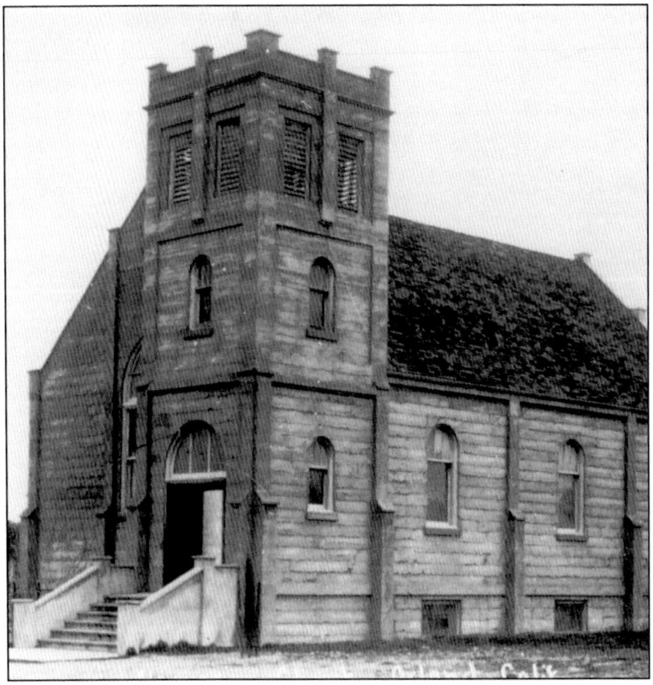

In 1896, six Norwegian American families left Calumet, on Michigan's Keweenaw Peninsula, to relocate northwest of Orland in the "Norwegian Colony." The Norwegian Evangelical Lutheran Church of Orland, chartered in 1902, had its beginnings in the homes of these settlers. In 1915, construction began on a permanent church at the southeast corner of A and Colusa Streets. The building was completed in the 1930s. The name of the congregation was changed to First Lutheran Church in 1932. (Courtesy Thelma White and Special Collections, Meriam Library, California State University, Chico.)

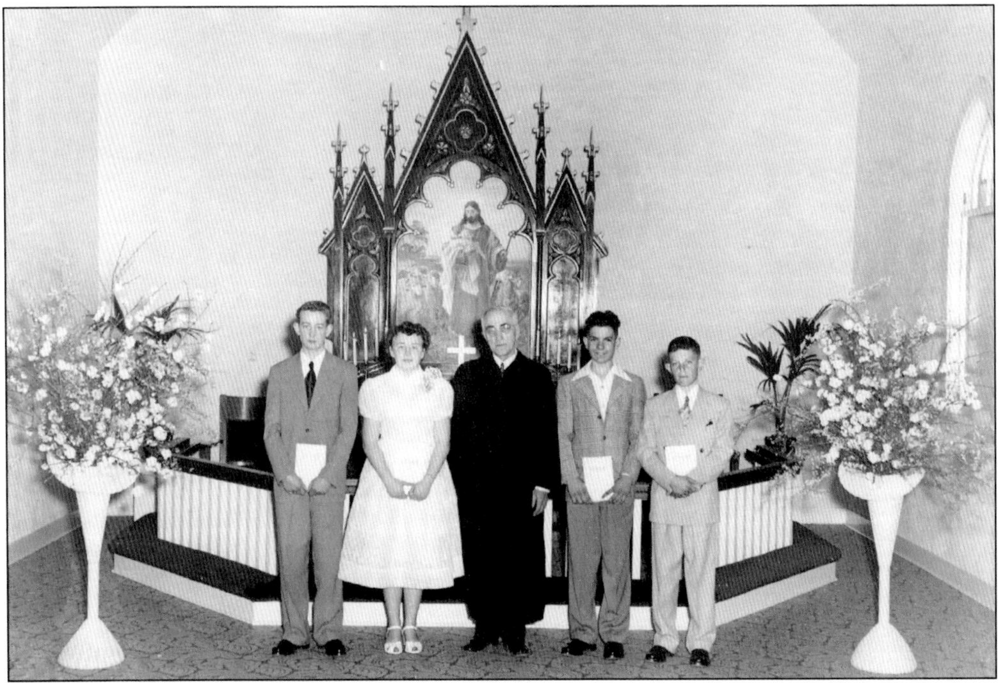

The ornate altar in Orland's First Lutheran Church was designed and built by Arne and John Osterli of Sacramento. The brothers were born in Norway, where they learned to be carpenters before immigrating to America in the early 1900s. The youth of the church purchased the altar in 1926 and had it assembled in the church. Pictured from left to right are the 1951 confirmands—Roger Hunt, Janette Holvik, Pastor Henry Thorpe, Donald Askeland, and Glen Peters. (Courtesy Bev Askeland.)

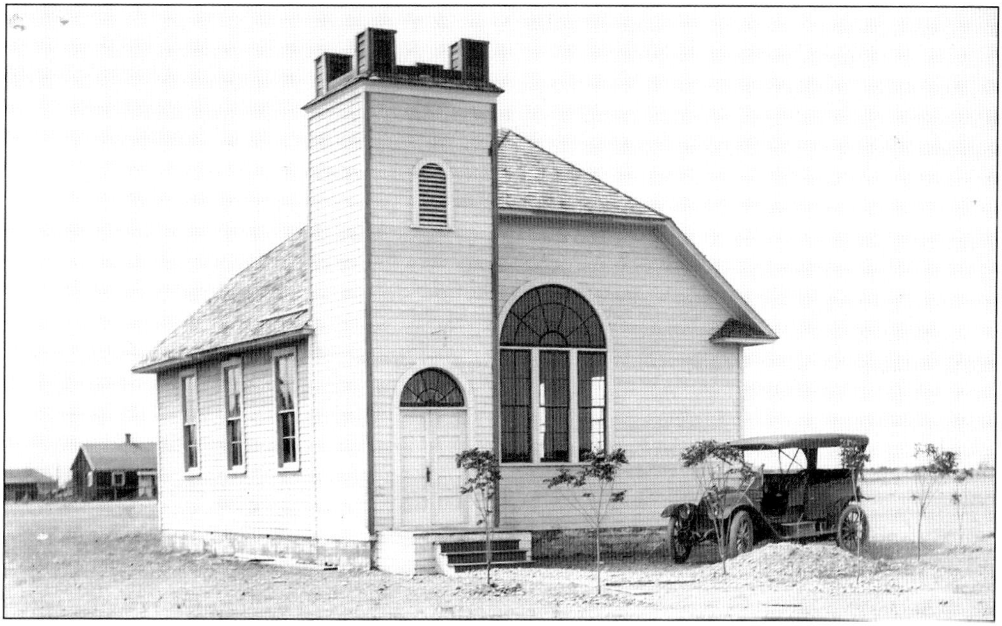

A three-day revival was used to mark the dedication of the Swedish Evangelical Free Church at the corner of A and Swift Streets. The meetings started on Friday and concluded on Sunday (April 27, 1913) with the formal dedication. The church was valued at $1,000, and K. Hendrickson was temporarily filling the pulpit. In 1920, the building was moved onto a lot directly across A Street and purchased by the Seventh-Day Adventist Church.

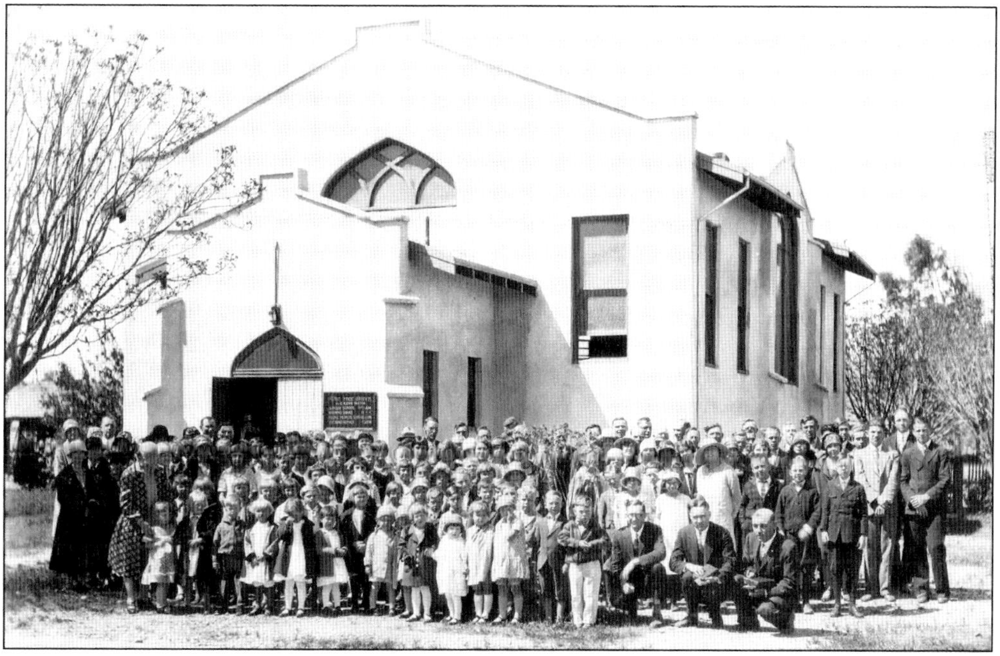

In 1918, the cornerstone of a new Evangelical Free Church was laid, but it was not until 1925 that the building was completed. The congregation worshipped in the basement rooms for a number of years during the completion of the main auditorium. Pictured is the Sunday school in 1927. (Courtesy Evangelical Free Church.)

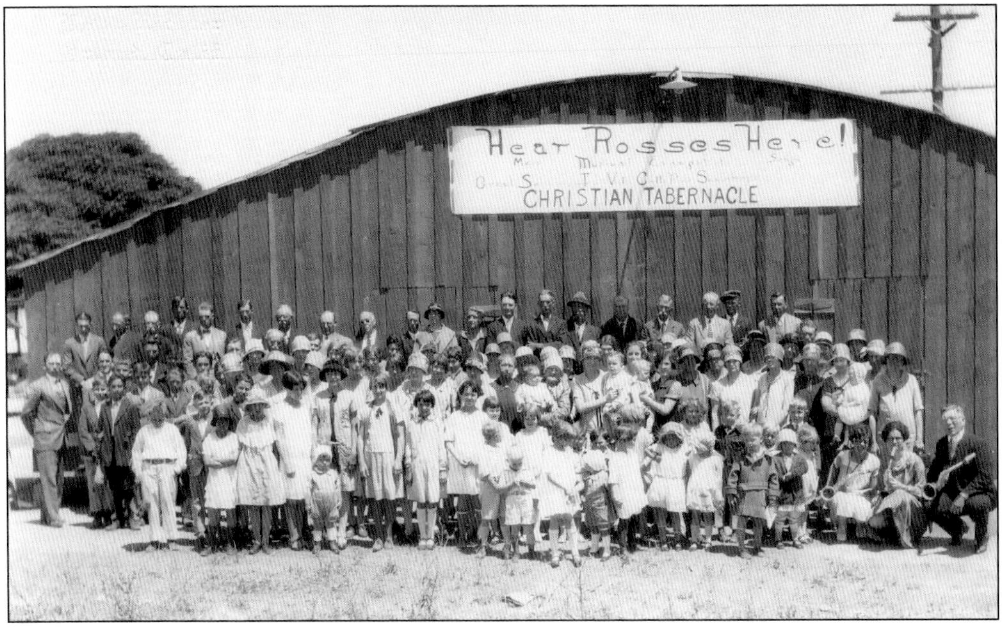

The First Christian Church of Orland was organized in 1925 and purchased lots at the northeast corner of Walker and A Streets in early 1927. On the property's east portion, a 40-by-60-foot wooden tabernacle was erected in April 1927. The following week, the Reverend Floyd Ross Evangelistic Company of Portland, Oregon, started a five-week revival. A permanent church was built west of the tabernacle and dedicated February 12, 1939. (Courtesy Arleen Hibdon Allen.)

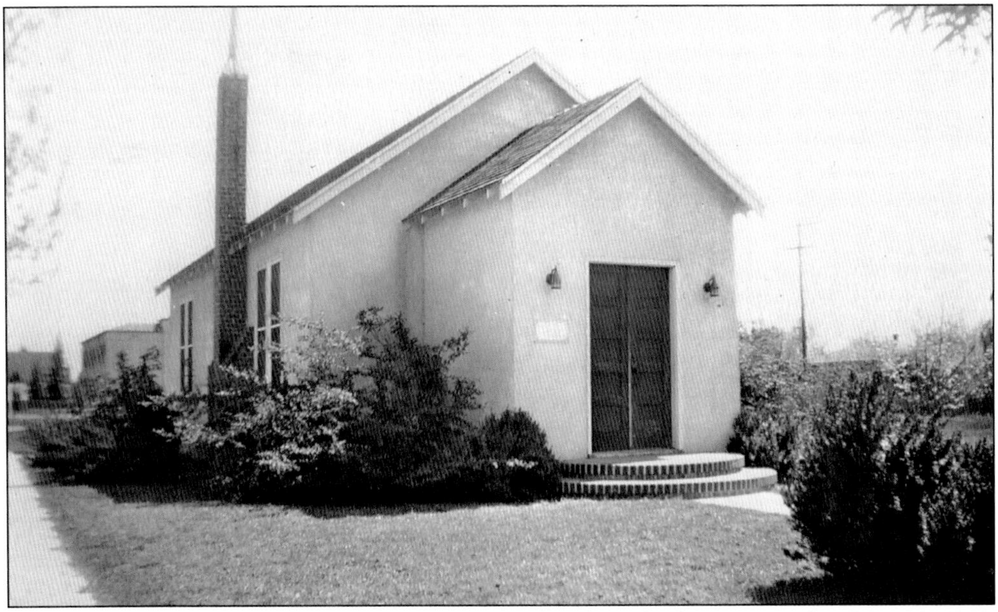

The dedication of the Orland Christian Science Church took place on Sunday, May 23, 1943. The building had been completed in 1939 and the landscaped grounds finished in 1942. Located at the southeast corner of Third and Mill Streets, the dedication was deferred until the church was free of debt. (Courtesy Judy Beck Serrano.)

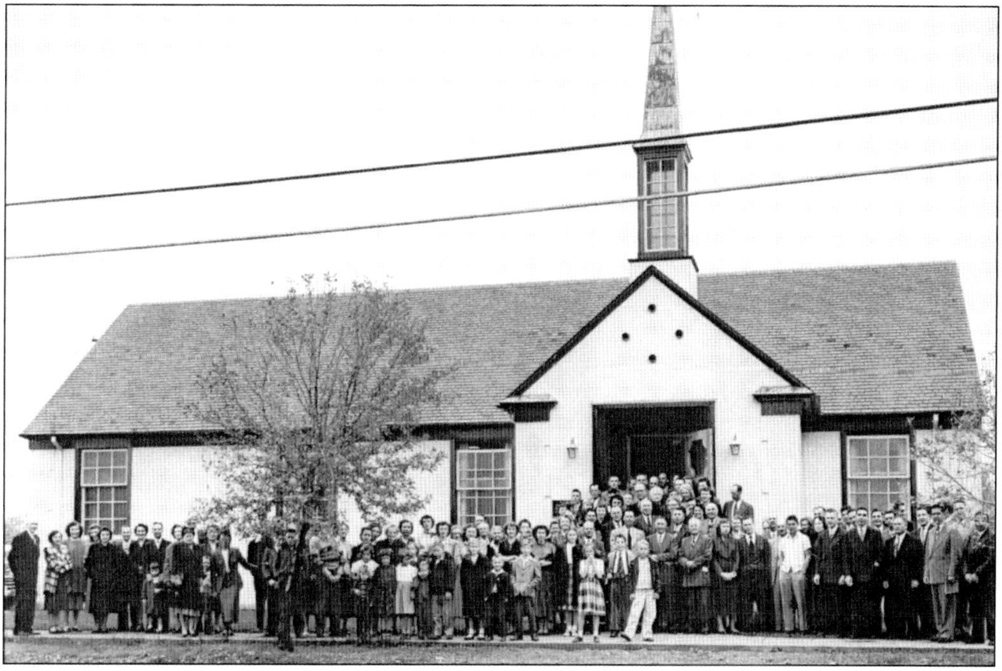

The first branch of the Church of Jesus Christ of Latter-Day Saints in Orland was organized in 1920 with J. I. Tolman as the first branch president. Meetings were held in the hall over the Bank of Orland and later in Bullock Hall before ground was broken February 20, 1950, at Walker and A Streets for their own chapel. The one-story stucco building with approximately 2,300 square feet of floor space was constructed at a cost of $30,000. Work was under the direction of branch presidency, Stephen R. Angus, Junius Heaton, and Dwayne J. Parker. Laurence Wortley of Redding was constructing engineer. The newly completed chapel was first used in July, and church dignitaries conducted the dedicatory services at 1:30 p.m. on November 19, 1950. A musical program was held that evening featuring tenor solos by Darwin Johnson of Fresno, a popular radio and concert singer. (Courtesy Berta Ramsey.)

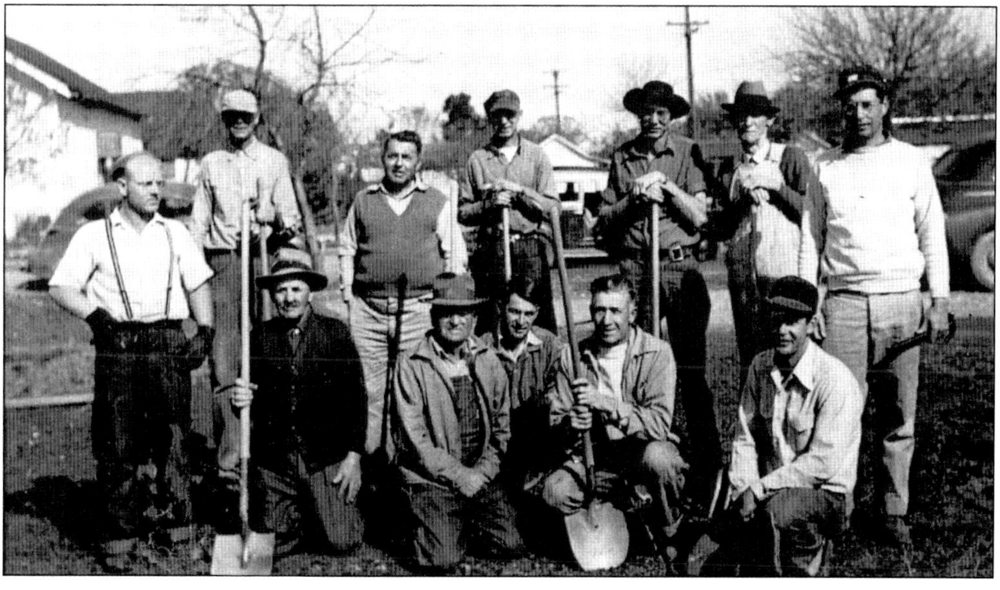

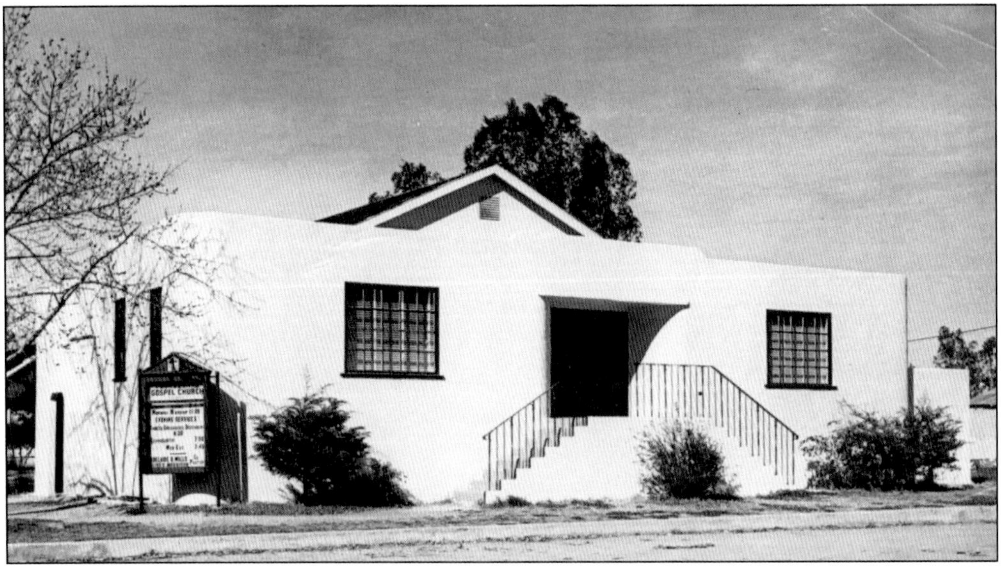

Construction on the Bible Way Mission Church began in March 1928 at the northwest corner of Seventh and Tehama Streets. A large proportion of the work on the concrete basement and 32-by-48-foot superstructure was done by church members. The new edifice was dedicated April 29, 1928, at a special Sunday afternoon service. The group joined the International Church of the Foursquare Gospel, Inc., and the charter was granted on June 26, 1929. (Courtesy Greg Gebhart.)

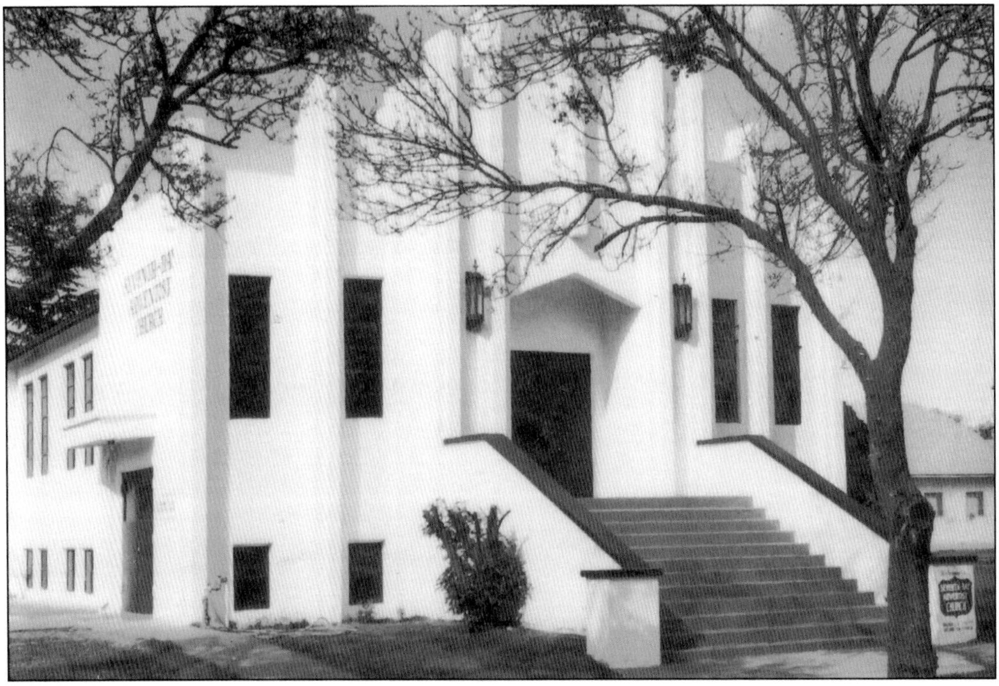

Ground was broken for the new Seventh-Day Adventist church at the corner of A and Walker Streets on February 22, 1951. The congregation started using the $33,000 modern structure in January 1952. In March 1921, the Adventists purchased the lot containing the old relocated Swedish Evangelical Church on A Street and used the building for the next 31 years. Prior to this time, they had been meeting in the Lake School. (Courtesy Jose Torres.)

Eight

Amusement and Entertainment

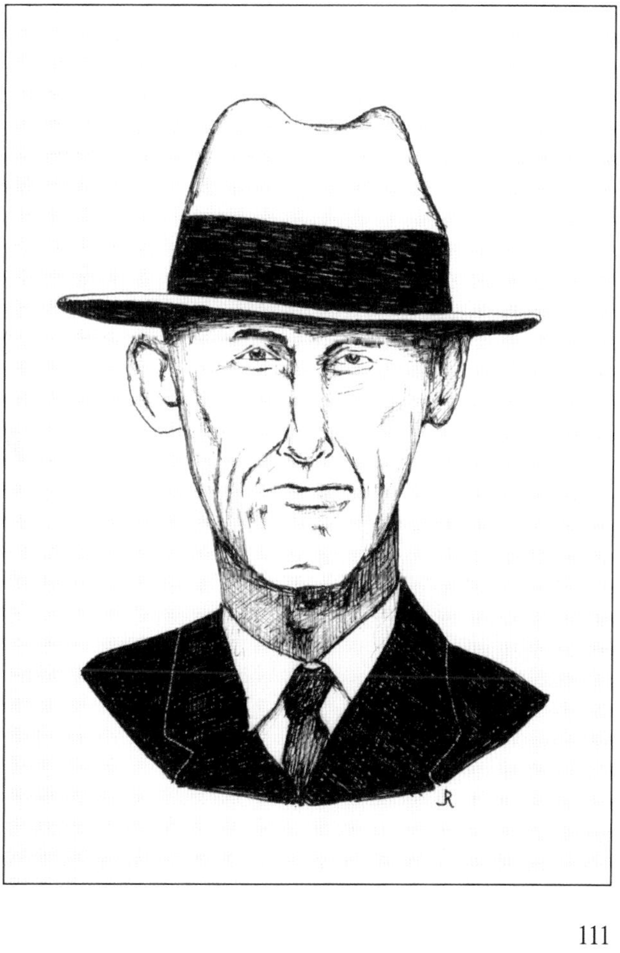

Drs. Charles and Hanna Bihler came to Orland in May 1921. The following year, they moved their chiropractic business into their home at the corner of Walker and East Streets. The Bihler home was the site for the organizational meetings in February and March 1923 that created the Orland Municipal Band. Charles was the band's president and bass drummer for over 20 years. As a rabid baseball fan, he served many years as the official scorekeeper for the town's baseball and softball leagues. When the local baseball field property exchanged hands and was lost during the Depression in 1932, Charles Bihler became a driving force for a new 17-acre municipal playground east of the high school. On October 6, 1947, the Orland City Council named the baseball park Bihler Field in appreciation for his efforts. He passed away on the morning of June 14, 1963.

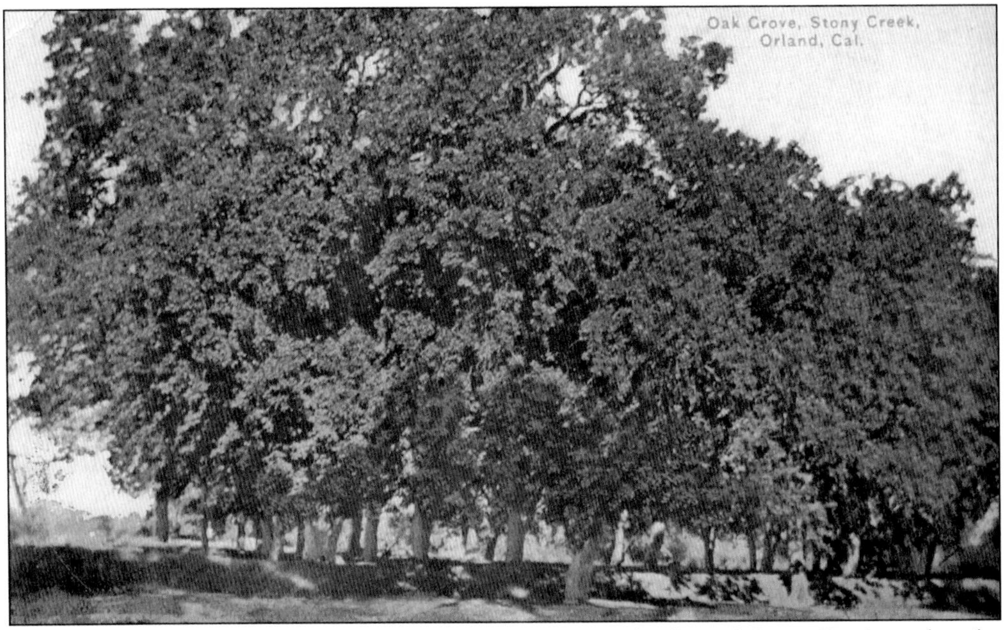

Greenwood Grove was a natural park located between Hambright and Stony Creeks and to the east of the railroad tracks. It was the site for most community picnics, reunions, and Fourth of July celebrations. Hiram A. Greenwood was a community-spirited citizen who owned extensive property north of Orland and also four miles south of town. The popular grove of valley oaks was used until the mid-1920s.

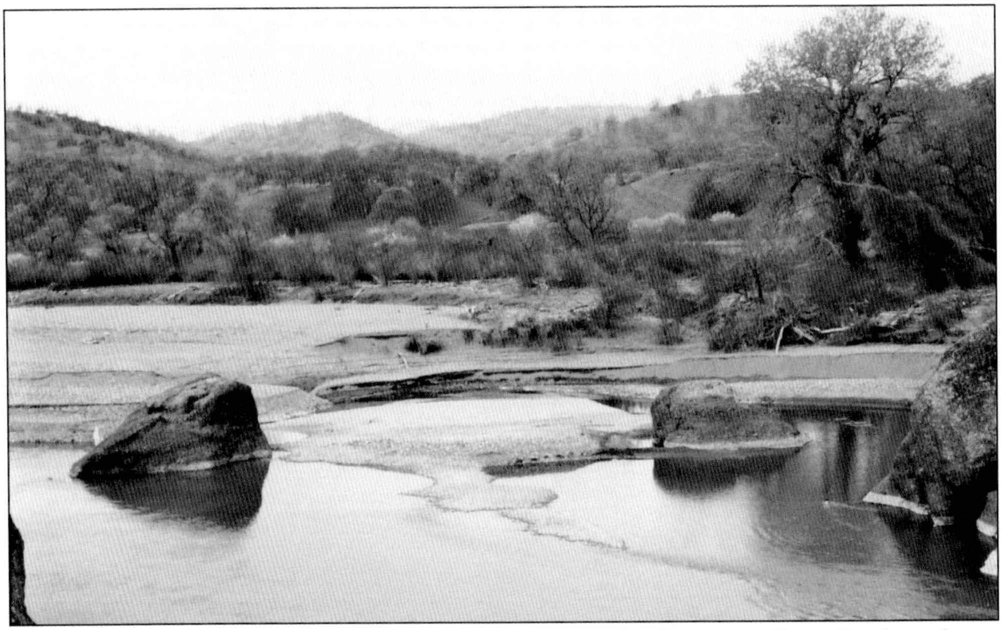

Julian Rocks is a narrow passage through a prominent rocky ridge that crosses Stony Creek southwest of Orland. Where the creek comes through, the gap is only about 15 feet wide with six-foot cliffs on either side. This constriction of Stony Creek has been considered as a possible dam site since the 1870s and as a highway bridge site since the 1920s. It was also a favorite summer swimming hole for those who did not mind encounters with rattlesnakes. (Courtesy Andrew Barron.)

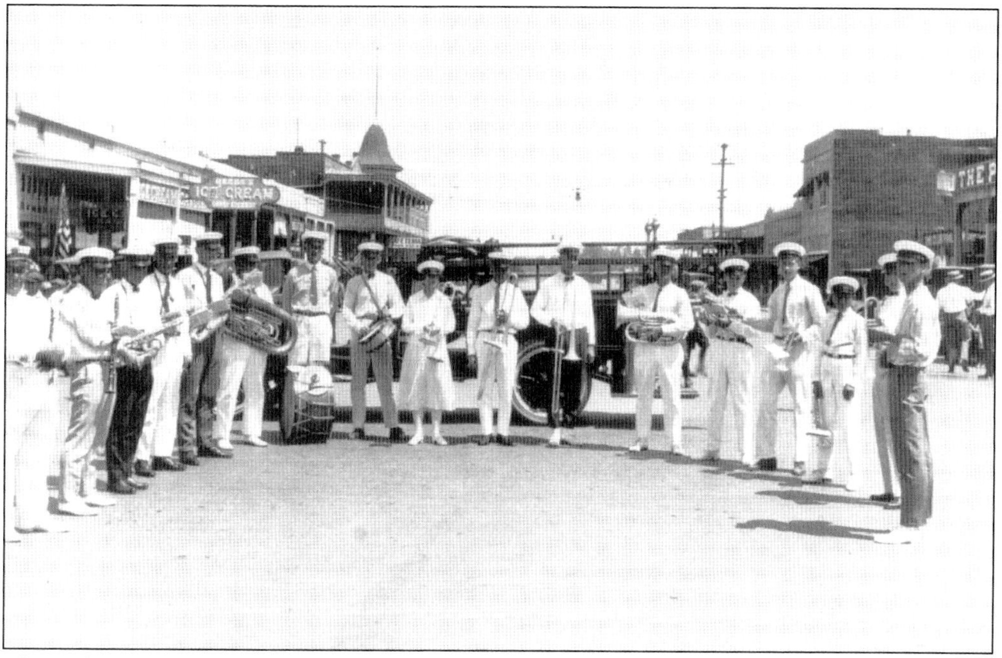

The Orland municipal or town band was formed and dedicated to furnish music of a pleasing quality for all public occasions. Between the years 1923 and 1945, a total of 206 musicians played in the band and received 25¢ per practice session. The band also traveled to neighboring towns and played on the back of a flatbed truck to advertise Orland and Glenn County Fairs. (Courtesy Special Collections, Meriam Library, California State University, Chico.)

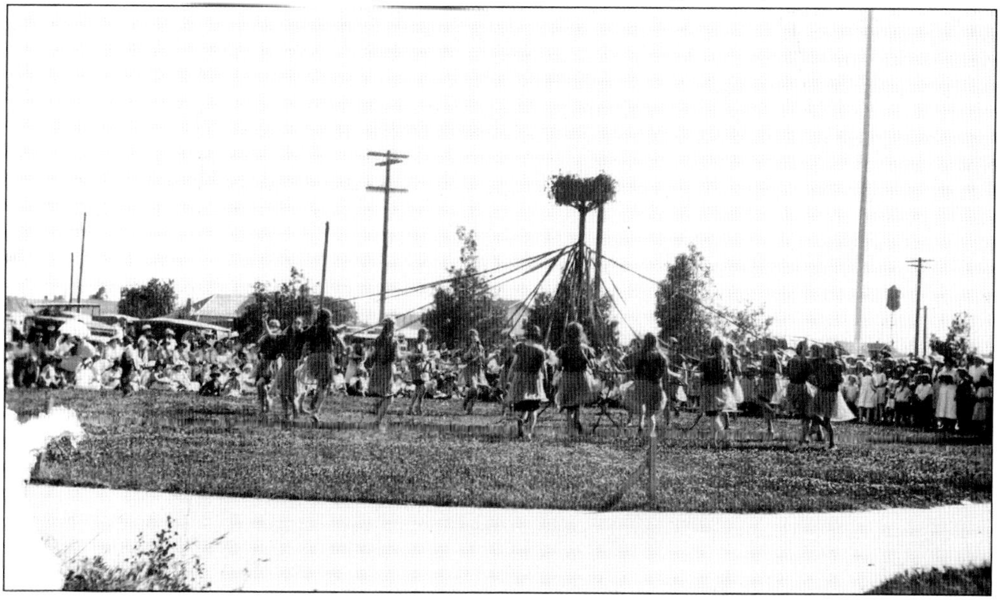

May Day (May 1) has been a spring festival celebrating the renewal of nature for thousands of years. A tall wooden pole with numerous long colored ribbons attached at the top served as the maypole. As part of the May Day celebration, schoolchildren danced and plaited the ribbons around the pole, then retraced their steps exactly to unravel the ribbons. This photograph was probably taken in the 1920s. (Courtesy Orland Alumni Association.)

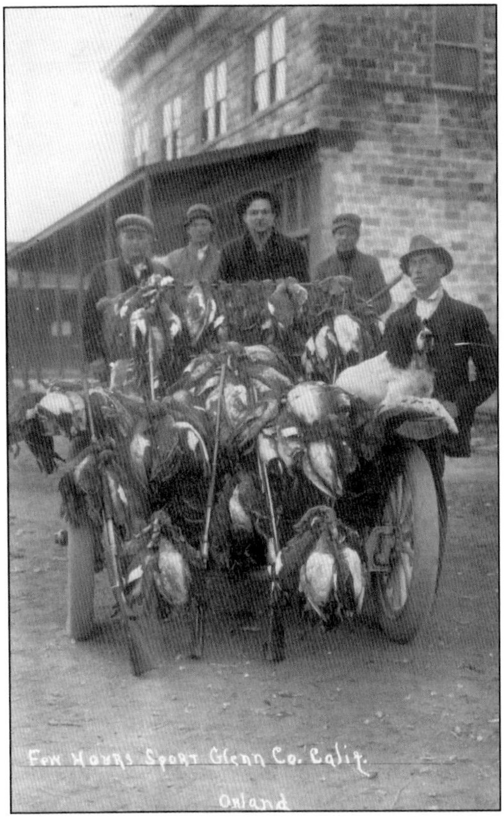

The land of Orland was presented in early promotional literature as a "sportsman's paradise." Ducks and geese were plentiful in 1907 when this photograph was taken. The hunters on George Barceloux's first automobile, from left to right, are Ed Green, Magnus Peters, George Barceloux, Joe Bender, and Walter Steuben.

Blacktail deer may be hunted in season on public land in the Mendocino National Forest. Trips to hunting and camping sites, like Government Flat and Kingsley Glade, have been annual activities for many hunters and their families. Nancy Jane was one of Jack Bucke's favorite pack animals and is shown bringing out the day's kill. (Courtesy Jack Bucke.)

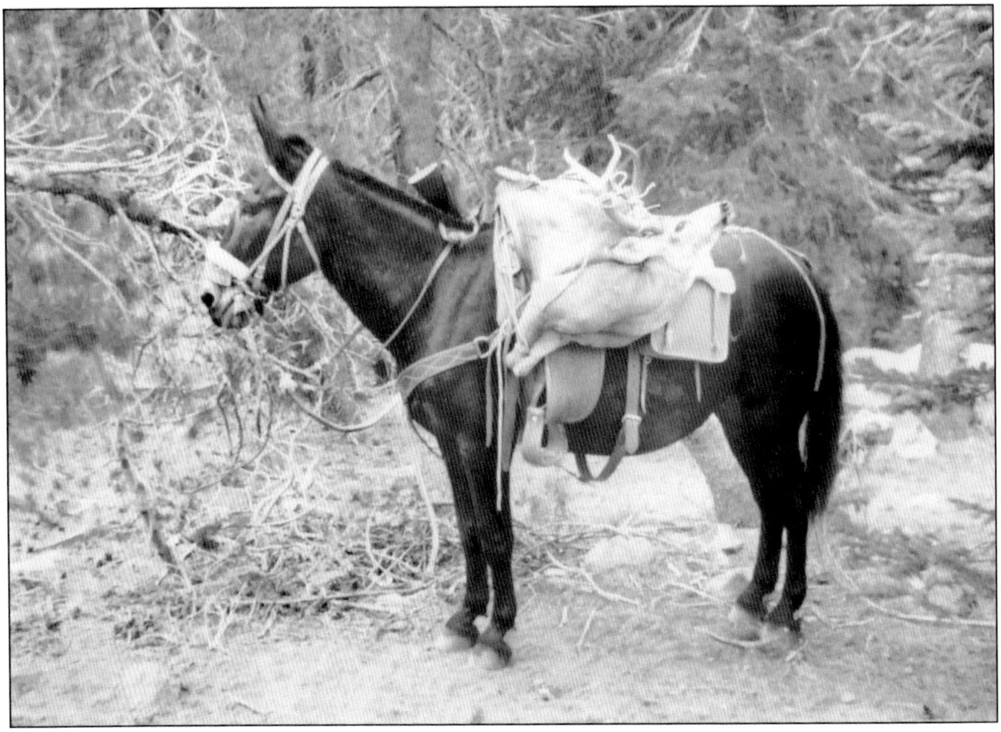

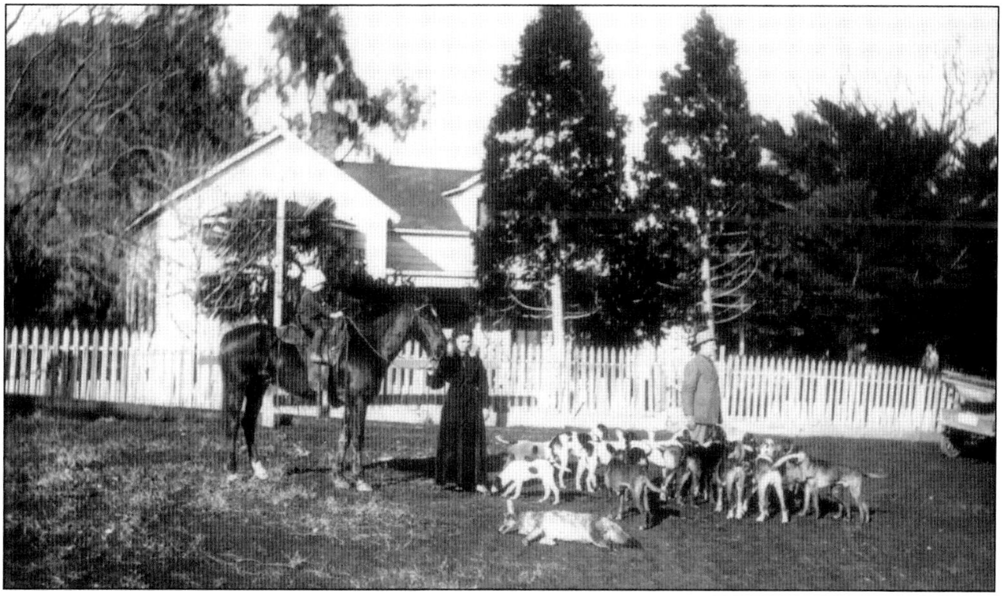

Allen T. Moore was a prominent Orland rancher and civic leader. When he arrived in California from the Midwest in 1889, he had only his horse, a rifle, a few cents in his pocket, and four dogs. He loved fine dogs and entered thoroughbred animals in various dog shows, winning numerous prizes. His registered foxhounds, shown after a hunt, were probably the best in Northern California. Moore was also Orland's most famous bear hunter. (Courtesy California History Room, California State Library, Sacramento, California.)

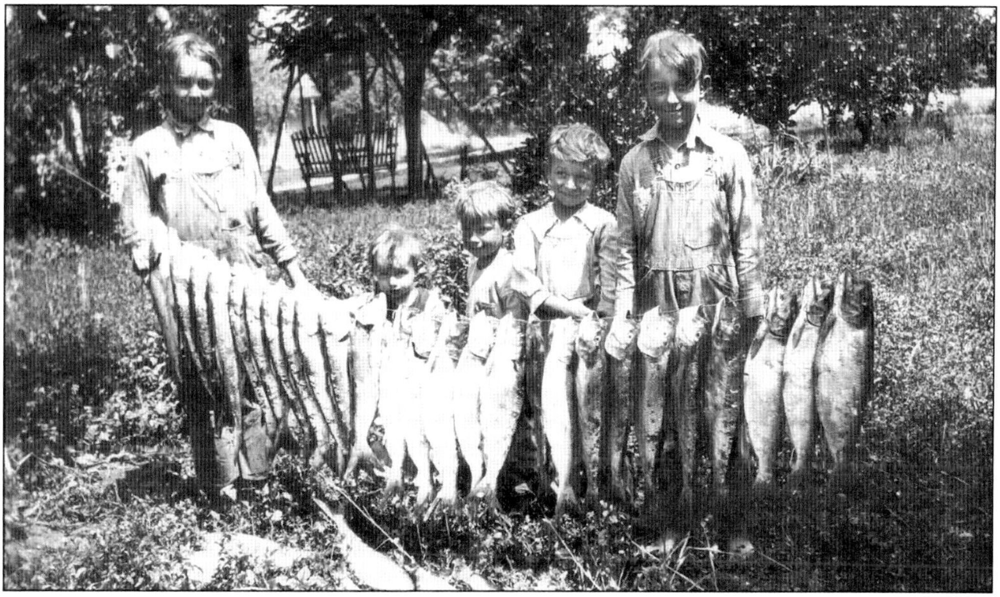

Shad were often caught at night from the banks of the Sacramento River. This string of fish and those in the foreground were one night's work by John Slyh and Bob Vonasek in the early 1930s. Bob Vonasek's children pictured are, from left to right, Alfred, George, Robert "Buddy," Paul, and Harry. Trout were annually sent to Orland in the 1920s for planting in the western mountain streams. The fry (young fish), approximately 100,000 in number, came by train from the Sisson (present-day Mount Shasta City) Fish Hatchery. (Courtesy Jim Slyh.)

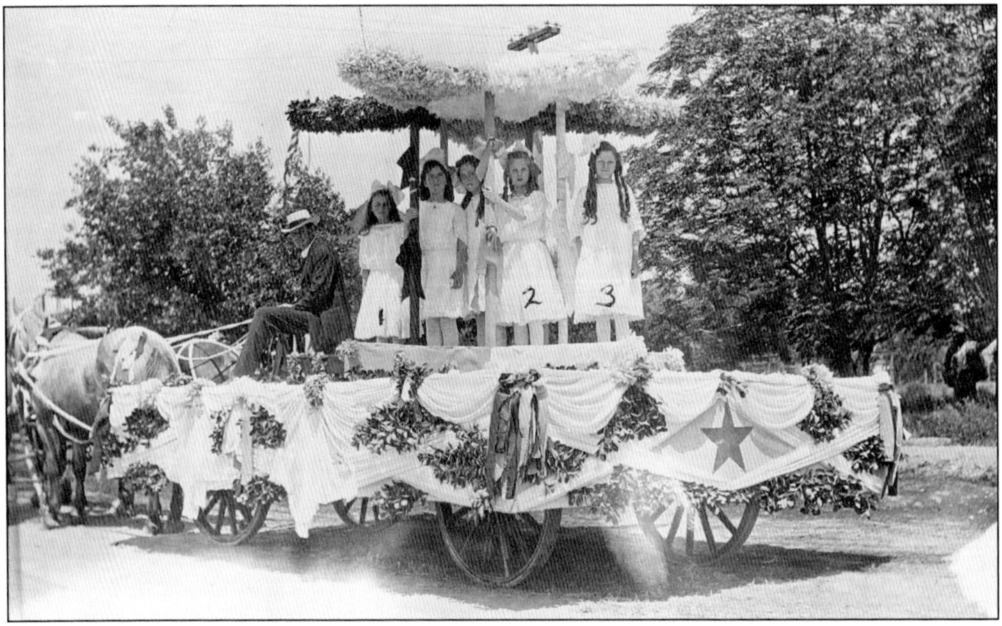

The Irrigation Jubilee was Orland's biggest celebration of the 20th century, held June 16–17, 1911. A crowd of 5,000 were on hand to mark the completion of the U.S. Reclamation Service's Orland Project. Postcards and 20,000 booklets were prepared to promote the big event. The first division of the parade included City of Orland and reclamation officials, the Second Regimental Band of Chico, the royal float, and civic leaders in automobiles. Division II included the Orland Cornet Band, commercial floats, and fraternal floats, including the Eastern Star entry pictured above. Division III included private automobiles and conveyances, and jerk-line mule teams. Simpson and Clark's team pulled three wagons loaded with grain, and the Cushman Brothers' three wagons were loaded with wool, pictured below. (Above courtesy Arthalyn Kublick; below courtesy Joe and Shirley Erickson.)

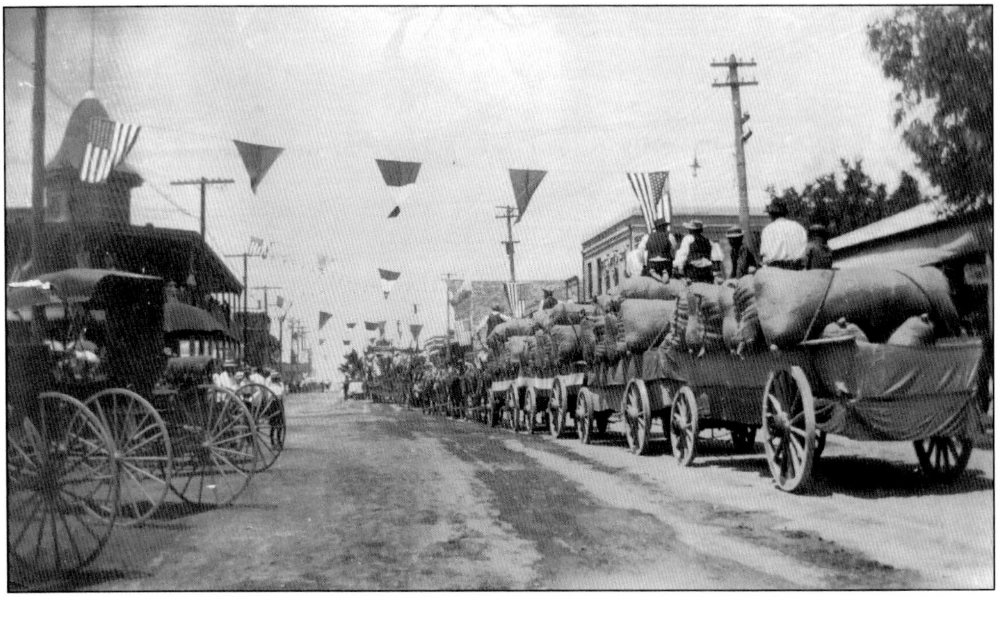

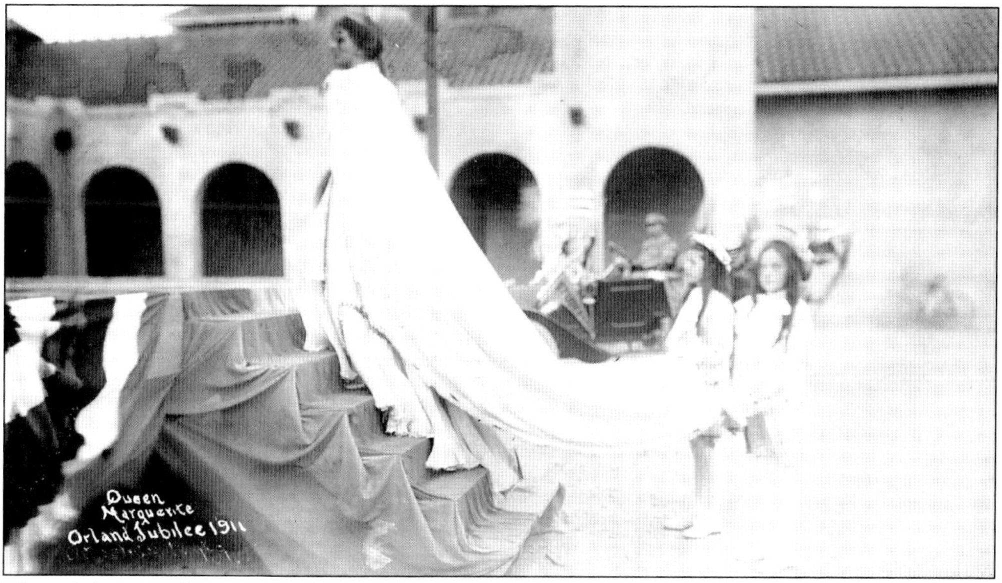

The jubilee parade came to a halt at the grammar school where a large platform with a throne had been erected. Master of ceremonies was W. A. Greenwood, and Dr. S. Iglick had been appointed coronation officer. With guards, maids, flower girls, and pages at her side, Marguerite DeArmond was crowned queen of the Orland Irrigation Jubilee and given three hearty cheers by her subjects. Those participating in the royal court included (maids) Mary Masterson, Grace Griffith, Delpha Judd, and Opal Brown; (pages) Vernon Sperlich and Elizabeth Mattoon; (guards) Wade Bates and Rollo Harelson; (flower girls) Dorris Birch, Lucille Sperlich, Alta Schmidt, Marie Liefred, Willa DeArmond, and Jessie Hiatt; and (crown bearer) Anvinette Bates. Speeches by Mayor Daniel Sturm and four other dignitaries followed the coronation. The afternoon activities included lunch, music, a carnival, baseball games, and open-air dancing in the evening. (Both courtesy Rovilla Christian.)

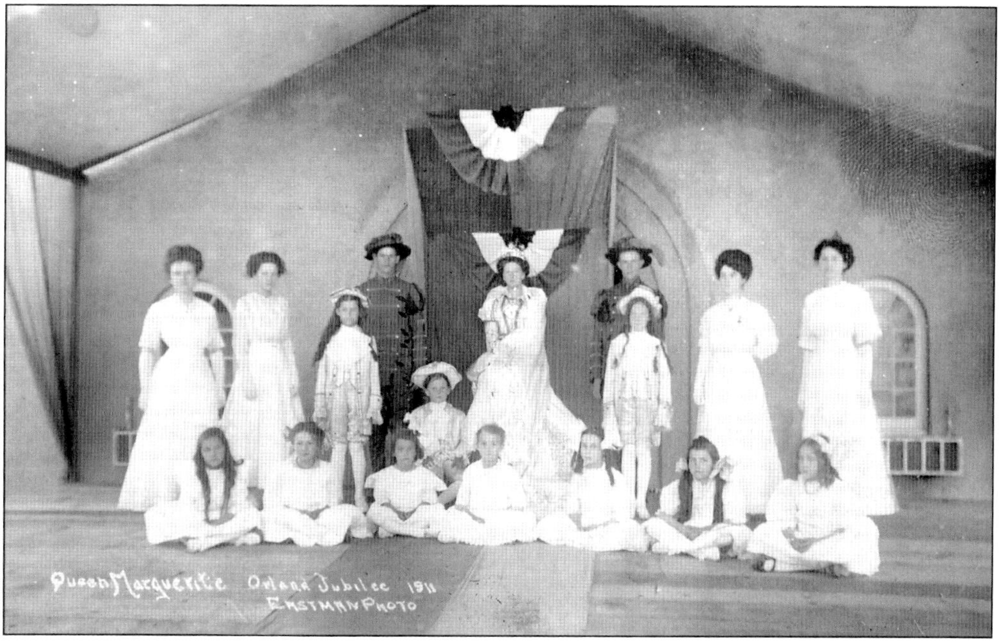

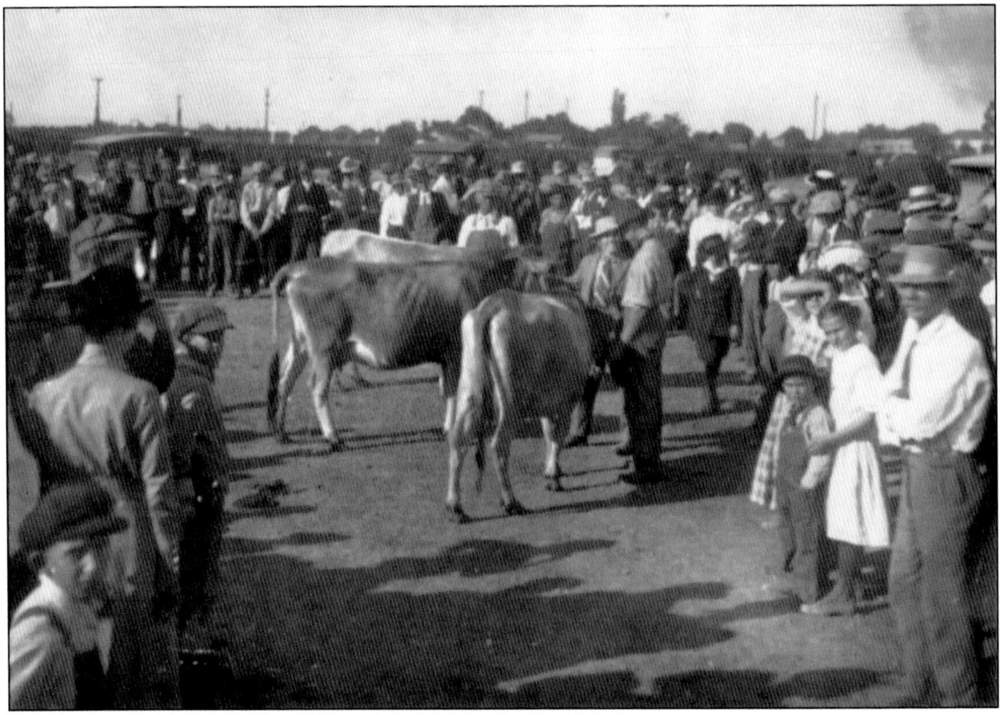

On October 21, 1916, the Orland Center of the Glenn County Farm Bureau staged a one-day program of showing and comparing livestock owned by area farmers. Several experts from Davis were on hand to evaluate the 70 dairy cows, 60 hogs, and 30 horses. The Saturday event was held on the town's ball field and was attended by 500 people.

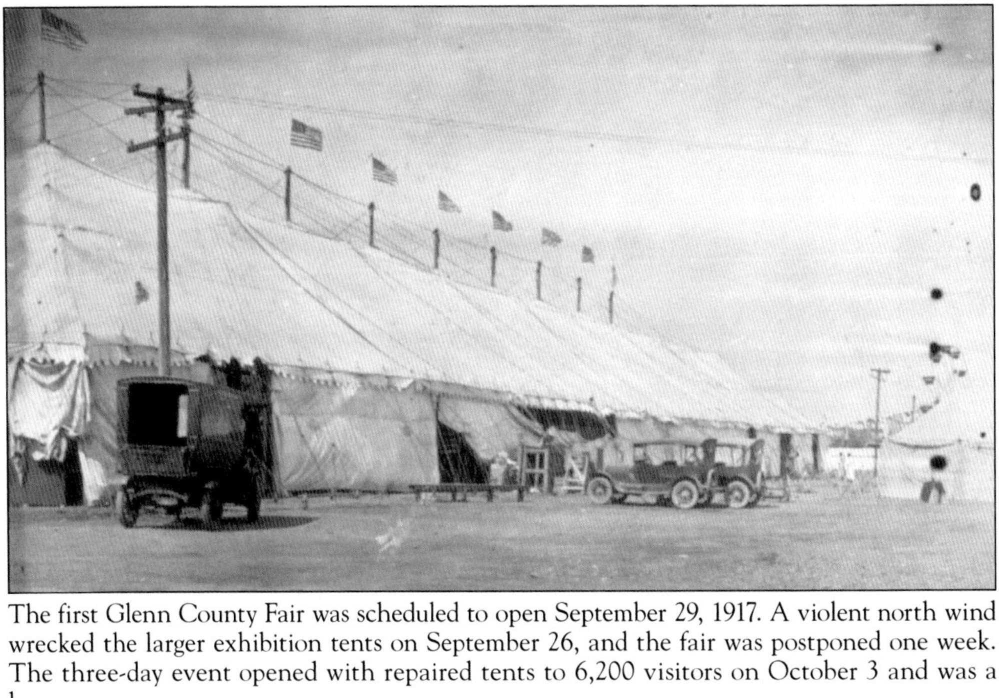

The first Glenn County Fair was scheduled to open September 29, 1917. A violent north wind wrecked the larger exhibition tents on September 26, and the fair was postponed one week. The three-day event opened with repaired tents to 6,200 visitors on October 3 and was a huge success.

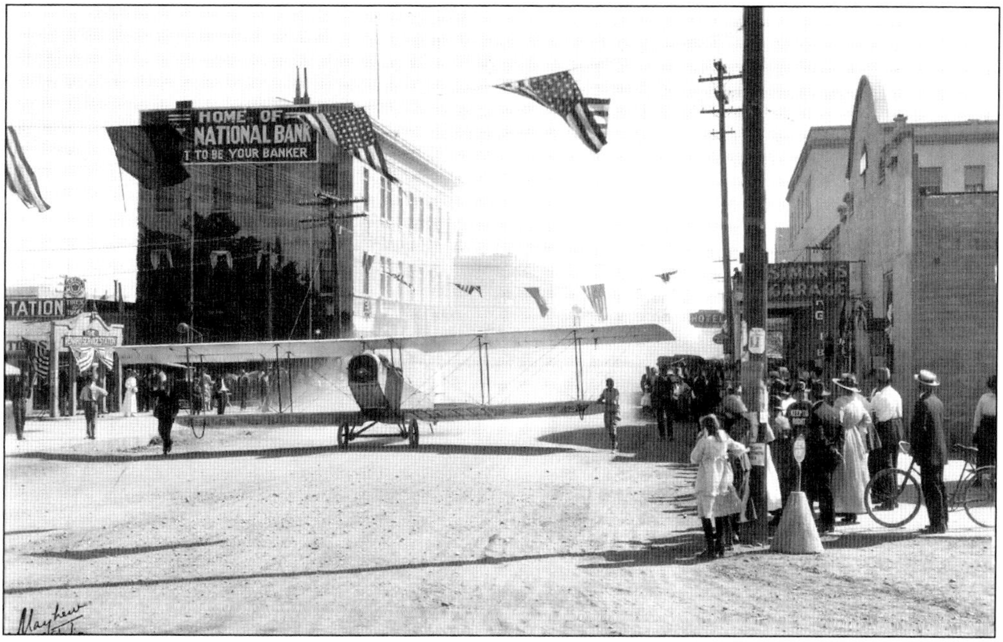

Parades through downtown Orland have been a popular tradition since the first Glenn County Fair in 1917. Hundreds of schoolchildren from the local and rural districts practiced marching and sometimes made costumes before participating in the big September event. Barnstormer Clyde Pangborn is shown leading the 1920 parade down unpaved Colusa Street.

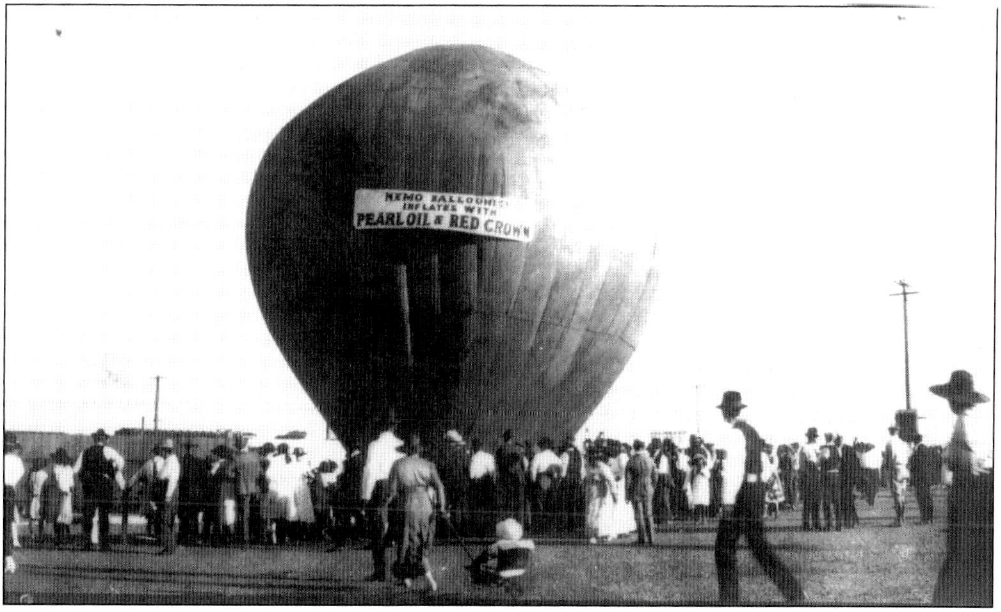

"Bigger and Better Than Ever" was the theme for the fifth Glenn County Fair, held September 19–24, 1921. Major attractions included daily upside-down airplane flying over the fairgrounds followed at 4:00 p.m. by the balloon ascension and parachute drop. While attendance was down slightly, it was deemed the biggest and best fair to date.

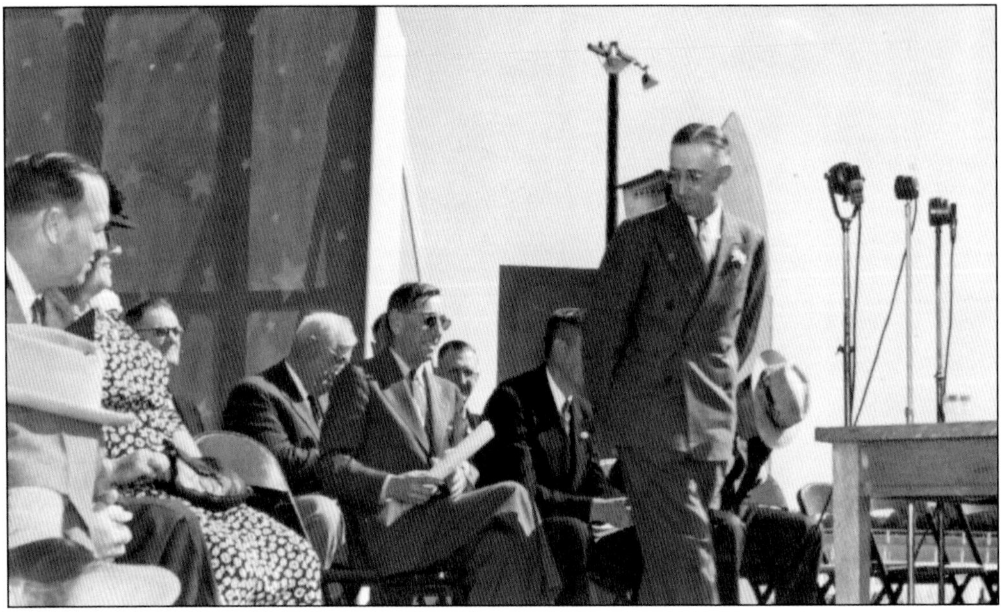

"Meet Me at the Forty in Forty-One" was the slogan for the 1941 fair at the new permanent fairgrounds. The 40-acre site had been purchased for $1,400, and the work of building a model fairground was done by the Works Progress Administration. The first structures completed included the entrance gateway, the exhibit hall, cow barns, a poultry shed, a grandstand, and a track. Later the WPA would construct the horse barns. The $200,000 home for the fair was dedicated on September 16, 1941, in front of a huge crowd packed into the grandstand. Fair director L. W. Wigmore made the surprise announcement that the new exhibit hall was to be officially known as Flaherty Hall to honor the longtime president of the fair board John Flaherty. The fair was not held during the years of World War II. Shown are two photographs taken during the opening day of the 1941 Glenn County Fair.

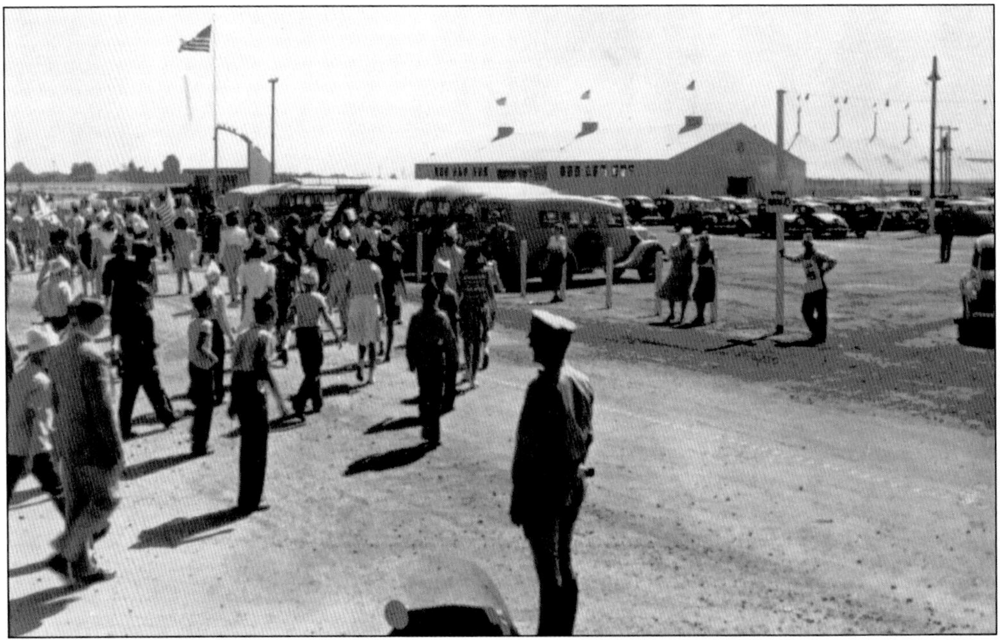

In the late 1950s, the Glenn County Sheriff's Posse sponsored an annual stampede that brought top cowboys and rodeo stock to the weekend event, held each May at the fairgrounds. Festivities included a queen contest, a parade through Orland, two rodeo performances, a rodeo grand entry parade, and an evening dance at the Barn. Pictured is Duke Williams during the bareback bucking horse event about 1963. (Courtesy Bruce Gilmore.)

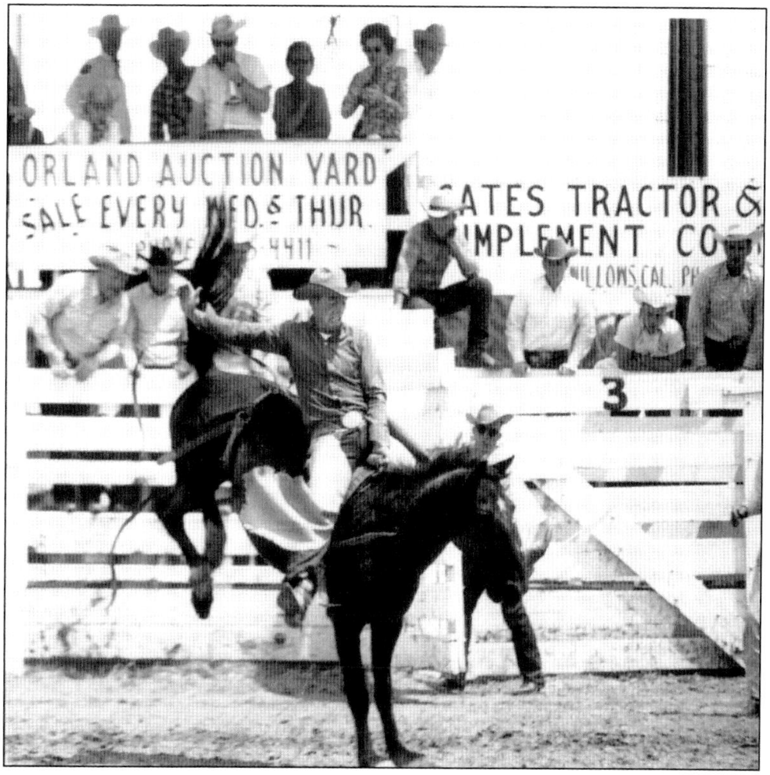

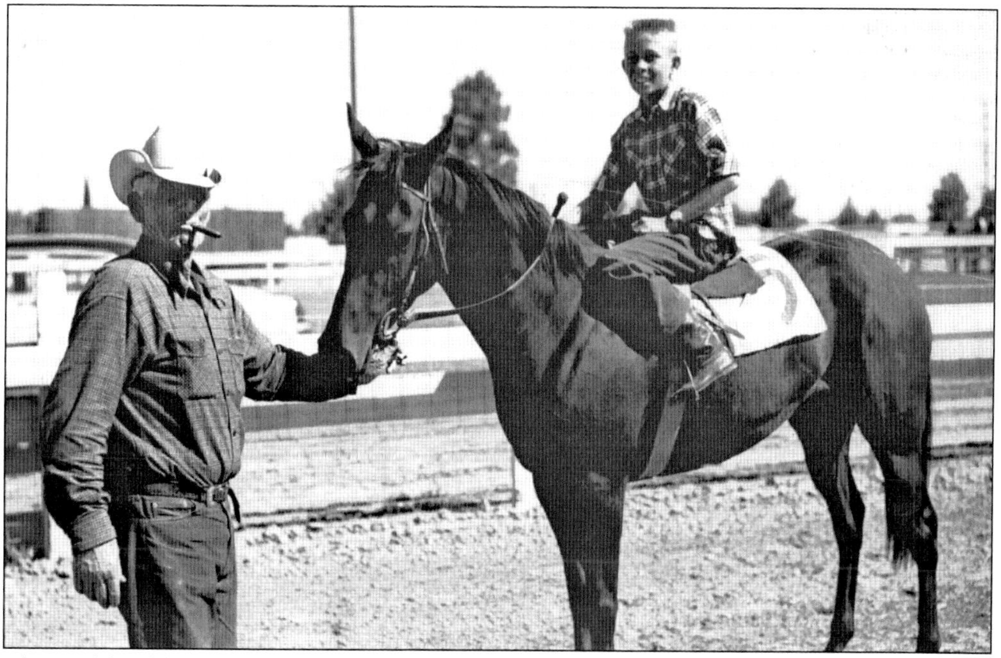

Thoroughbred horseracing was a featured attraction on the one-half-mile track at the Glenn County Fairgrounds during the 1950s and early 1960s. Cleo Johnson was a local horse breeder and trainer at the 1953 fair when this picture was taken. Bobby Wall is the jockey on Johnson's Thoroughbred. (Courtesy Bruce Gilmore.)

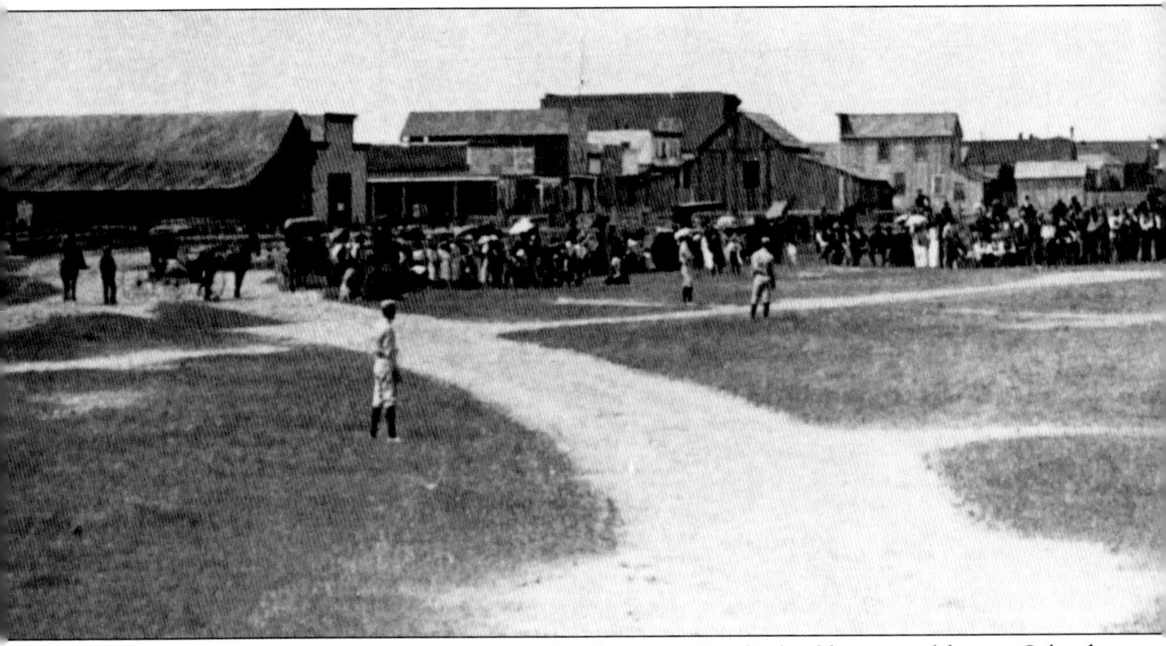

Baseball was taken seriously in the 1890s and early 1900s. Hundreds of frantic and fanatic Orland fans attended games to watch the local team play the national pastime. Pictured is an early playing field between Fourth and Fifth Streets and south of Colusa Street. Other diamonds were

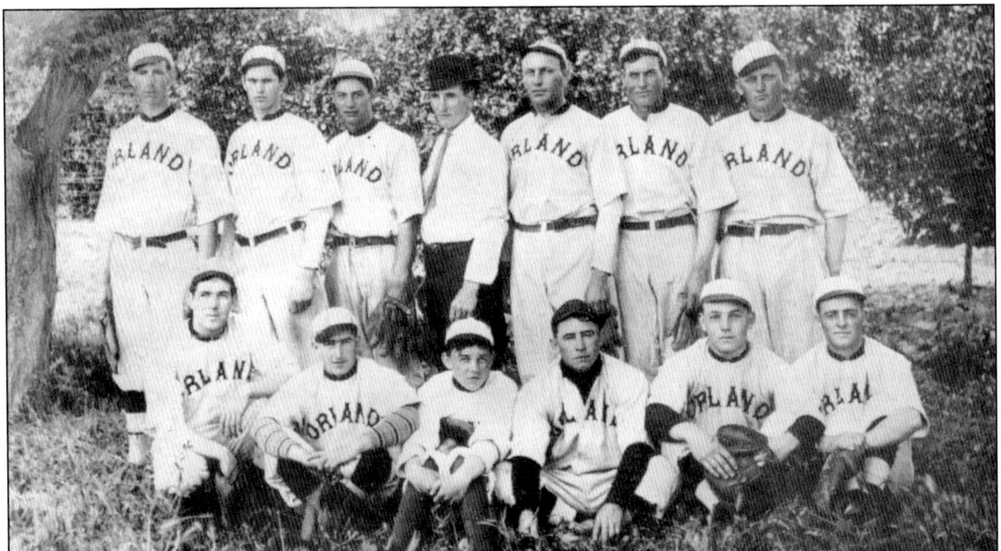

The town baseball team played almost every Sunday from April through July 1912. The Orland Bearcats played games against Arbuckle, Chico, Corning, Los Molinos, Oroville, Redding, Willows, and Woodland. The 1912 season opener was against Roy Brownell's Wonders from Floyd. Pictured from left to right are (first row) Marcus Masterson, Howard Mecum, unidentified, Earl Pearcy, Dud Martin, and Kenneth Morrissey; (second row) Bob Kooney, Rolo Harelson, Bob Aitken, unidentified, Fred Benton, Charles Thode, and Curley Schlagle.

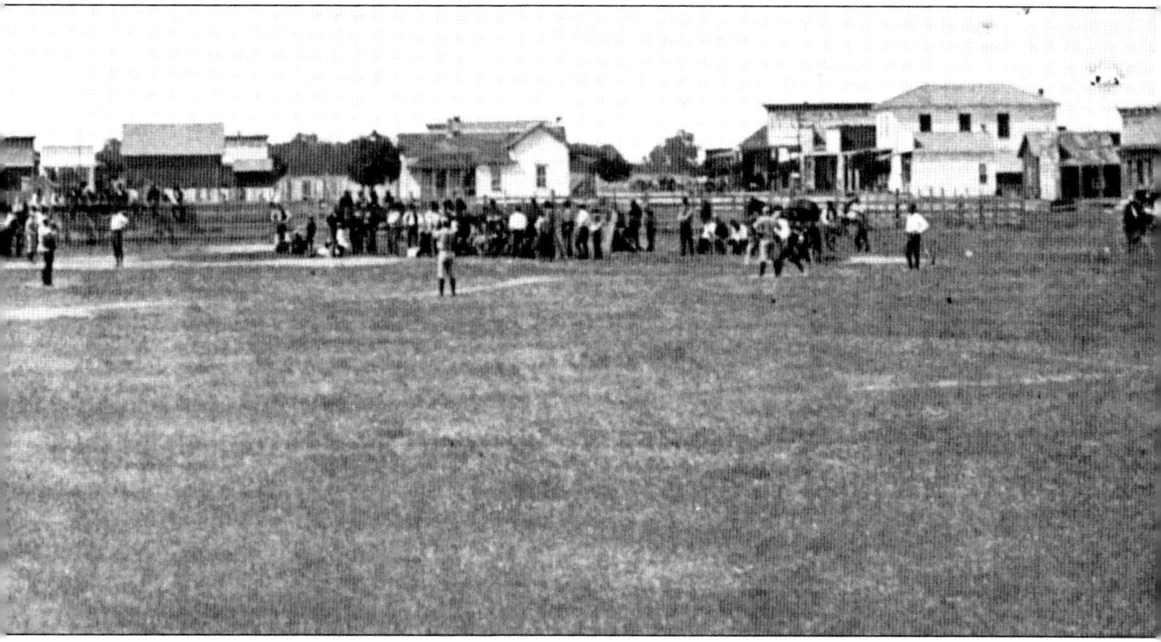

located at Greenwood Grove and the fairgrounds southwest of town. The town water wagon was used to help prepare the field for Sunday afternoon games. (Courtesy Thelma White and Special Collections, Meriam Library, California State University, Chico.)

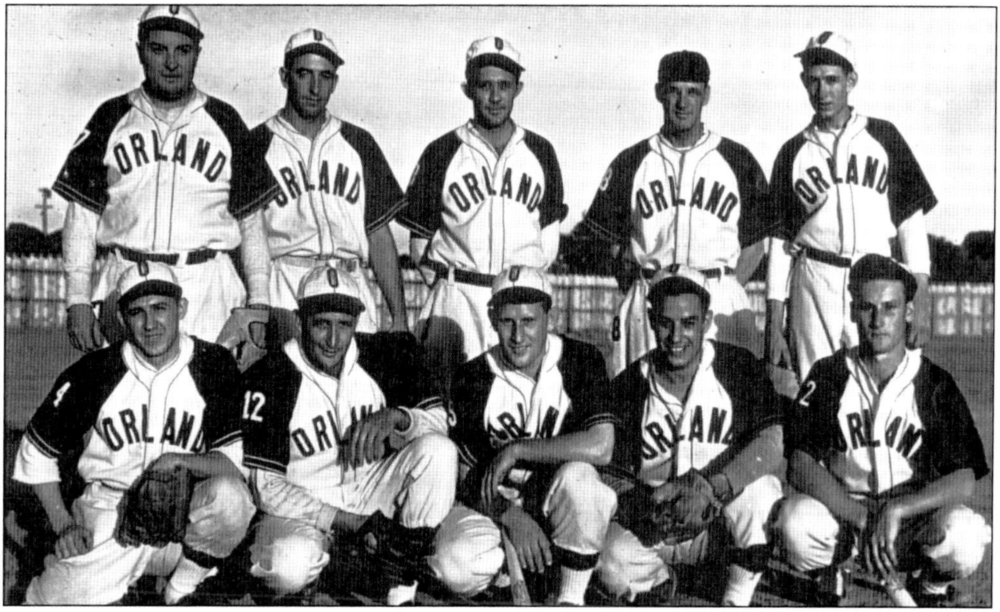

The Orland Tigers were the 1941 champions of the Golden Empire League. Other teams included the Chico Cubs, Cottonwood Bees, Red Bluff Bobcats, Shasta Dam Builders, and Yuba City Bears. Members are, from left to right (first row) D. M. "Buck" Gleason, Joe Holvik, Alden Hinz, Leo Guareno, and Leroy Winters; (second row) H. C. Speck Schonborg, Pete Holvik, Gus Franke, John Cox, and Dale Sievers. Not shown are Harry Bruckenstein, Glenn and Ralph Gunn, Curt Hibdon, Les Jones, Marvin Lake, G. Parlin, Steve Passafiume, and Jimmie Smith. (Courtesy Evelyn Gleason.)

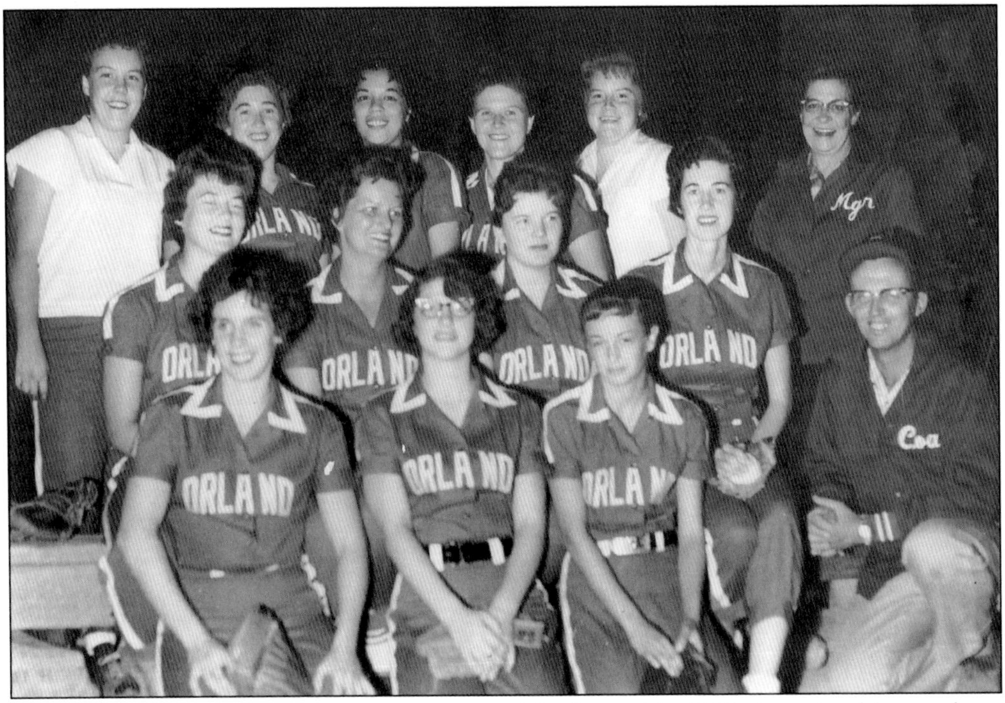

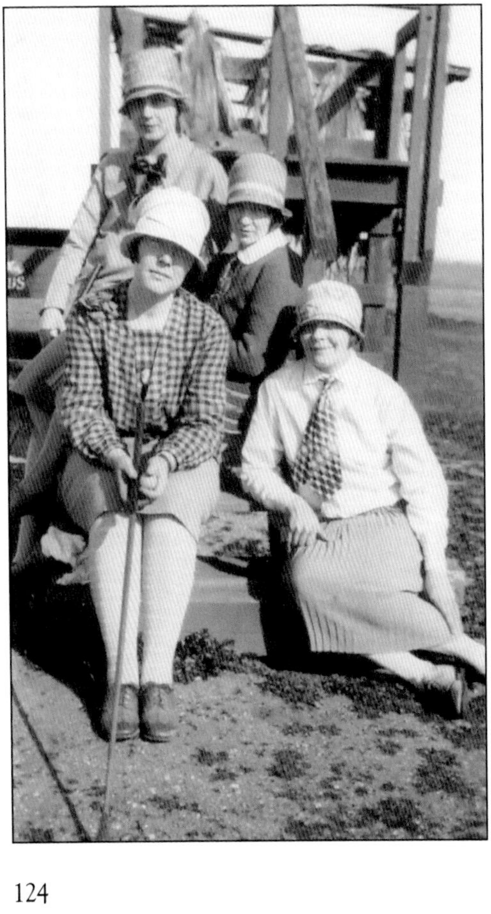

Members of the 1961 championship squad of the Sacramento Valley Girls' Softball League are, from left to right, (first row) Barbara Maas, Lorraine Salvagno, Phyllis Qualls, and Irvin Merrifield; (second row) Janet Dixon, Esther Sabin, Helen Kaber, and Marlene Holland; (third row) Billie Rodriques, Anne Myers, Si Pata, Fay Hanson, Mary White, and manager Berdena Reeder. Not present are Prudy Wright, Darlene Bernard, Betty Newman, and Ronnie Bernard. (Courtesy Fay Hanson.)

The Orland Golf and Country Club was formed in 1926 when several businessmen got together and purchased 105.5 acres of land three miles west of town and built a nine-hole golf course. Membership was $50, and dues were $10 per year. Females could originally only be associate members. Shown from left to right are (first row) Margaret Guilford and unidentified; (second row) Esther Guilford and unidentified. (Courtesy Mark Guilford.)

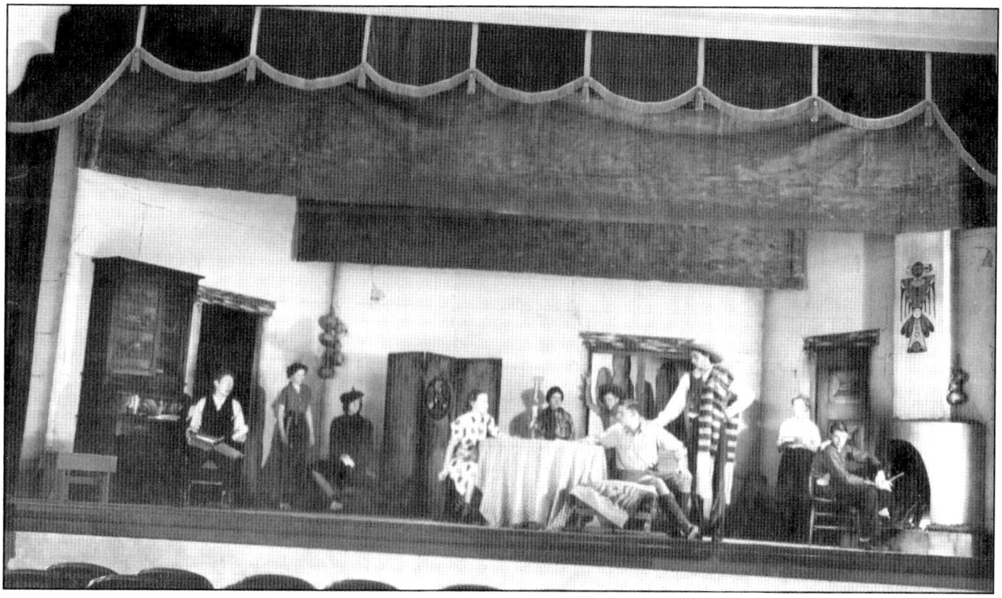

Orland audiences enjoyed theatrical performances in a number of venues over the years, including the Orland Opera House, the grammar and high school auditoriums, and the Memorial Hall. *The Good Bad Man* was staged by the junior class in May 1938 at the Memorial Hall and played to good reviews. The sets were professionally prepared by woodshop teacher Ralph Parker, art instructor Helen Gakey, and their Orland High students. (Courtesy Orland Alumni Association.)

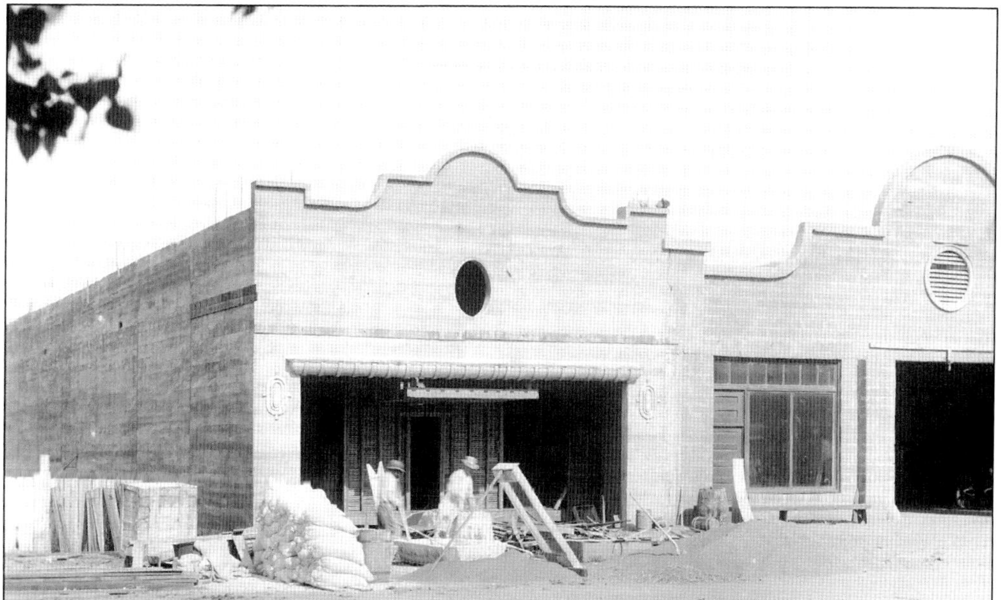

The Pastime was an early-20th-century Orland moving-picture show house, while the Aerdome was an early open-air picture establishment set up in the summer months. The Orland Theater was built on Fourth Street around 1913. The first talking picture shown on the screen was *The Long, Long Trail* starring Hoot Gibson. The date was February 14, 1930, and admission was 15¢ and 35¢. The longtime manager of the Orland Theater was C. A. Pendleton.

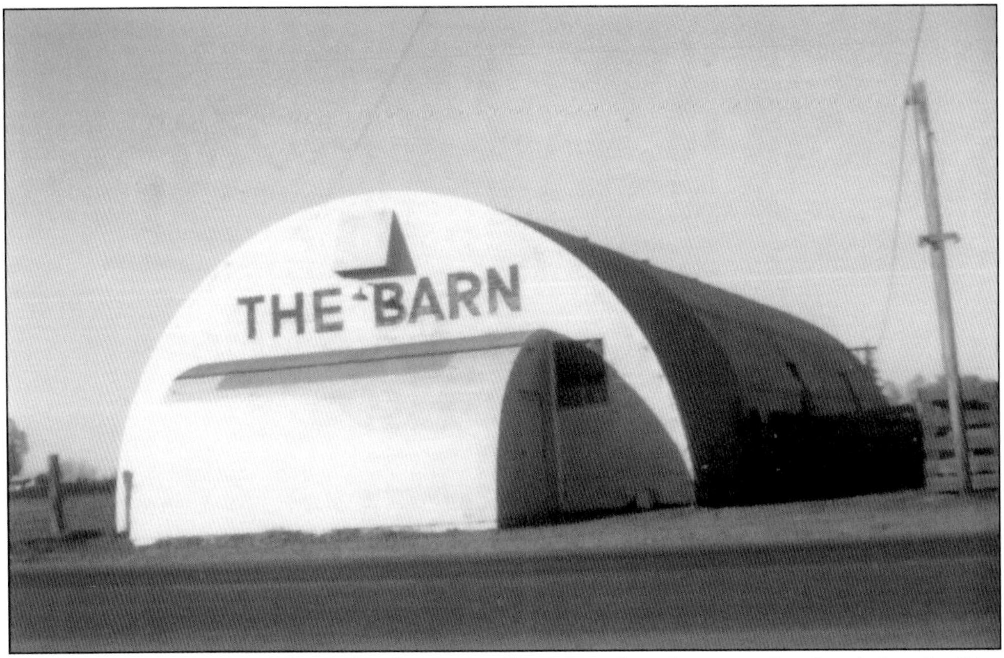

Ivan Stockton, owner of the Orland Auction Yard, loved to dance, so he decided to build a dance hall on his property near the corner of Eighth and South Streets. Following World War II, wood was not available, so he used a Quonset hut. The Barn opened about 1946. The popular dance hall had a very highly polished concrete floor and a stage at the north end. Burlap was placed across the ceiling, but the acoustics were described as "terrible." (Both courtesy George and Lana Trovao.)

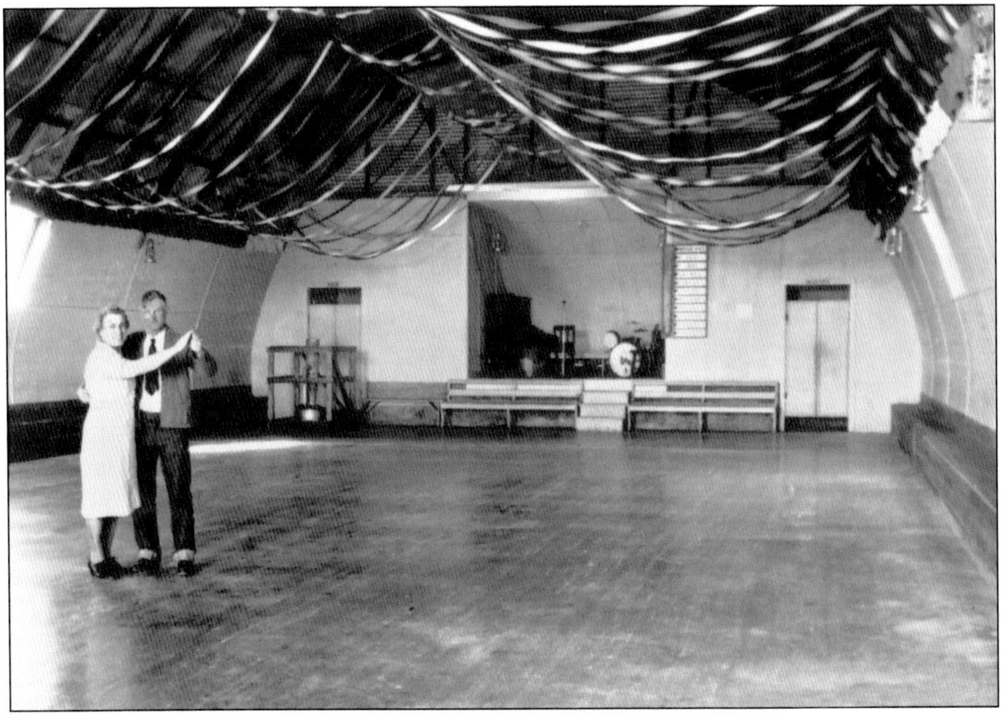

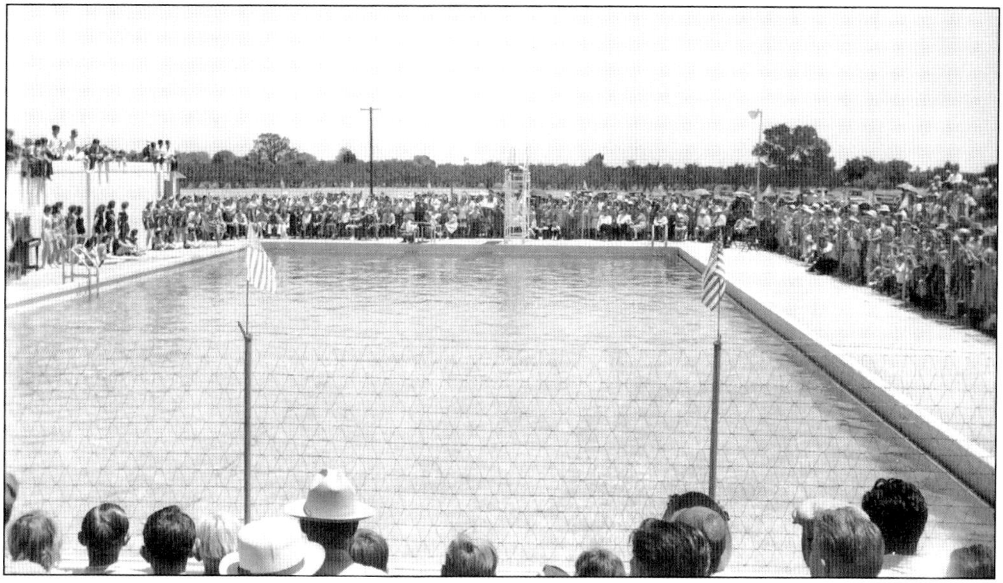

The dedication of Orland's city swimming pool took place on May 27, 1939. The Works Progress Administration had built the pool, baseball fields, and a playground in the new municipal park. The ceremonies were handled by Jim Moran as president of the Orland Boosters Club. The program included a bathing beauty pageant, speakers, and an exhibition by national diving champions.

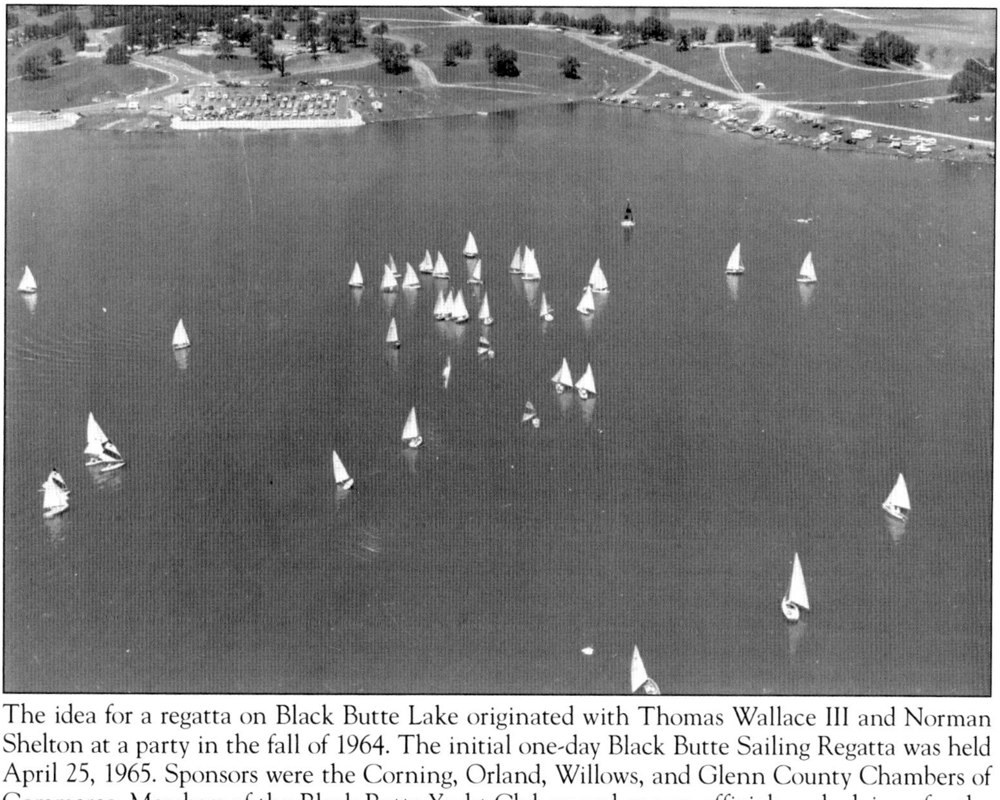

The idea for a regatta on Black Butte Lake originated with Thomas Wallace III and Norman Shelton at a party in the fall of 1964. The initial one-day Black Butte Sailing Regatta was held April 25, 1965. Sponsors were the Corning, Orland, Willows, and Glenn County Chambers of Commerce. Members of the Black Butte Yacht Club served as race officials and advisors for the regatta. The last regatta was held in 1980.

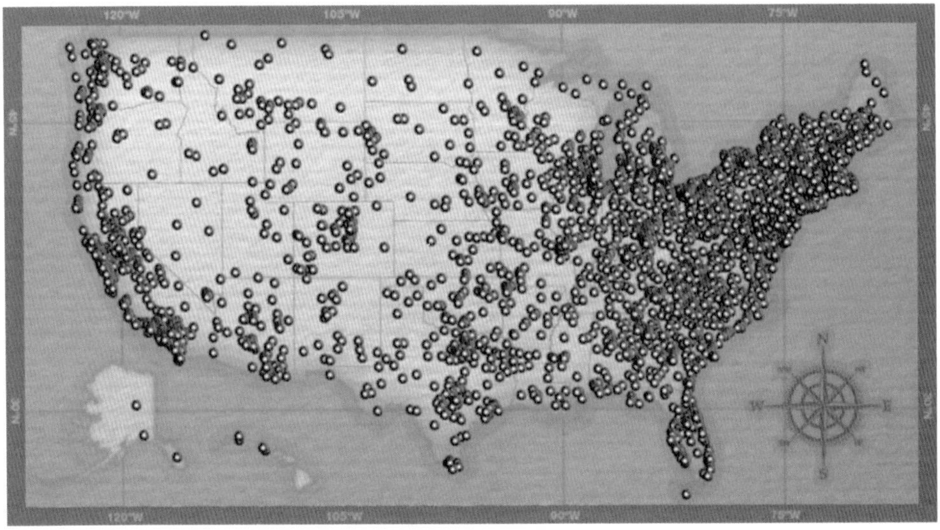